THE
OTHER SIDE
OF
THE RIVER

BY ALEX KOTLOWITZ

Alex Kotlowitz

ANCHOR BOOKS
A DIVISION OF RANDOM HOUSE, INC.
New York

THE
OTHER SIDE
OF
THE RIVER

A Story of

Two Towns,

a Death,

and America's Dilemma

All dates, place names, titles, and events in this account are factual. However, the names of certain individuals have been changed in order to afford them a measure of privacy.

FIRST ANCHOR BOOKS EDITION, FEBRUARY 1999

Copyright © 1998 by Alex Kotlowitz

All rights reserved under International and Pan-American Copyright Conventions. Published in the United States by Anchor Books, a division of Random House, Inc., New York, and simultaneously in Canada by Random House of Canada Limited, Toronto. Originally published in hardcover in the United States by Nan A. Talese / Doubleday in 1998. The Anchor Books edition is published by arrangement with Nan A. Talese / Doubleday.

Anchor Books and colophon are registered trademarks of Random House, Inc.

The Library of Congress has cataloged the hardcover edition of this book as follows:
The other side of the river: a story of two towns, a death, and America's dilemma/Alex Kotlowitz.—1st ed.
p.   cm.
1. Saint Joseph (Mich.)—Race relations—Case studies. 2. Benton Harbor (Mich.)—Race relations—Case studies. 3. Hate crimes—Michigan—Saint Joseph—Case studies. 4. Murder victims—Michigan—Saint Joseph—Case studies. 5. McGinnis, Eric, d. 1991. I. Title.
F574.S26K68   1998
977.4′11—dc21   97-18247
CIP

ISBN 0-385-47721-X

Book design by Jennifer Daddio
Map designed by Jeffrey L. Ward

www.anchorbooks.com

Printed in the United States of America
10

For Maria—

And in memory of my mother,

Billie Kotlowitz

CONTENTS

The Race Card: A Tale in Three Parts

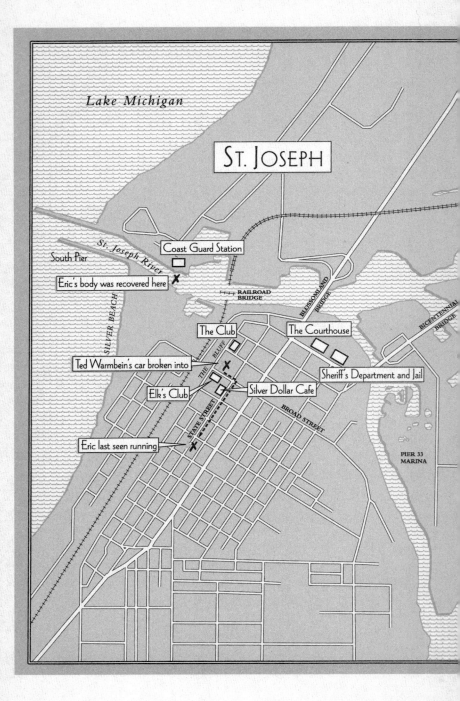

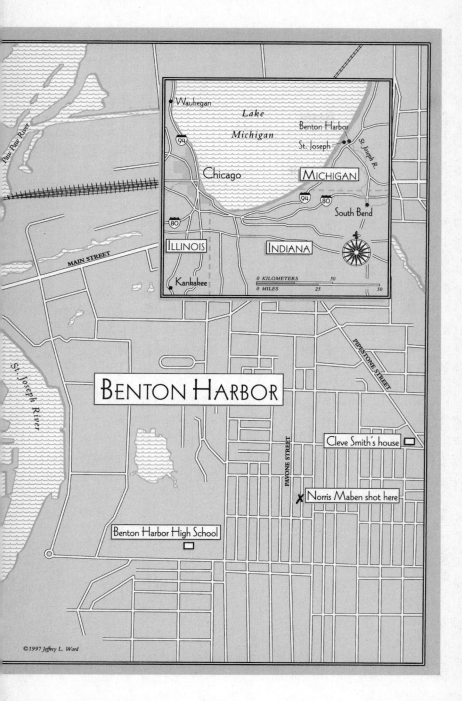

Waukegan

Lake
Michigan

94

Chicago

Benton Harbor
St. Joseph

St. Joseph R.

MICHIGAN

94

80

South Bend

ILLINOIS

INDIANA

Kankakee

0 KILOMETERS   50

0 MILES   25   50

PIPESTONE STREET

MAIN STREET

St. Joseph River

BENTON HARBOR

Cleve Smith's house

PAVONE STREET

✗ Norris Maben shot here

Benton Harbor High School

©1997 Jeffrey L. Ward

THE BODY

This much is not in dispute.

On Wednesday, May 22, 1991, at the day's first light, a flock of seagulls noisily abandoned their perches along the two cement piers jutting into Lake Michigan. Like rambunctious schoolchildren, they playfully circled above the mouth of the St. Joseph River here in southwestern Michigan, absorbing the warmth of the new day's sun. The seas were calm; the sky, partly cloudy.

Almost exactly one hour later, first-year Coast Guard seaman Saul Brignoni, hosing down a concrete walkway alongside the river, teasingly shot a blast of water at a covy of gulls resting on the embankment and spotted what appeared to be a muddy strip of driftwood floating twenty yards from where he stood. Minutes later, he received a cryptic radio call from the crew of a nearby dredging boat. "We got something out here you might want to take a look at."

Brignoni and two colleagues pushed off in their twenty-two-foot Boston Whaler and on closer inspection discovered that the flotsam was the bloated body of a fully clothed teenage black boy.

Using a seven-foot-long boat hook, they carefully prodded the discolored corpse onto a large metal litter, turning their heads to avoid the putrid gases that rose from the body, along with the early morning mist from the river.

They then motored back to shore, where they laid the body, face down, on the wooden deck by their barracks and doused it with a nearby hose, cleansing it of some of the river silt. Three St. Joseph police officers soon arrived. While two asked questions of the Coast Guardsmen, making certain to stay upwind of the body, the third officer circled the corpse like a buzzard over its prey, snapping pictures with a 35-millimeter camera. After getting shots of the boy's short-sleeved shirt, a blue-striped baseball jersey that read MCGINNIS, Detective Dennis Soucek had his fellow officers carefully turn the body over. He knelt to get close-ups, focusing on the dead boy's stonewashed USED jeans, a popular brand, which were unbuckled and unzipped, exposing blue-striped bikini shorts. He snapped shots of the victim's upper body, the arms and hands still caked with mud; the skin, yellowish, almost green in places, was scraped away on the left forearm. He took photos of the boy's head, which was so swollen that the face looked separated from the skull, as if someone had stuffed cotton in the cheeks, the chin, the forehead, and every other part of the head. Only the ears retained their normal size, and in proportion to the other features seemed small and insignificant. The red lips puckered out like a fish's, and there were marks around the neck, two bloody lines that looked like rope burns. There were other matters the camera caught as well: a silver ring with a turquoise stone, a pinky fingernail painted pink, and unlaced high-top Nikes.

Nearby, Jim Dalgleish, a weedy-looking reporter for the *Herald-Palladium,* the local newspaper, turned his eyes from the scene, his worn Nikon hanging around his neck. Dalgleish, who, like other reporters at the small paper, doubled as a photographer, had heard over the police radio about "a floater" in the river and had sped over in his pickup. Drownings are common occurrences around here, sometimes as many as three to four in a year. The area, after all, is surrounded by water. The St. Joseph River slices through the county, its languid surface hiding a sometimes tricky current. The narrower and shallower Paw Paw River feeds into the St. Joseph just upstream from the Coast Guard station; its mucky bottom once devoured a car that had swerved off the road, trapping the driver. And just two hundred yards downstream from the Coast Guard station, the St. Joseph empties into Lake Michigan, which at times can rise up in a fury, whipping eight-to-ten-foot swells onto the two piers. The force of those waves has swept fishermen and foolhardy teens into roiling water where even the strongest of swimmers have a difficult time staying afloat. Dalgliesh, who hadn't the stomach to look at the puffed-up bodies of floaters, only glanced at this particular corpse; he did snap some photos after it was placed on an ambulance stretcher, a white sheet covering it from head to toe.

The body was taken to Mercy Hospital for an autopsy. The incident was, the police believed, probably a drowning.

Like a swollen snake, the St. Joseph River lazily winds its way north from Indiana through the hilly cropland of southwestern Michigan, eventually spilling into the clear waters of Lake Michigan, where it is 450 feet across at its widest. It is here, near its mouth, that this otherwise undramatic chute of water becomes a formidable waterway, not because of its currents but because of what it separates: Benton Harbor and St. Joseph, two small Michigan towns whose only connections are two bridges and a powerful undertow of contrasts.

South of the river on a hill sits St. Joseph, a modest town of nine thousand that resembles the quaint tourist haunts of the New England coast. Vacationers on their way from Chicago—it's a two-hour drive—to the northern woods of Michigan stop here to browse the downtown mall, shopping at the antique stores, art galleries, and clothing boutiques. Its beach, just a short walk down a steep bluff from the downtown, once boasted an amusement park, but, reflecting today's more environmentally conscious world, now stands bare, its acres of fine sand and protected dunes luring families and idle teens during the summer months. The town is made up of both blue-collar families and professionals, many of whom work at the international corporate headquarters of Whirlpool, one of the area's major employers. In recent years they have been joined by affluent Chicagoans looking for second homes. For those in Benton Harbor, though, St. Joseph's most defining characteristic is its racial makeup: it is 95 percent white.

Benton Harbor lies just across the river. It is a larger town, with a population of twelve thousand, and although, technically speaking, it is the other sibling in the much-used name the Twin Cities, it couldn't be more different from St. Joseph. Benton Harbor is 92 percent black and is dirt poor. It is, as a result, shunned by the citizens of St. Joseph, whose children are taught from an early age that they're not to venture into Benton Harbor because of the gangs and the drugs. A state legislator once publicly warned visitors to lock their doors when driving through the city's downtown, whose empty movie theaters, potholed streets, and vacant stores stand as an inverted image of the mall across the way. And it is suggested from time to time that the local airport, just north of Benton Harbor, should be relocated so that visitors wouldn't have to drive through the wreckage of the town to get to St. Joseph. For the people of St. Joseph, Benton Harbor is an embarrassment. It's as if someone had taken an inner-city neighborhood—indeed, the typical family income is one fourth that in St. Joseph—and plopped it in the middle of this otherwise picturesque landscape. A further reminder of the relentless differences was put forward in 1989, when *Money* magazine anointed the Benton Harbor metropolitan area, which includes

St. Joseph, the worst place to live in the nation. Everyone, of course, blamed Benton Harbor for the rating.

It is here, where the St. Joseph River opens into Lake Michigan, providing sustenance for spawning salmon and seasoned sailors, that this story begins. And it's here—at the beginning—where people began to disagree.

2.

A PRELUDE

My interest in the death of Eric McGinnis borders on obsession. I've come to realize this after conducting over two hundred interviews, after scouring, countless times, the six-inch-thick police report, after listening to the opinions and reasoning offered by forensic pathologists, toxicologists, homicide detectives, and civil engineers, after navigating the St. Joseph River, after hanging out in bars and on basketball courts, and after playing and replaying in my mind the last moments when Eric was seen alive.

Eric, at least what I knew of him, called to mind the friendships I've been lucky to forge over the years, relationships I treasure. I've known teens like Eric who, in the throes of adolescence, can be marvelously engaging and formidably beguiling. And so my obsession may be explained, in part by my familiarity with the terrain. Eric's death stirred me. I thought perhaps I could restore some dignity to another faceless name and help put closure on the mystery surrounding his death. I wasn't prepared, however, for the sudden and precipitous shifts in the landscape. The terrain wasn't as familiar as I'd thought.

I never knew Eric. Nor did I know his family or friends until after his death. But the three-by-five color snapshots of his bloated body haunt me, one photo in particular, in which his arms are splayed at his side at awkward, impossible angles, one wrist turned away from his body, almost as if he had died trying to mock the body-bending acrobatics of a contortionist. I flinch at the image of his battered face, which, because of the decomposition and its ballooning, seems without form or character. When I close my eyes and conjure up that photo, what I see most clearly is the single blade of grass along Eric's left cheek, extending just above one eye. It is as if the camera had focused on that at the exclusion of his features. Everything else is a blur: his eyes, set deep in their sockets; his hair, caked in mud; his mouth, puckered out as it is, without expression.

A father, I close my eyes and picture that blade of grass on the cheek of my daughter or stepson. It's too painful, too trite an exercise. How can I comprehend the darkness, the internal chaos of losing a child? I try to imagine. But I become nauseated and dizzy. And quickly pull myself out of such contrived but no less disturbing wanderings. What must it be like for Eric's mother? Her only child. Her most reliable companion. Her dining partner. Her fellow Pistons' fan. What must it be like not knowing how her son, playful and talkative, impish and open, could end up dead in the river? And after he was last seen in the all-white town. Chased by an angry man. While a deputy sheriff watched. The questions pile up, so fast and so high that at times I feel lost as I stand by them. What about the untied shoes and unzipped pants? His missing coat? But when I become distracted, I remind myself that I have to stay focused, as the camera did on that blade of grass, on only one inquiry: How did Eric end up in the St. Joseph River?

The theories abound. I've heard them all—or so I think until I pick up one more stone, which reveals a patch of earth muddier than the last. Each time I aim for the truth, home in on it, the target blurs and sways, so that as I near it, the bull's-eye all but disappears. Or, at times, as I approach what I think are facts, the bull's-eye multiplies, each taking on a different shape and hue, so that, as my vision darts from one to the other, I don't know where to land. The facts become elusive. Such is the story of race. Such is the story of Eric's death. Truth becomes myth; myth becomes truth. And your perspective—myth or truth, truth or myth—is shaped by which side of the river you live on. In the end all that matters is what *you* believe. Or so it seems.

I first heard about Eric's death in the spring of 1992, almost a year to the day after the discovery of his body. At the time—I was writing for the *Wall Street Journal*—the verdict had just been rendered in the Rodney King case. Not guilty. With those two words, Los Angeles's black community exploded, its rage surpassing the imagination of even the most liberal of whites. As I'm apt to do, I wandered away from the story of the day, the conflagration in Los Angeles, and traveled to less choppy waters. I'd like to believe it's a good journalistic instinct, but it has as much to do with my fear of competition, of being placed face to face with reporters who may be more agile and composed under deadline and whose reporting will expose what I've missed.

So it was that I ended up in Benton Harbor and St. Joseph, when I probably should have been in the eye of the storm, two thousand miles away. But when it comes to racial matters, the storm cuts a wide swath. Having convinced an editor at the *Journal* to give me a few days, I drove the two hours to what are called, without irony, the Twin Cities, unsure whether I'd find anything to write about.

I had been here four years earlier to write about what I called our forgotten cities, small, out-of-the-way, impoverished places like

East St. Louis in Illinois, and Camden in New Jersey, and Benton Harbor. On my first day in Benton Harbor, I stopped in the town's library, a usually lively place that runs a bustling video-rental operation (in addition to lending books, of course), to peruse recent issues of the local newspaper. There, Barb McKee, a librarian of twenty-seven years and a Benton Harbor native, told me the story of Eric. And so I spent the next two months researching and writing an article for the *Journal*—and the next five years digging into the events surrounding Eric's death. I drove to the towns regularly, sometimes staying for only a day, other times for a stretch of weeks. For two summers, my wife and I rented a home nearby.

People in the two towns would often ask which side of the river I was staying on, wanting to gauge my allegiance. But the question most often asked was: "Why us? Why write about St. Joseph and Benton Harbor?" So I would tell them that, while the contrasts between St. Joseph and Benton Harbor seem unusually stark, they are, I believe, typical of how most of us live: physically and spiritually isolated from one another. I do not mean to single out these two towns or their people, for I can see much of myself in the good intentions of most residents of St. Joseph and empathize with the anger and wariness of the residents in Benton Harbor. I've come to realize that most of us would like to do right, but, as was said of the South's politicians during Jim Crow, race diminishes us. It incites us to act as we wouldn't in other arenas: clumsily, cowardly, and sometimes cruelly. We easily fall on one side or the other; we circle the wagons, watching out for our own. There's comfort, of course, among the familiar.

I should make it clear from the outset that Eric's death did not drive a wedge between the two communities; that wedge had already been driven deep. Nor did it complicate relations between the races; they were already twisted and knotted in ways that local residents had become resigned to. It did, however, serve as a defining moment for the towns. The discovery of Eric's body shattered any illusion that they shared much more than the St. Joseph River.

A quarter of a century after race was part of everyday public discourse, it haunts us quietly, though on occasion—as in the Rodney King beating or the O. J. Simpson trial or Eric McGinnis's death—it erupts with jarring urgency. It is at these moments of crisis, during these squalls, that we flail about, trying to find moral ballast. By then it is usually too late. The lines have been drawn. Sabers rattle. Accusations are hurled back and forth across the river like cannon fire. And the cease-fires, when they occur, are just that, cease-fires, temporary and fragile. Even the best of people have already chosen sides.

In the tumultuous weeks and months following the discovery of Eric McGinnis's body, as the police tried to find out how he had ended up in the river, the contour of relations between the two communities came into focus: the mistrust, the misunderstanding, and the fear—even of the truth. Eric's death became a kind of Rashomon of the races, with relations between the towns distorting the perceptions of what happened on the night he disappeared.

The events surrounding Eric's death should ring familiar to all of us, both black and white: the confusion and the understanding, the despair and the hope, the disconnections and, indeed, the connections. With all that in mind, I set out to find out how Eric ended up in what is the towns' strongest connection of all, the river.

homes, built by the river captains, merchants, and mill owners, the monied class of the time. But what makes St. Joseph so alluring (and difficult for other cities to replicate) is its waterfront—or, more accurately, its waterfronts: Lake Michigan to the west, the curling St. Joseph River to the north and the east. So seductive is the setting that in recent years there have been a number of suicides in and around these waters, which seem to offer a gentle exit from an otherwise burdensome world. One elderly man, on a powdery beach at the south end of town, disrobed and left his clothes, wallet, and keys in a neat pile on the sand. He apparently swam into the lake; his body was found a few days later when it floated back to shore. Another man jumped into the river fully clothed. And a young woman put a gun to her mouth in a Holiday Inn room that she had selected for its magnificent view of both the lake and the river; in her six-page note, she described that panorama and the many peaceful strolls she'd taken on the beach.

On my visits to St. Joseph, I would often take a hike after lunch, walking north of downtown, past the Whitcomb and an outdoor band shell, down a steep paved road, to a manicured arboretum inhabited, year round, by a gaggle of friendly mallards. I would sit on a wooden bench there and gaze at the murky, seemingly still waters of the river. It narrows here (though it's still three hundred feet across), ballooning both immediately downstream and upstream. Upstream, between two drawbridges, it has been widened and dredged to allow ample room for Great Lakes' freighters to turn around. Still farther upstream, beyond my view, the river narrows and curls south, wedging the town between river and lake. Down-river, following the current, the St. Joseph passes beneath a railroad swingbridge, past the new Waterfront Condominiums (which sell for as much as $300,000), and past the Coast Guard station. Finally, it abruptly zigzags right and then left, before flowing between two piers, which, like welcoming hands, stretch out into the waters of the lake. At the tip of the northern pier is a red-and-white lighthouse so quaint in appearance that it was chosen to adorn a thirty-two-cent stamp. Here, in late spring and summer, I could admire the parade of sailing sloops and pleasure craft with names like *Playmate, Prime Time, Obsession,* and *Guilty.* Their owners and friends would wave to us landlocked voyeurs and show off their tan bodies or, on occasion, the large corpses of coho salmon and steelhead, which were planted in the lake to satisfy the hunger of Michigan's sport fishermen.

But more popular than the riverfront is St. Joseph's lakefront, on both sides of the river. A sliver of the town, including the Coast Guard station, sits north of the river, cutting off Benton Harbor from Lake Michigan. St. Joseph's prime real estate, though, is due west of the downtown, down a grass-covered bluff and over railroad tracks that serve freight as well as Amtrak passenger trains. There lies Silver Beach, an expanse of fine sand spreading out like butterfly wings. In the summer, it is packed with both locals and out-of-town vacationers, most of whom hail from Illinois and, with some disdain, are commonly referred to as FIPs, or Fuck'n Illinois People. (On the first interstate overpass in the county, traveling north from Chicago, someone has spray-painted "Go Home FIPs.")

The beach abuts the river's mouth, separated by the southern pier, and is the site of volleyball and triathlon tournaments, picnics and teenagers' parties. On some days, when the westerly winds have died down and the sky appears as smooth as the sand, the lake resembles the Caribbean, its waters a transparent blue, its bottom carpeted with hardpacked sand, which the sometimes powerful undertow forms into small ridges in the shallows.

St. Joseph residents feel proprietary about Silver Beach, their crown jewel, so in the spring of 1992, when the city put high-peaked tin roofs on the restrooms near the top of the bluff, the citizenry rose in protest. They deluged local radio stations with phone calls. Three hundred signed a petition. They appeared en masse at a city commission meeting. The *Herald-Palladium* ran front-page stories. The reason for the outrage: some felt the roofs would block the view of the lake. Nor did they like the color, aqua blue. They thought it cheesy.

On a summer day four years after the discovery of Eric McGinnis's body, I pulled into St. Joseph's downtown and parked across from City Hall, a worn, two-story red-bricked building, one of the few tired-looking edifices in St. Joseph. As I crossed the street toward the police department, housed on the second floor, I could make out the tin bathroom roofs and the placid, inviting waters of Lake Michigan in the distance.

Upstairs, I entered the unassuming rooms of the St. Joseph police, a department of twenty officers. Janet, the department's secretary, greeted me. "Go right on back," she directed. "Lieutenant Reeves is expecting you." I wandered down a long hallway and stuck my head in Jim Reeves's wood-paneled office, filled with all the paraphernalia one associates with law enforcement: his framed criminal justice degree from Michigan State University, a black-and-white photo of a fellow officer who died of a heart attack while on duty, and an aerial shot of St. Joseph and the river. On his window sill were two psychedelically-decorated bongs recovered in raids. But Reeves, who would just as soon have been home with his two young children instead of chasing criminals, also had on the shelf behind him an armful of photos of his family, a copy of the *Anarchist's Cookbook* (a gag gift from a friend), and a trophy from an annual golf tourney he sponsors to raise money for the Special Olympics. There was also a signed photo from Burt Reynolds ("Jim, Good Luck, Burt Reynolds") and a book entitled *People Skills*.

Reeves, the phone pressed to his ear, motioned me in. "I'm a straightahead man," he said into the receiver, sounding unmistakably like *Dragnet*'s Joe Friday. "If I can get this resolved, that would be great. All I have to do is collect the facts." He had recently recovered from what may have been a minor heart attack (the doctors put him on an exercise program and low-cholesterol diet), and his complexion was a bit pale. He had a slight paunch, which he was now committed to losing, but it wasn't all that noticeable on his compact five-foot-seven frame. Reeves favored colorful ties, usually with a gold motif, and brown penny loafers, usually with the pennies. And he sported a well-groomed mustache. All of which conspired to make him resemble a baker more than a cop.

As he finished the phone call, still saying his good-byes, he leaned over his gray metal desk to welcome me. The few papers there were neatly laid out; a business card Scotch-taped to the front of the desk served to identify this modest office as his. "So what brings you into town?" he asked rhetorically.

I was here to question him yet again about Eric's death, but as I had learned during the past years, it was not a subject Reeves enjoyed discussing. Often when I brought it up, he rolled his eyes— unconsciously, I thought; I knew he'd have preferred to talk about some other topic. On that morning, the opportunity quickly arose when he noticed me eying three identical composite sketches tacked to the wall. They were of a black man who looked to be in his mid-twenties, his face marked by a pencil-thin mustache, a receding hairline, and an abundance of freckles. Attached to each composite was a color Polaroid of three different men, each of whom to one degree or another resembled the penciled portraits. Reeves proceeded to tell the story behind them.

A ten-year-old white girl, daughter of a local pastor, had filed a complaint with the police department saying that a black man had come by St. Peter's Church one evening while she was drawing on a computer in the church's office. The adults were in the sanctuary, attending an Easter-week service. When the man asked for directions to the basement, she took his hand and led him down the stairs, where, she alleged, he grabbed her by the throat and tried to drag her into the dark boiler room. She resisted, biting his hand, kicking him in the shins, and then letting loose with an ear-piercing scream. He relaxed his grip long enough for her to run upstairs to her mother, who called the police.

These were highly charged allegations, particularly in light of the friction between St. Joseph and Benton Harbor. The next day the *Herald-Palladium* ran on its front page the composite sketch, accompanied by a headline: GIRL ESCAPES ABDUCTION AT SJ CHURCH. Reeves, who considered himself a fair and thorough officer, approached the case with caution. He immediately saw the potential explosiveness of the charges: a black child-molester on the loose in a white community. St. Joseph residents would have had little doubt that the accused was from across the river. "I worried there'd be tension between the two communities," he said. "We just don't need any more poison in the system." Reeves pursued his leads quietly, avoiding the press as he searched for anyone resembling the description given by the girl.

Reeves pointed to the first photograph, of a man with a passing resemblance to the sketch. He had a mustache, though it was bushy and uncombed, and his face, like the drawing's, was round. But there the likeness ended. He had a full shock of hair and no freckles. The girl's father, the minister, had told Reeves that there was a black man named Kevin Hall who came around the church regularly, begging for money. In fact, he had been by the sanctuary the day before the alleged incident. Reeves knew Hall. He was a heroin addict who frequented St. Joseph and was suspected of petty crimes, including filching urns from the local cemetery. Reeves brought him into the station and took a Polaroid. The girl was unable to pick him out of a photo line-up. What's more, Hall had no history of violent behavior.

The second photo, that of Jeremy Johnson, showed some resemblance as well. Again, the suspect had a mustache and in this case shortly cropped hair, but he had no freckles. Johnson, who was mentally impaired, had become a fixture in downtown St. Joseph, known primarily for his toilet fetish. He would ask to use the bath-room of a downtown business and often remain for twenty minutes to an hour. Despite such odd behavior, the police knew Johnson to be a gentle and harmless man. Again, Reeves took a Polaroid; and again the girl could not identify him in a photo line-up.

Reeves handed me the third photo, that of Warren Sharpe. It was a match; the similarities were unmistakable. Like the composite, Sharpe had a thin mustache, a receding hairline, and, perhaps most notably, a face peppered with freckles. A security guard at a local grocery store had recorded Sharpe's license plate and alerted Reeves when he noticed Sharpe in the checkout line and remembered the picture in the newspaper. Reeves drove to Sharpe's home, and when Sharpe opened the door, he could barely contain his excitement. "I figured I had this case wrapped up," he recalled. He showed Sharpe the sketch.

"Who's that?" Reeves asked, somewhat mischievously.

"That's me," replied a perplexed Sharpe, who was also struck by the resemblance.

Sharpe, it turned out, worked as a supervisor on the night shift at a local factory. Nearly twenty co-workers could testify to his whereabouts on the night of the incident; he had an ironclad alibi. Nonetheless, Reeves took a Polaroid; again, the girl could not pick it out of a line-up.

By this time, Reeves had begun to doubt the girl's allegations. Little parts of her story changed with each telling. Early on, she had said the black man poked his head in the office where she was playing on the computer; later, she said she went out to see who had come through the church's side door. What's more, she seemed generally undisturbed by the incident; she even recounted it, with some embellishments, during show-and-tell at school. Reeves also noted that the child seemed unsettled by the family's recent move from Minnesota; she had repeatedly told her teachers that she wanted to move back. Did she think this a way to force her family's return? "I don't believe anything happened, not as she reported it," Reeves said. "It's very important to collect the facts no matter how they fall. And here she says it's a black man who grabbed her. We're getting back to the bogeyman thing. It could have been volatile." But it wasn't. The case quietly disappeared from public view. And though Reeves considered the case closed, he kept the sketches and the photographs tacked to his wall as reminders that even what seems like indisputable evidence may be suspect. In addition, he admired the free-hand artistry of the young patrolman who doubled as the department's portraitist. The drawings served to decorate his spartan office.

Reeves is a respected small-town cop, praised by both other officers and by citizens for his sense of humor and his gentlemanly attitude toward the people he serves. He relies on that waggery and charm in his work.

Indeed, Reeves prides himself on his ability to deal courteously with all kinds of people, a conceit that sometimes borders on boastfulness. He became friends with Warren Sharpe, and refers on numerous occasions to his close friendship with Joshua Ndege, a Zimbabwean immigrant, whom he had once arrested and who runs a computer-training business. He keeps his home phone number listed so that people can easily reach him to talk about their troubles. It was, in fact, his civility that his second wife, Denise, first noticed. Denise, a devout Christian Scientist, was the department's secretary. Her shyness and modesty—she wore long, unrevealing skirts—made her an easy target for the antics of the predominantly male department. Once, someone strung together all her paper clips; another time, she came to work to find everything glued to her desk. Reeves, she said, treated her respectfully. Partly, though, that was because Reeves had been warned by his superiors to keep away from her; he would have been a bad influence, they felt. Reeves, recently divorced, was going through a confusing time. "Let's just say it was fast cars and fast women," he says. "I was burning the candles at both ends." He was dating several women concurrently and drove a limited-edition Camaro. But it wasn't really his style—and he wanted Denise to know that. "I had to show her that there was a side to me that many people around here didn't see, kindhearted and sensitive," he says.

Reeves loves practical jokes. Knowing of Denise's passion for junk food, he bought her a case of potato chips and had a local Pepsi distributor stop by to ask Denise where she wanted her cases dropped off. They went on their first date in February 1984 and were married a year later. The marriage has mellowed Reeves, who is now marked more by his earnestness than his highjinks.

Reeves doesn't have the swagger and bravado of his big-city brethren (he often leaves his gun behind in his desk drawer), though that's not to say he's without ambition. Ever since I met him, in the summer of 1992, I've known that he has wanted to become the town's next chief of police; the current head was nearing retirement. There were others in the running, including the one other detective, with whom Reeves has had a somewhat icy relationship. "Jim is political for a police officer," says one area law enforcement official. "I think he has big plans."

The "McGinnis case," as it came to be known, was Reeves's first involving a possible homicide. It's not that he wasn't trusted in the department or that he wasn't senior enough; there's only the one other detective. It's just that such cases are rare in St. Joseph. In the preceding forty-three years, the city had experienced only three murders, all crimes of passion. There was one twenty-five-year pe-riod in which the city didn't record a single homicide. Reeves's cases for the most part have been, at least by big-city standards, picayune: check forgery, burglary, embezzlement, and the occa-sional assault. One afternoon in his office, I found him scrolling through his computer, looking at recent incidents. Among them was

"Randy Yales and Peter Sabal attempted to skateboard down the Park St. hill and failed. Both were transported to 3320 Lakeshore Dr. to seek treatment of their minor injuries." St. Joseph's city council had recently banned skateboarding and Rollerblading downtown. Such are the concerns of Reeves and his colleagues. Police in surrounding towns say they would never work in St. Joseph. Too boring. There were some in law enforcement who felt Reeves was in over his head in the McGinnis case. When it came to conducting a major investigation, "I just don't think Jim has a clue," offered one colleague.

On the morning of May 22, 1991, Reeves, dressed in khakis and a short-sleeved shirt, was gathering his clubs in preparation for a day of golf, when, shortly before eight, Chief Ted Fleisher called to inform him that a body had been found in the river. "My first thought was that maybe someone had fallen off a ship," says Reeves, who recalled that the river was being dredged, as it often is in the spring. Moreover, in the days leading up to the Memorial Day weekend, pleasure boats make their first outing onto the lake, and freighters enter the harbor carrying gravel for local cement companies.

As he drove along the river bank on a road aptly named Marina Drive, an ambulance passed in the opposite direction, carrying, it turned out, the corpse. So by the time he arrived at the scene, the three officers, their job done, were getting into their cars. The fact that the body had been removed before his arrival irritated Reeves, though the truth is that he also felt some relief. He hates dealing with drownings. "I don't like dead bodies," he says. "And I don't look forward to talking with parents."

After debriefing the officers at the Coast Guard station, Reeves returned to his office, where he began phoning police departments in the area to ask about any reported missing persons. Jim Coburn, an officer with the Benton Township police, stuck his head in. "My nephew's been missing since Friday," he said. The boy's father, Coburn explained, had dropped him off at a teen nightspot called the Club in St. Joseph the previous Friday night. He never came home. "His name is Eric McGinnis." Coburn agreed to go to the morgue to identify the body.

"It was when he told me that Eric had been to the Club that I got more anxious about the case," recalls Reeves. "A lot of thoughts went through my mind. A black kid was last seen at the Club in St. Joseph. What happened? I'm thinking maybe he was shot or stabbed and dumped into the river." He was also concerned that the public, particularly in Benton Harbor, would jump to conclusions. Fearing the potentially explosive nature of the case, he proceeded cautiously, making sure that everything was done properly. He checked that a full report had been filed and double-checked that someone had taken photos of the body both at the Coast Guard station and at the morgue. He also called Detective Soucek at the local hospital to inquire about the autopsy. Although it hadn't been completed, Soucek told him that the staff had taken from the boy's pants a set of house keys and a bundle of soiled bills, totaling $49. Reeves dutifully recorded it all.

When Coburn returned, his eyes filled with tears, Reeves knew they had the identity of the boy. Coburn told him that the ring found on Eric's left pinky had been given to him by his father. "Jim," Coburn said, "I'm ninety percent sure. He's all swelled up. I'm ninety percent sure."

Word quickly spread of the body's discovery, and by midday everyone knew. That afternoon's *Herald-Palladium* ran a photo on page three of the sheet-covered body under the headline GRIM TASK.

Reeves wanted the case solved swiftly to prove to Benton Harbor that a white cop would take the death of a black teenager as seriously as he would one of his own. And he wanted to prove himself in his own department, as well. But this was not an incident that would pass quickly or quietly, and as the case unfolded, raising only more questions, the mystery seeped into the lifeblood of the two towns.

"I was concerned primarily with the local newspaper and [radio station] WHFB because I'd received a telephone call from a black reporter at WHFB," recalls Reeves. "He told me who he was and asked for some inside information. I said I didn't have any. He said, 'Is it true that Eric had a rope around his neck?' Unfortunately, we have reporters who, if they can't report the news, make it up. I knew the news about Eric's recovery was out there and that people were beginning to speculate. I thought, 'Oh, shit.'"

4.

FAMILY

Not long after my visit to Reeves, I was driving by a fenced-in former factory site in Benton Harbor, now an expanse of broken bricks, rubble, and weeds, and noticed a red-tailed hawk perched on a charred slab of wood. Hawks are majestic birds and at rest seem mightier and larger than they do in flight. This one looked out of place in the urban setting, but the barren lot contained a motherlode of mice, an essential part of the red-tail's diet. Moreover, Benton Harbor, urban as it is, is bordered by Lake Michigan to the west and fruit fields to the east and north, enticing terrain for birds of prey as well as other wildlife. I've spotted rabbits and raccoons running along the town's streets at dusk, and there is the occasional sighting of coyote, fox, and deer, which, because of home construction in surrounding rural towns, are being pushed out of their natural wooded habitat.

I pulled over and got out of my car to admire the bird, which seemed unfazed by my arrival. As I stood there, a young black boy, maybe eleven or twelve, rode up on his bicycle, evidently curious about what had caught my attention. "Shhh," I told him, putting my finger to my lips while gesturing toward the bird. He seemed unimpressed.

"It's a red-tail hawk," I explained. "Do you know what he's doing here?"

"Looking for mices?" he answered uncertainly.

I nodded. As we stood there, gazing at the statue-still predator, I asked the boy whether he had heard about the case of Eric McGinnis.

"Who's that?" he asked.

"The boy they found in the river. Do you remember hearing about that?"

"Oh, yeah."

"What do you think happened to him?"

"He got thrown in the river," he said with the utmost certainty. "He was dating a white girl."

The hawk spread its wings, apparently unsettled by the company, and took off, as did the boy on his bike. I was left with one more concise explanation for Eric McGinnis's death. I had got in the habit of asking virtually everyone I met here if he or she knew Eric or had any idea what happened to him. Not because I was looking for new theories—I had plenty of those—but because I hoped that eventually I might stumble across someone who had a nugget of information, however small or seemingly insignificant, that would help me understand the reasons for his death. But by now, four years after the discovery of his body, I knew what to expect. The people of Benton Harbor, young and old, liberal and conservative, whether they had been personally acquainted with Eric or not, were convinced not only that he had been murdered, but that he had been murdered by a white person.

———

Eric was sixteen when he died, too young to leave a distinct legacy, too old to be completely innocent. The *Herald-Palladium* reported that he had belonged to the NAACP, had participated in Junior ROTC, and had sung in his church's youth choir. In fact, Eric was a fairly typical teenager: insecure, self-involved, and at times self-destructive. But in adolescence—and in death—one becomes all things to all people. In this case, Eric became a symbol, a reference point. When his body bobbed to the surface, so did years of pent-up mistrust and anger—on both sides of the river. Only a few weeks before his death, the nation had viewed a dark, grainy videotape of Los Angeles police officers pummeling and kicking the motorist Rodney King. That people would later see this beating as something more—proof of police brutality—or something less—an isolated incident of police carrying out their official duty—was not lost on the people of Benton Harbor and St. Joseph. They came to view the death of Eric McGinnis as something more—the murder of an unarmed black child—or something less—the accidental drowning of one more careless teen in the waters bordering the towns.

Almost everyone in Benton Harbor and St. Joseph recalls one photo of Eric, which appeared in the *Herald-Palladium:* the photo his mother placed on his casket at the funeral. In the portrait, Eric, handsome, lanky, and broad-shouldered, stares confidently into the camera with an ever-so-slight grin. His closely cropped hair, high cheekbones, and bushy eyebrows give him a distinguished look. Adding to the effect is his posture; he's leaning forward on what appears to be a tabletop, his chin resting thoughtfully in his left palm. His complexion contrasts with the white turtleneck and the gold chain hanging around his neck. Eric looks surprisingly self-possessed for a sixteen-year-old, though his mother points out that he was posturing for the J. C. Penney photographer, who pleaded with him to sit still and remain focused on the camera.

This framed picture now sits in Ruth McGinnis's living room, and on different visits I've found it in different places: on the glass coffee table, on a bookshelf, and on the television set. It's as if Ruth wants the effect of an active son in her house; Eric, almost everyone agrees, was a bundle of energy. He had trouble remaining in one place, which is why, his mother suggests, he so loved to dance—and why he may have got into trouble the night he disappeared.

Ruth is a cautious, private woman, who, four years after her son's death, still finds it hard and sometimes impossible to talk about him. There were days when I would arrive at the appointed time and Ruth would excuse herself, saying she didn't want to talk then. And there were periods, sometimes months, when she didn't return phone calls. It was too painful, she'd say. The memories too fresh. She felt Eric's absence, and two months after his death she moved out of the two-bedroom home she and he had shared. "The memories were just tearing me apart," she told me. "It kept bothering me, though, because once I moved, I kept thinking he doesn't know where I am. And I swear, Alex, I'm not kidding you, in that one bedroom I was lying in my bed—a king-size, always have had one— and I woke up one night and he was right there. I could see him, and he had a smile on his face. I just freaked. I mean I woke up and he was just like, just as clear as day. And then when I batted my eyes, of course he was gone. I don't know how some people manage. It eats you alive."

Ruth works as a supervisor at Modern Plastics, a family-owned maker of ignition and brake parts; she began there twenty-one years ago, one of only two black women employees at the time. She fought, unsuccessfully, to form a union, but because she was much liked both by her co-workers and management, despite her efforts to organize her colleagues she was promoted to quality-control supervisor, in charge of five employees, including her mother. She is presently the firm's highest-ranking black employee.

Ruth comes from a highly respected Benton Harbor family. I should qualify that: a highly respected *black* Benton Harbor family. Though not publicly acknowledged, it is understood that there is the black Benton Harbor—and there is the white Benton Harbor. That distinction has everything to do, obviously, with race—but also with time. For the first half of this century, Benton Harbor was predominantly white and the more prosperous of the two towns.

Benton Harbor proper is 4.4 square miles and unfurls along the St. Joseph River like a flag in the wind, so the town is bordered by the waterway to the south and to the east. As the river curls south, so does the town. Benton Harbor took full advantage of its access to the river, and in 1858 dredged a shipping canal, which extends like a finger into the downtown. Fruit-growers and foundries could now easily load boats and ship their goods to Chicago and other cities along the Great Lakes.

Fruit was for many years the area's sustenance. The region's raw, ragged hills and proximity to Lake Michigan makes it prime terrain for growing fruit. The hills allow the cold air to drain away from the trees, and the lake moderates the climate in the spring and fall, when there might otherwise be false warmings or early freezes. For many years, Benton Harbor boasted the world's largest outdoor non-citrus fruit market; area farmers sold their cherries, apples, peaches, grapes, and apricots there. Fresh produce is still so large a commodity that the local newspaper carries weekly bushel prices.

Benton Harbor also became home to a flurry of manufacturing activity, most of it centered on the automobile—foundries and parts plants, primarily. Heath Company made its do-it-yourself radio kits here, and Whirlpool, the nation's premier maker of washing machines, began here and still maintains its international corporate headquarters just north of the town.

The town prospered, too, as a vacation destination for Chicagoans looking to escape the hot, sticky urban summers. The *Roosevelt,* a steamer, made daily voyages from Chicago to Benton Harbor; most people came to visit the House of David, a quasi-religious

29

cult, which had built an amusement park and an elaborate miniature railroad. They also came to watch the House of David's semiprofessional baseball team, whose members sported waist-length beards and were nationally renowned for their extraordinary talent. The town also boasted a number of splendid downtown hotels, including the Vincent, where Al Capone and his henchmen would hole up, renting an entire floor. Residents still tell stories of Capone motoring down the town's streets, his bodyguards riding shotgun, as he waved to passersby.

The town also supported a number of Jewish summer camps and resorts; in fact, the Jewish population was substantial enough to sustain three synagogues and two kosher meat markets. The Jewish Agricultural Society had enticed a number of recent Jewish immigrants to buy land here and become farmers. The six-pointed star serves as a persistent historical signpost for Benton Harbor. It adorned the Jewish temples, of course, and it became the House of David's icon, so an oversize electrical six-pointed star greeted visitors at the entrance to the cult's amusement park. And now the Black Gangster Disciples, a street gang, marks its territory by spray-painting, on abandoned homes, street signs, and even the walls of the library bathroom, its symbol, a six-pointed star. The symbol's ubiquitous presence can be confusing. A rabbi new to the area saw a six-pointed star spray-painted on the side of a convenience store; the star had been defaced by a rival gang. Unaware of the icon's new symbolism, the rabbi immediately urged her congregation to confront what she thought was anti-Semitism in the community.

In the summer of 1953, Bennie Bowers, Ruth McGinnis's father, joined the migration of blacks from south to north, traveling from Middleton, Tennessee, to Flint, where, a distant relative had told him, there was an abundance of jobs in General Motors' sprawling plants. Ruth, his oldest child, was six at the time. He landed a job on the assembly line at Buick, but housing was so scarce—he and his family squeezed into one bedroom in a house with six other families—that in four months he went to Benton Harbor, moving everyone in with his sister in public housing. There, he took a job at the Superior Steel Casting Company at $1.11 an hour, and eventually bought a wood-frame home on Buena Vista Street, a quiet, tree-lined lane that, until the mid-1960s, was a mixture of black and white families.

In the 1960s and 1970s, a combination of forces not at all unique to Benton Harbor drained the town of its prosperity: a newly constructed mall lured clothiers and department stores from the downtown; global competition killed off many of the foundries and auto parts plants; urban renewal scattered the black populace, which, for the most part, had remained in a low-lying area by the river called the Flats; and, finally, whites, uneasy with their new neighbors, fled, many of them simply skipping over the river to St. Joseph. Institutions followed, including the newspaper, the YMCA, the hospital, even the local FBI offices. Each had its own reason for moving, which at the time made sense, but in the end, after they'd drifted off, like geese going south, the reasons sounded more like excuses. The final blow, one deep in symbolism, came in 1982, when members of Benton Harbor's oldest church, the First Congregational Church of Christ, split on the decision to move. The debate became so heated that friendships ruptured and families divided, and in the end half the congregation, along with the minister, left for St. Joseph and started their own church.

It has since been said that even God fled the black tide by crossing the river.

Ruth raised Eric in a Benton Harbor much different from the one she'd known as a child. By the time Eric was born, whites made up only 13 percent of Benton Harbor, down from 75 percent twenty years earlier. And the city was so poor that its five police cars had been repossessed; the police had to, as a result, drive cars belonging to the city's building inspectors and carry hand-held radios. The fire department's one pumper used a garden hose. In 1981, there was even talk of disbanding the city government and contracting out essential services. The main boulevard, once host to Sears and two other department stores, had become a strip of burned-out storefronts and surprisingly few vacant lots; it was too expensive for the city to demolish the structures. St. Joseph residents referred to the town as "Benton Harlem" (while those in Benton Harbor called the town across the way "St. Johannesburg").

Situated halfway between Chicago and Detroit, Benton Harbor has become a refuge for young men and women running from troubled families, gangs, and the law in these larger cities. It is also an obvious business expansion site for drug lords, who, despite the city's small size, can retain some anonymity. It's common knowledge that the Benton Harbor police department is so understaffed that its officers have little time to investigate anything other than the most heinous crimes, usually murders. During one of my visits, I learned that the department's lone detective barely had time to pursue the city's recent homicide, the eighth in as many months. The three hundred cases on backlog included alleged rapes, shootings, and petty larcenies. Property crimes, the lowest priority, weren't even included. "If you ain't bleeding," the detective told me, "you ain't going to make it on the list."

Ruth, like many parents here, has struggled to keep these forces at bay. She and Eric's father, Excell, were divorced when Eric was an infant. For the child's first four years, Ruth lived close to where she had grown up. But in the winter of 1981, she awoke to a desperate voice outside her window. "Somebody help me. Please, somebody help me." She opened the front door, and there lay a man, shot in an argument, dying in a snowdrift in her front yard. Soon afterward, Ruth moved into Benton Manor, an apartment complex technically in Benton Township, but with a Benton Harbor address and just a short bike ride from the town's main drag. The neighborhood, despite its proximity to the town, is more rural than urban; some of the roads remain unpaved, and Lake Michigan sits a quarter-mile away. And the complex itself, with its red-brick rowhouses, manicured lawns, and fenced-in play area, is handsome and tidy, and removed from the noisier life of the town proper.

"Most of the kids don't like it out here, because there's nothing to do," says Ruth. "It's too far away. But we adults love it. We have a lot of curfews out here, a lot of rules. They keep people out of trouble, and you know where your kid is. Eric liked it okay at the beginning. As he got older, of course, he wanted to go on the other side of town."

Ruth got the news from her uncle Jim Coburn. It was Wednesday, and Eric had been missing since Friday night, when his father had dropped him off at the Club. At first Ruth thought her son may have driven to Grand Rapids with some friends; the school year was nearing completion and spring had arrived, so the teens were celebratory and restless. Or maybe, Eric's friends suggested, he had rented a hotel room for himself and his girlfriend, something he had done before. But when Saturday morning came and went, and Ruth had heard nothing from Eric, she called the police to report him missing.

That Saturday evening, she says, "was the hardest part of my life, just waiting to hear something." Sunday dragged. Each phone ring, each knock on the door, each car pulling into the complex, made Ruth hopeful. Word spread. Some of Eric's friends handed out his photos to local stores. Monday, Ruth returned to work, barely able to focus. "I was climbing the walls," she says. By Wednesday, she was so distraught that she left work in the morning to visit the assistant principal at the high school, Ken Overley. Had he heard anything? Could he question some of Eric's friends? He said he would. On the way home, Ruth stopped at the Coburns', where she joined Jim's wife for a cup of coffee. "I'm still not quite falling apart, thinking maybe he's just out having a good time," she recalls. When Jim came by the house a few minutes later, she knew. "You found Eric, didn't you? He's dead, isn't he?" she asked. Jim nodded. "I'm sorry."

Ruth remembers being unusually collected. "I've got to call my mom and sister," she thought to herself. When she arrived home, she placed pictures of Eric all around the living room, on the television, on the coffee table, even on the kitchen counter. She then took out her Bible and opened it to the 23rd Psalm, which she used to read to Eric during trying times, when she didn't have the money to buy him a new pair of shoes or after he'd flunked driver's education for the third time.

> The Lord is my shepherd; I shall want nothing
> He makes me lie down in green pastures,
> and leads me beside the waters of peace;
> He renews life within me,
> and for his name's sake guides me in the right path.
> Even though I walk through a valley dark as death,
> I fear no evil, for thou art with me,
> thy staff and thy crook are my comfort.

With the Bible in one hand and Eric's picture in the other, she rocked back and forth, her eyes tightly shut. She can't recall what images rolled through her mind; the days following the discovery of her son's body are all a haze now, so thick and disorienting that Ruth hesitates to revisit them. She vaguely remembers friends and relatives coming by the apartment, alternately hugging her and asking whether she needed anything. One of her younger brothers, Bennie Bowers, Jr., a state trooper, drove in from Kalamazoo. Her closest friend, Louise Strand, hurried down from Grand Rapids. Her minister, the Reverend Alfred Johnson, came over. As did friends from work, both black and white. But Ruth felt disembodied, as if she were watching this happen to someone else, and it was someone else who had lost a son. At one point, she felt so hemmed in by the people and the noise that, unnoticed by her visitors, she walked out the front door, picked up a branch lying beneath a pine tree, and began to swing it gently at the ground. As if she were wielding a divining rod searching for water, she carved wandering lines in the dry dirt along the roadside. Walking slowly by the modest wood-frame houses, she thought, "Why me? I should never have let him go over there." In the late afternoon sun, a neighbor plowed ground for a garden; another sat on his front stoop. They certainly had no idea of the weight bearing down on this lone woman, walking aimlessly, her stick stirring up small dust storms. But to Ruth "it just felt like everybody knew." About a hundred yards down the street, where the unpaved Lafayette Road meets Madeline Avenue, she paused and picked up a golf ball–size stone, which she heaved into the woods across the way, aiming for a cluster of rusted-out junk—two metal barrels, a washing machine resting on its side, and a set of boxsprings. "I wanted to hit something. Do something." The rock ricocheted off a tree. Perhaps it was the hollow sound of stone against wood or the emptiness about her, but Ruth began to cry—for the first time. She couldn't stop. And as she turned to go home, now eager for the company of friends and family, she mumbled over and over, "I can't believe it. I can't believe it. I can't believe it."

There are many difficult moments for a police officer, but certainly none more distressing than having to deliver news that someone's child has died. That's what Reeves thought he was doing when he drove out to see Ruth. He could remember, all too vividly, the time a teenage boy was hit and then dragged by a pickup truck outside St. Joseph High School. Reeves, who had been the first on the scene, took it on himself to visit the boy's father, who, it turned out, had already heard of his son's death. But the father asked Reeves to tell his ten-year-old daughter; he himself didn't have the strength. Reeves remembered the discomfort he felt, sitting at the foot of the girl's bed and watching her face grow long and weary as he delivered the news. He recalled this moment as he drove to Ruth's.

Ruth stood in the doorway, her gaze direct and, like the girl's, already weary. It was clear to him from the moment he caught her silhouette in the screen door that she already knew. Her head, her shoulders, her arms, all of her seemed to be battling, unsuccessfully, the weight she carried. Her body dragged. Her profile—the round face, the full, shapely lips, the high cheekbones—blurred by the screen door, looked familiar, though he couldn't place it. Reeves reached out to take her hand, sandwiching it between his own. "I'm so sorry, I'm so sorry, I'm so sorry," he repeated clumsily, unsure of what else to say.

The two shuffled into the living room and sat side by side on the couch. Reeves held Ruth's hand again and told her what he knew, which at that point wasn't much. Her son, he said, had been found floating in the river by the Coast Guard station; a medical examiner would perform an autopsy later that day. Reeves asked Ruth to describe the clothes Eric had been wearing; he wanted to confirm that they had identified the right boy. Ruth described it all, including the turquoise ring, which had been given him by his father. She also mentioned a long green winter jacket, made by Task Force, a brand popular among black teens. She remembered it well because she had bought it for him the previous Christmas and had commented to Eric, before he left for the Club, that it was too heavy for such mild weather. Also, Eric, who had high tastes in fashion, had had a friend's mother sew on it a fake fur collar cut from a ragged piece he had bought at a tag sale for a dollar. "He wanted it to be different," she said. Reeves made note of it. No coat had been found with the body.

"Can you tell me when you last saw him?" he asked.

"Friday night," she replied, kneading a ball of Kleenex. "Eric had been staying with his dad. He called me around five o'clock and asked, 'Mom, if Dad takes me, can I go to the Club?' I said, 'Sure.' Then he asked, 'Would you give me five dollars?' I said sure to that, too. Then I called him back and said, 'You be sure on your way over here you stop and get me a sandwich.' And he said, 'Yeah, no problem.' So they came through here around a quarter to nine. I'll never forget the time, because I'm a diehard Pistons' fan, and I was watching the game. That's the reason I wanted him to bring me a sandwich, because I didn't want to get up and leave. And he brought me a hamburger and fries from Henry's and I gave him five one-dollar bills. He asked, 'How do I look? Do you like my new cologne?' And I told him he looked nice. He was dressed real nice. I asked him why he had that big heavy coat on. He told me, 'It might get chilly, silly.' He asked me about his haircut. I said, 'You look really nice. You have a good time and stay out of trouble.' He said, 'Oh, I will.' I said, 'If you don't have a way home and your dad can't pick you up, you call me. I'll be here.' Usually if there was a group coming back they'd all ride together. And then he looked at me and says, 'Remember I love you. And don't say I never done anything for you.' And he teased me about the game. 'The Bulls are going to kick their butt.' Yeah, we used to argue so much about the games. That was it until his dad called me Saturday and wanted to know if Eric was here."

Reeves told Ruth that they had found some money on Eric.

"How much?" she asked.

"Forty-seven dollars," Reeves mistakenly told her. It was actually $49.

As Reeves thanked Ruth and again offered his condolences, she handed him the picture of Eric in the white turtleneck. It was the only look he would get of Eric, since he didn't plan to attend the autopsy; he didn't have the stomach for it. Reeves admired the handsome boy in the photo. Ruth melted into the couch. "Are you sure?" she asked. "Are you sure?" She breathed deeply and quickly, pulling in air as if she too were drowning. "My baby. My baby. My baby." Reeves took her hand.

"What really bothered me," Reeves said later, "was that Ruth was about my age, and seeing what she was going through, I got to thinking about my own daughter. That's a terrible thing, to lose a child. Parents are supposed to go before their children. I went home that night and just hugged Makenna, held her in my arms.

"Also, we didn't have any answers except that the body was Eric's. She asked all sorts of questions, but all I could do was tell her what I knew. We were waiting for the autopsy report. I really thought there'd be some logical explanation as to what happened. Right away when you have a young black man floating in the river who was last seen in a predominantly white community, you can visualize anything happening."

"This might sound strange," Ruth told me, "but it was about four or five days after Eric had died, I was in the basement where we used to live, and it was like he was talking to me, telling me what had happened. I know that sounds weird. A lot of people go, 'Yeah, right.' But I don't know if I wanted to believe something so badly, now that I think back about it. I wrote down what I thought he told me and put it in an envelope. 'I got into some trouble and was chased. Things that you didn't know about.' I couldn't put it all together because there was just bits and pieces. 'There is somebody else involved' . . . I couldn't put a face with it . . . So I ended up tearing it up."

5.

AND FRIENDS

The skullcaps pulled low over their heads hid the tears. These friends of Eric's, maybe fifteen or twenty teenage boys, gathered on the freshly mowed lawn outside Ruth's home. They bounced from foot to foot, their hands deep in their pockets, their heads deep in their shoulders. A few brandished wooden canes, a fashion statement at the time, waving them around like the long swords of ancient warriors. Ruth could hear the loud, blustery talk through her open living room window.

"Eric ain't deserve this."

"You know them motherfuckers covering up something over there."

"Ain't that the truth."

"They knew what was going on."

"Man, they probably got something to do with it."

They shook and cursed and grumbled some more, and then one of them suggested, "Man, we should go over that bridge and do the same to them." There were shouts of encouragement and talk of the havoc they could wreak. Smash store windows. Burn down the Club. Storm the high school. Just plain put the fear of God into those people across the river.

Ruth donned her coat and walked into this sea of angry adolescent faces. Her presence brought an immediate calm. The canes came down by their sides. Their high-pitched threats drifted harmlessly into the wind. "They were just waiting for me to say, 'Go get them,' " she recalls. "They were ready to go over there and tear down every store. But I didn't want another child killed. I was hurting so bad, I was thinking of every other mother coming back and saying, 'If you hadn't done this, my son would be alive.' I couldn't live with that . . . I just wanted answers. Answers. I just wanted answers."

One boy told Ruth, "Mrs. McGinnis, this ain't right." The others, in chorus, nodded in agreement and nervously pawed the ground with their feet. Tears rolling down her cheeks, she pleaded with them. Don't go into St. Joseph. Don't seek revenge. Don't hurt someone else. "Guys, I'm going through so much now," she told them. "I know. I miss Eric, too."

"No, Mrs. McGinnis, they wrong," one boy responded, politely but firmly. "See, they didn't want us over there in the first place. That's why they did this."

"We don't know what happened," she told them. "We're just trying to wait and see, and besides I don't want any of you guys hurt. Let the police do their work. They'll get to the bottom. Please."

The boys, heeding Ruth, hung around for much of the afternoon, recalling Eric and damning St. Joseph for its whiteness, its prosperity, its smugness. For these boys, the neighbors across the way were the enemy.

Rumors about Eric's death flowed fast. There was the report that he had been found with a noose around his neck, that his hands had been tied behind his back. A rumor that the relatives of a white girl he dated had done him in. That an older white man, seen chasing him down the street, had forced him into the river. One story had it that a group of white boys, agitated that Eric had dared to dance with a white girl, beat him and pushed him into the river. There was even a rumor that Eric had committed suicide.

At Benton Harbor High School, students learned of Eric's death when it was announced over the PA system during sixth period. As they had done on Ruth's lawn, young boys filled the hallways, surging with bravado, boasting of what they planned to do to St. Joseph. Word spread that one group intended to go over the bridge en masse. One boy strutted through the hallways, pounding on the thin metal lockers with his fists, screaming, "Kill the white people! Kill the white people! Kill the white people!" A white student—there were roughly a hundred in the school—eating lunch outside was coldcocked by a black teen. Two other white students were jumped after school.

The school administration called an assembly for the next day to allow students to let off steam. The students seethed. One boy went to the microphone and announced, "I don't like white people. Never liked white people. If they die, they die." When an administrator suggested that they calm down and give Eric a moment of silence, Donnie Allen, a close friend of Eric's, rose from his seat and shouted, "Fuck that! We know who killed him. Let's get them. Let's blow up that club." The students roared their approval.

Bennie Bowers, Ruth's brother and a Benton Harbor High School graduate, took the stage. Though not in his state trooper's uniform, at six-foot-four inches and a highly sculpted 250 pounds Bennie cut an impressive figure. Moreover, he'd been a football and basketball star here, earning athlete-of-the-year honors when he graduated in 1976. He knew these halls well. He also knew Eric well. On weekends Eric would visit Bennie and his wife and two children in Kalamazoo, an hour's drive from Benton Harbor. Just hang out. Shoot baskets. Eat pizza. Work on stereos. Play with Bennie's kids.

Bennie had been told that some of the kids were talking of marching into St. Joseph. He had seen one boy walking around outside the school with a cane in hand, and that worried him. He warned the students at the assembly: "A naïve police officer hears gun and he sees a kid with a cane, and bang-bang the kid's dead. This is the wrong way to go about it. It's not going to bring Eric back." The students grew quiet as Bennie continued. "There'll be an investigation," he promised. "We don't know what happened. But you can't go and take this in your hands. Let the police do their job. They'll find out what happened to Eric. Just let 'em do their job. They'll get to the bottom of it. I'll make sure of that." He told them that he had viewed the photos, and contrary to what students had heard, there was no noose. He then pleaded that anyone who knew anything about the night Eric disappeared should talk to him. The NAACP had posted a $600 reward for information.

Students continued to ask questions, their emotions still high. "What are the police going to do if a white kid gets thrown into the river?" one asked. "People would be upset, and here we're asked to be quiet."

"Man, you know it's racial. You know that."

"We got to throw one of them in the river."

The next day, three young black men armed with a pipe and a revolver brutally beat a white couple necking at Tiscornia Park, a pristine Lake Michigan beach just north of the river. Two friends of Eric's cornered a white woman pushing her cart in a grocery store aisle and taunted her in whispered tones with "Nigger killer, nigger killer." Five black youths interrupted a girls' softball practice at a local parochial school, threatening to assault the players. And a man who refused to give his name called the St. Joseph police dispatcher.

"That shit will continue to happen unless we get some information about Eric McGinnis. Next time someone will get hurt seriously," the voice said.

"What's your name?" the dispatcher asked calmly.

"Don't worry about my fuck'n name, bitch. You might be next."

Benton Harbor parents told their children, particularly their sons, not to go into St. Joseph—and that if they did, to exercise great caution.

Meanwhile, occasional carloads of young white men sped through the streets of Benton Harbor. One car followed Donnie Allen down a residential street until it came abreast of him. A white man leaned out the window and hollered, "We're going to get you. We're going to get you motherfuckers." Wheels squealed. Donnie ran.

A Benton Harbor patrol officer saw a carload of white teens tooling down Empire, a notoriously dangerous strip, and hollering out the window, "It was just a nigger; don't get upset about it!"

For their part, St. Joseph residents girded for the assault. The Club closed down after getting word that carloads of blacks were on their way to shoot up the place. Parents kept their children home from school. And the police, on high alert, patrolled the high school's graduation practice.

"This was a time bomb ready to go off," says Reeves. "That river is a real hindrance, a real divide."

One night I had a dream that the St. Joseph River was boiling, the bubbles huge and menacing, the steam thick and suffocating. The water, as it swashed along the banks, flowed over, forcing onlookers to flee its blistering rush. In the dream, the river spilled just into Benton Harbor. But in the case of Eric McGinnis, the scalding river flooded both shores—and people on both sides fought it the only way they knew how: by rallying their forces, by retreating, by taking refuge behind a high wall of rhetoric. The adversary, each side believed, lurked on the other side of the roiling river. But there were reasons that went well beyond Eric's death.

6.

THE SHOOTER

The shooting of Norris Maben, a twenty-one-year-old petty thief, occurred a year and a half before Eric's death. Those who wanted to believe that Eric had, indeed, been killed—and killed at the hands of whites—needed to look no further than the killing of this young black man. The facts seemed evident: he was shot by a white policeman, Marv Fiedler. But the truth was more elusive. Fiedler, for all his years on the force, should not have been on the street pursuing a suspected killer. Particularly by himself. He was too old. Too slow. Too nice.

If Jim Reeves can be characterized as a small-town cop, then Fiedler was a small-town cop from an earlier era, when a police officer swung a nightstick in one hand and carried chewing gum for the neighborhood kids in the other. At fifty-seven, he had spent over half his life as a police officer in Benton Harbor; it was his only law enforcement job. In those years of tooling around in a patrol car he had put on weight, and had a soft look about him. His head, reaching out from his hunched shoulders, gave him the appearance of a tortoise in search of food. His oversize glasses, outsize ears, and a left eyebrow that jumped when he spoke accentuated his physical awkwardness, and his gravelly voice, no doubt the result of his three- to four-pack-a-day habit, had a John Wayne tone to it, but without the bravado. There was, as with Reeves, nothing daring about Fiedler. In fact, his fellow officers called him Mother Marv.

They ragged on Fiedler for being nosy and maternal. "He always needed to know everything. He'd look over your shoulder if you were typing," recalls a former police clerk. He'd send officers on assignment, and before they'd even left the parking lot, his voice would crackle over the police radio: "Now be careful," or "Did you remember the warrant?" Once a rookie cop reported over his patrol car radio that he was taking a boy into custody. Fiedler ordered the rookie into the station. "You don't use the word 'boy,' " Fiedler lectured. "But he was maybe six or seven years old," the man argued. "I know what you mean, but other people might not."

His busybody and sometimes bumbling nature made him the butt of practical jokes. Someone once taped *Mother Marv* over his nametag. Oblivious of his altered ego, Fiedler wore the tag all day, to the stifled chuckles of the other officers. Another time, a fellow patrolman placed an envelope in an overhead light fixture. "Marv was always picking up stuff," recalls Gary Ruhl, now the county's undersheriff. "They knew he was the only person in the world who would try to get that envelope." Sure enough, Marv kept glancing up at the fixture as he went in and out of the station during his eight-hour shift. Before going home, he craned his neck one last time, turning his head this way and that way, trying to assess the contents of the mailer. The intrigue was too much. He climbed up on a chair, removed the light fixture, retrieved the envelope, and tore it open. The paper inside read: "Fuck you, Mother Marv." As always, he took the ribbing good-naturedly; he walked away, mumbling, "Those guys are messing with me again."

Fiedler was, by almost all accounts, a genuinely good-hearted person. He occasionally bought dead-bolt locks for residents too poor to afford them. He once gave gas money to a stranded motorist. "I've seen suspects cuss and rant and rave, and Marv would say, 'Now, brother, you don't want to talk like that,' " recalls the former clerk. "They'd be shaking hands before he left."

When Fiedler responded to domestic disputes where alcohol was involved, he'd walk around the house collecting the half-filled wine or liquor bottles, and then flush the contents down the sink. "Ignorant oil," he'd call it. "It pissed people off," says Tim O'Brien, a fellow officer.

Officers joked about Fiedler's inept handling of a gun. No one, they say, wanted to stand next to him during shooting practice, because he would mistakenly hit their targets. "Marv couldn't intentionally hit a human being with a gun. He drank so much coffee, he just had a natural shake," says Milt Agay, who at one point was the department's firing range officer. "Marv couldn't get the bullets where he was supposed to get them. You'd have run him through five times before he'd qualify." Says Dale Easton, a former Benton Harbor officer, "He was one of the worst shots in the department. He drank so much coffee, smoked so many cigarettes, his hand would shake on the range."

I tell you all this for a reason. No one could believe that Marv Fiedler could or would kill a man, even someone he thought was wanted for murder.

Benton Harbor residents greeted the new decade with anxiety. The last few months of 1989 had been frightful. Drug gangs, modeled after Chicago's notorious Disciples and Vicelords, had taken hold, giving this small town a big-city feel. And these gangs, in turn, were being challenged by outsiders from Detroit. Over the preceding twelve months there had been nine murders, an unusually high number for a city of twelve thousand. And the worst was yet to come. Almost all the victims were black—as were their killers. The shootings in Benton Harbor had become so frequent that Dan Levy, then an assistant county prosecutor, remembers hearing the occasional gunshot echo from across the river as he walked from his apartment in downtown St. Joseph.

Fiedler reported for work at 6:45 A.M. on Thursday, January 18, 1990, a bleak winter day, the temperature just above freezing, a blustery, arctic wind blowing down from the north. The Benton Harbor police station sits at the foot of a bluff, a couple of blocks off the town's main street. It is like a bunker, an unimpressive, one-story brick building, angular and squat. The front lobby is the size of a walk-in closet; a visitor who needs to speak with an officer waits on one of two cracked plastic chairs stuffed into a corner too dark to permit reading. Behind bulletproof glass sits the dispatcher, with her radio equipment and a color TV usually tuned to daytime talk shows. The squad room, toward the back, consists of a labyrinth of metal desks hidden by piles of reports and files. A stereo plays an endless selection of pop songs.

The new year, though young, looked to be no safer or calmer than the previous months. In the first two and a half weeks of January, the police received, on average, two calls a day of gunfire, mostly from one of the public housing complexes and a neighborhood eight blocks from the police station. I've walked in that neighborhood many times and over the years have attempted to count the vacant or fire-damaged homes, but it's a moving number. One two-story building I've seen with plywood over the windows—and then off—and then on again—and even on the last occasion there seemed to be some activity in the shuttered house. In spring and fall, because the drainage system clogs, rainwater creates small ponds a foot deep. It's not to say that some of the homes aren't well tended. A few houses stand out like tulips in a field of weeds. One is painted fluorescent yellow; another, lollipop purple. At one bungalow, the elderly owner constructed a white picket fence by hand, the boards nailed at slightly skewed angles, though now one three-foot-long section is down, run over by drug dealers and gang members using her back and side yards as a shortcut from one street to the other.

The streets are not easily navigable. Some potholes are so wide and deep that the city has placed orange barrels in them to warn motorists. Many alleyways have become dumping grounds for household junk—box springs, chairs, tables, dressers, televisions— that create an obstacle course. And if you're on foot, you have to contend with stray dogs that roam around in packs, hungry and tired. They have been such a problem that animal control officers at times become small-game hunters, shooting wild dogs on sight.

In this neighborhood just three months earlier, on the evening of September 13, Pat Gibson, a seventeen-year-old, was shot to death as she walked toward her home. Photos taken at the crime scene show her lying on her side on the cracked sidewalk next to an overturned shopping cart, her white jogging suit curiously unstained by the puddle of blood around her head. Somewhere, according to the police report, is a bag of potato chips she'd been eating, but I can't find it in the picture. Nor can I locate the bullet entry in her forehead. Nor can I place where she is in Benton Harbor, though the police report tells me it's on the 200 block of Lake Street. The police in the weeks preceding this shooting had made a number of substantial drug busts here; they'd seized eleven handguns, eleven cars, a kilo of cocaine, and $25,000 in cash, and had arrested some of the top echelons of the Black Gangster Disciples, which controlled drug traffic in the neighborhood. The problem, though, as the police soon learned, is that success, in the most traditional sense of police work, often creates only greater problems. With one gang in tatters, two gangs, the Corleones and the Best Friends, both from Detroit, arrived in town to fill the void, and began, in the most brutal of fashions, to claim the distribution of crack on streetcorners and from homes here on Benton Harbor's south side. Several Black Gangster Disciples had been shot by the arrivals from Detroit.

On this particular evening, Gibson, who had been strolling with two friends along the street, said good night and headed in the opposite direction for home. Witnesses say they heard four, maybe five gunshots. Gunshots are so common here that neighbors can distinguish the sounds, and they identified the weapons as a handgun and a shotgun. The police had an immediate suspect, Tracey Hibbler, a twenty-eight-year-old Benton Harbor native, whom they knew well. Hibbler had been arrested for a series of crimes, from carrying an open beer can in his car to assault with intent do great bodily harm, for which he served time in prison. According to Earlene Parks, who said she was an eyewitness, Hibbler approached Pat Gibson and demanded $10 owed him so that he could buy a rock of crack. When she refused, so the account went, Hibbler pulled out a 9 mm handgun and shot her. The Benton Harbor police put Hibbler's name out across the wire, warning that "he should be considered armed and dangerous."

January 18 posed nothing out of the ordinary for Marv Fiedler. At about one-thirty in the afternoon he responded to a 911 call; a teenage girl had been accidentally shot in the chest by a boyfriend who was cleaning his .22-caliber pistol. When Fiedler arrived at the home of the victim, he handcuffed the boyfriend and took him back to the station.

As Fiedler booked the suspect, near the end of his shift, Alice Palmer, the sister of murder victim Pat Gibson, called the dispatcher to say she had spotted Tracey Hibbler. He had apparently fled town after the killing, though the Benton Harbor police heard only a few days earlier that he had returned to the area. Palmer reported that Hibbler was walking along the 700 block of Pavone, three blocks from where Gibson had been killed. With only two uniformed officers on duty and the lone detective tied up on the recent accidental shooting, Fiedler, who ranked as a lieutenant, volunteered to handle the call. In most towns or cities, a police officer would never attempt to arrest a suspected murderer by himself or herself, but here in Benton Harbor, which could afford only two road officers on duty, the department was left with little choice. Fiedler's partner stayed to process the assault suspect while Fiedler sped over to Pavone, ten blocks from the station. The dispatcher passed on a description of Hibbler; she told Fiedler he was wearing a blue jeans jacket with a fur collar, black sweat pants, and a brown hat with a brim. Fiedler was also told that Hibbler wore his hair in braids.

When Fiedler got to Pavone, a lone man was standing on the streetcorner. No, he told Fiedler, he hadn't seen anyone wearing a brimmed hat. Fiedler slowly circled the block, past the boarded-up homes and wreck-filled lots, when he saw two young men duck into a two-story brown clapboard house. It is like so many homes in Benton Harbor: sickly. When I visited the house two years later, I found half a dozen window panes missing from the front porch and a basketball-size hole punched into the foundation; to the left of the hole, by the front steps, a black scorch mark reached to the front door, as if someone had tried to set the place on fire. The roof, inexplicably, had become a kind of miniature junkyard, though the only objects on it I could clearly identify were two bicycle tires. And like so many of the homes here, this one-family house had been converted into two apartments, one above the other.

I've tried to imagine what Fiedler was thinking that afternoon as he drove up to this dreary house on Pavone to arrest Hibbler. Had his time in Benton Harbor made such a potentially dangerous call seem routine? Or, knowing that Hibbler was suspected of shooting a teenage girl, was he on edge, anticipating a violent confrontation? Or did Fiedler, ever affable, think he would be able to coax the murder suspect to give himself up? What happened next, though, is, according to public record, fairly clear.

He spotted a short man, dressed in dark clothing, and wearing a small brimmed hat. "I thought that was Tracey Hibbler, who we had the warrant for," Fiedler later testified. "That's who I thought it was." He gave the dispatcher his location and got out of his car at the house the men had entered. After walking up the makeshift front steps, three unpainted two-by-fours nailed loosely in place, he knocked on the first-floor apartment door. A young boy, maybe five or six years old, answered. Had he seen two men enter? The boy nodded. Did he know where they went? The boy pointed upstairs. "At that point, I told him to go back into the house," Fiedler later testified.

He trudged up the dark stairwell, knocked on the second-floor apartment. A large middle-aged woman, Tina, opened the door, which led directly into her spare, tidy kitchen. "Where are they?" Fiedler asked.

"No one's here."

Fiedler told her of his conversation with the boy downstairs. The taller of the two men quietly walked into the small, crowded kitchen and placed himself behind the neatly set Formica table, which took up most of the room and separated him and Fiedler.

"Do you have any ID?" Fiedler asked.

The man produced a driver's license attesting to the fact that he was Sam Buchanan. "Is there anyone else here?" Fiedler inquired, craning his neck to look into the living room.

"No. No one else here."

Another man, much shorter, walked into the kitchen. "What's your name?" Fiedler asked.

"Maben."

Fiedler spotted a rusting butcher knife, twelve inches long, lying on the kitchen table. Tina, it turned out, used it as a security measure; with the blade stuck into a crack in the doorframe, the handle acted to barricade the door. "I grabbed the knife and either handed it to her or laid it on top of the stove," Fiedler later testified, "but I got it away from in front of him . . . I believed it was Tracey Hibbler."

"Can I see your ID?"

"Don't have any," the young man replied.

Fielder clumsily reached with his right hand toward the man he thought was Hibbler so that he could pat his coat pockets for a wallet or possible gun. But before he could reach all the way, the suspect grabbed Fiedler's arm and flung it to the side, momentarily knocking him off balance. As he tried to regain his footing, the suspect bolted from the kitchen through the living room and into the back bedroom, and before Fiedler could even give chase, he heard the shattering of glass. He ran to the bedroom. The suspect had vaulted, head first, through the closed window, landed on the back porch roof, and then dropped fifteen feet onto the patchy grass in the backyard. He then sprinted diagonally away from the house toward the muddy, rutted alley.

Fiedler had shot his gun only once before while on duty, and that was in his rookie year, when his training officer ordered him to shoot a warning shot as they chased a stolen car, according to fellow officers. Fiedler testified that he yelled three times for the suspect to halt and that when the suspect got near the alley, between two bare trees, he stopped and turned toward the house and Fiedler. The suspect reached into his back pocket and then raised his hands as he looked up at Fiedler. Fiedler, immediately thinking that the suspect had reached for a gun, reacted so fast that he can't remember whether he held his .38-caliber Smith & Wesson six-shot service revolver with one hand or two. Or whether he kneeled or stood. "I thought he was going for a gun. I drew my gun and shot three times quick."

He dashed down the stairs, around the house, into the backyard, and knelt by the young man, who lay on his back, his arms stretched over his twitching shoulders. A gray brimmed hat, two quarters, and an orange keyring lay scattered beside him. Blood oozed from a small wound near the left nipple, just to the side of the heart. Fiedler felt for a pulse on the victim's neck. Nothing. A woman who lived nearby walked toward him.

"Oh, my God, that's one of the Maben kids," she said.

Fiedler froze, his gaze directed at the still body. "Shit," he muttered. "I shot the wrong kid."

He slowly rose and walked toward a nearby tree, kicking at a crumpled beer can in disgust. He pulled out his radio; "I shot somebody," he tersely told the dispatcher.

smiled and thought, "Now this is going to be good. Living here, right off the lake." But as he drove past the pleasant vistas, past the Mansion Grille Restaurant, past the Snow Flake, a Frank Lloyd Wright–inspired motel, past Monet's, a coffee shop, he got the uneasy feeling that he was, in fact, not in Benton Harbor. This was not as it had been described to him.

"And then I had to stop for directions, because it was taking me so long," he recalls. "I thought I was in Benton Harbor, but I didn't know. They said, 'No, you got to follow the road and you'll see the sign.' Well, I saw the sign and I turned, and as I hit the crest of the hill on the bridge, I said, 'Oh, Lord.' "

People joke that the Bicentennial Bridge is the longest in the world. I used to grimace whenever I heard that, a remark made more often than not by the people of St. Joseph, but I concede that, though the bridge is only a quarter of a mile long, it joins two landscapes so dissimilar that, even after you've made dozens of trips, the view can take your breath away. Traveling across that span was so unsettling that I got into the habit of scheduling interviews each day for only one side of the river. I couldn't manage—not quickly enough, anyway—to avoid some resentment and indignation each time I crossed the river. And it had nothing to do with race or political ideology. For each time I hit the crest of the hill on the bridge, I saw what the Reverend Johnson saw: a landscape so shriveled and stooped that it appeared near death—and yet, as I drove cautiously down the ruptured streets, as the smell of burned wood from another house fire wafted through my car window, as I passed the group of unkempt men aimlessly chatting by the downtown soup kitchen, I was reminded that this, for some, was home.

As the Reverend Johnson drove over the bridge down the town's four-lane Main Street, here's what he saw: two car dealerships (one of which has since closed), a vacant motel (now operating under the misleading name: The *St. Joseph* Riverwatch), the marquee of the boarded-up Liberty Theater, which, as if mocking its town, read WE—ME THE NEW B—ON HARBOR. Abandoned downtown stores had imploded, their innards piled high and some of the debris—bricks and twisted furniture—hanging halfway out the glassless display windows. It is a city so without resources that when a major street collapsed two years before Johnson arrived, the city could afford to fill it in only with dirt.

When Johnson left town the next day, he drove back over the Bicentennial, from Benton Harbor to St. Joseph, and as he learned, was *not* greeted by the latter's sprightly downtown. Instead, looming on a hill, like a watchtower, sat a concrete fortress: the sheriff's office and jail. Next to it, also built in an august style, was the county courthouse, an imposing square structure. Whether there was intention or not, the buildings stood as a warning, an admonition to those crossing into St. Joe: Don't forget where you are—and don't forget who runs this county. I've heard black teens whisper that the sheriff's department had a lookout tower so that it could keep tabs on them as they walked or biked or drove across the bridge into St. Joseph. Nothing of the sort existed, as far as I know, but buttressing the perception was the schoolyard-size recreational area for the prisoners jutting out from one end of the jail. It was encircled by a high wire-mesh fence topped with barbed wire, and in one corner stood a wooden guard tower, with a view not only of the yard but also of the bridge and all those who might cross it.

"If I lived in Benton Harbor, I'd think that building was there to keep an eye on us," said a white law enforcement official new to the area. "For the life of me, I can't figure out why they built the sheriff's office and the courts where they did. It's prime real estate."

"It's like the fortress on the river," said Bob DeWitt, a local radio reporter.

It's that citadel which featured in many of the stories conveyed to the Reverend Johnson by his middle-class congregants during his first months in town. These schoolteachers, factory workers, and city employees, despite their stable position, felt that if there was anywhere they didn't want to be, it was the courthouse. If there was anyone they didn't want to face, it was the police. They told the Reverend Johnson that the whites who ran the courts—all nine circuit and district judges and all but one prosecutor were white—and the whites who headed the sheriff's department, the St. Joseph police, and, for that matter, all the law enforcement agencies (except for Benton Harbor's), did not treat the blacks of the county justly. On one of his first visits to the courthouse, to pay child support, he remembers, "I was looking around for black people. I'd go to the clerk's office and all I could see were whites. I said, 'Where are the black judges?' I was saying, 'I know some black folks work here, but where are they?' "

Johnson heard of Maurice Carter, a black man convicted by an all-white jury of shooting an off-duty police officer in Benton Harbor in 1973. Carter is still in prison, serving a life sentence, but it has come out over the years that three prospective black jurors were kept off the jury, including one who allegedly had been excused for job reasons, though she had not requested to be removed from the jury pool. The case, over twenty years old, continues to haunt; it has been the subject of stories on CNN and CBS's *48 Hours,* and has become a cause célèbre for the *Michigan Citizen,* a statewide black newspaper.

Johnson also heard the tale of Floyd Caldwell, who is serving two consecutive life sentences for robbing at knifepoint in 1975 a former county judge and his wife. Caldwell, it turns out, may not have been identified by the judge and his wife in line-ups, but his petition for a new trial has been denied.

But it was the trial of James Rutter, the recently appointed Benton Harbor school superintendent and a member of the Reverend Johnson's church, which was freshest in everyone's mind. A year earlier, Rutter, a respected and admired community leader, had been repeatedly struck by a white cop. But, people reported between stifled giggles, the real story was the astonishing courtroom exchange between Rutter's attorney and the police officer.

Rutter, then the high school's principal, was returning from the hospital late one night with his thirteen-year-old stepson, Danny Franklin, and his brother-in-law. Danny had fallen off a moped and been injured. The three were zipping along in Rutter's Porsche down Napier Avenue, a four-lane thoroughfare that skirts Benton Harbor, when they were pulled over by Ed Siedenstrang, a Benton Township patrolman. Rutter allegedly had been driving fifty-five miles per hour, fifteen miles over the speed limit. Making matters worse, Rutter, who had been in a rush to get Danny to a doctor, had left his wallet at home. What happened next is in some dispute, but according to Rutter and other witnesses Siedenstrang whacked him three times with a nightstick on his thigh and then on his wrist, sending his watch into the street. Siedenstrang argued that he was acting in self-defense, since Rutter, a stocky man, had assumed a boxer's stance, his fists clenched in front of him. Siedenstrang also claimed that Rutter muttered that the only reason he'd been stopped was "because I'm a nigger driving a Porsche." The county prosecutor charged Rutter with resisting arrest. Black leaders picketed the Benton Township Hall, demanding the dismissal of Siedenstrang, who had been accused by others, as well, for using excessive force; they also urged the prosecutor to drop the charges. But the case went to trial and might have been forgotten had it not been for the testimony of Louise Wright, a childhood friend of Siedenstrang's.

A year earlier, Wright had asked Siedenstrang to accompany her to the Red Arrow Tap, where her estranged husband was drinking. She wanted the keys to their car. When they got to the Tap, Wright's husband asked them to wait for him outside. Wright testified, "So we—me and Eddie [Siedenstrang]—agreed to go outside and wait for him . . . I hadn't seen Eddie in a long time and we were hugging, you know. And I said, 'Golly, what brings you down

The exchange effectively undermined Siedenstrang's credibility, and an all-white jury acquitted Rutter of resisting arrest, though it did find him guilty of driving without a license and fined him $95. Benton Harbor residents delighted in repeating Siedenstrang's denial that he had ever heard "coon" used to refer to blacks.

So when Marv Fiedler shot Norris Maben a year and a half after Rutter's trial, the Benton Harbor community was thoroughly prepared to believe that another officer had gone coon hunting.

Minutes after the shooting, the Reverend Johnson received a call from a minister whose church was just around the corner from the incident. Johnson, dressed in his gray wool suit (he always wears suits, he says, because "you don't want to be mistaken"), hurried over.

Word had already spread. A cop shot a kid. Shot him in the back. Shot him at point-blank range. Shot him while he was cuffed. Men, women, and children gathered in the rutted alleyway. They stood shoulder to shoulder on the sidewalk and in the street, pressing against the yellow police tape hung from tree to tree like a spider web. They shifted and buzzed like captured flies. Twenty-five people. Fifty. A hundred. As many as a hundred and fifty at any given time that afternoon. The crowd rhythmically grew and shrank and grew as people came to see the body of Norris Maben, lying on his back on a miserable patch of grass in the backyard. The questions and declarations floated among the bystanders, suppositions passed from person to person until repetition made them facts.

"Hey, man, who been shot?"

"Do Dirty." (That was Maben's nickname.)

"You know, Maben."

"Hey, if it had been a white guy, he would have run out that door and tried to catch him. Hey, but he's a black man; a bullet could catch him."

"Shot him in the motherfuck'n back."

"What you gonna do?"

"Ain't make no sense. He didn't have no gun."

"Just another nigger to them."

For a long while, the crowd directed attacks at Tim O'Brien, the younger, more aggressive officer, who had been the first to arrive at the scene. They assumed he had killed Maben. Some in the crowd half-heartedly hurled sticks and small stones at O'Brien and the dozens of other officers who had come from other towns and townships in the county. Reeves, who was among them, sensed the growing unease of the crowd. He told O'Brien, "You'd better get out of here. You're going to get hurt." O'Brien left, hoping his departure would defuse the tension. But at nightfall, six hours after the shooting, firemen directed high-powered beams on the backyard as if they were lighting a theatrical performance, the chalk outline of the body taking center stage. The police performed their roles—collecting evidence, photographing the crime scene, interviewing witnesses—as the audience, faces barely perceptible in the darkness, grew more restless and brazen. The police, worried that the illumination made them easy targets, donned bulletproof vests and lent vests to the technicians from the Michigan State Police crime lab.

Off to the side of the crowd, on the sidewalk, Johnson conferred with other ministers, his lithe, tall frame towering over the others. Earlier they had approached the police, urging them to remove the body, which they had done. Now, Johnson urged the restless crowd to remain calm. "Go on home," he told them. "You can't do anything. There's nothing else to see. Go on; you're not going to do any good here." Once he realized that the people were not heeding his cajoling or his pleading, he walked through the gathering and asked the gawkers whether they had seen anything. Did Maben have a gun? Was he shot in the chest or the back? Where was the officer when he shot Maben? Johnson and the others did their own informal police work, hoping they could get a quick fix on the situation.

"Every police department was there," recalls Johnson, "scouring the community, going door to door. Had it all cordoned off. From the early reports, here you have this white policeman from the second floor looking down at this black male and shooting him. Running away; he's not a threat. If Maben was white, he wouldn't have shot him. He would have gotten on the radio and they would have blanketed the area. Stereotypes. Not being comfortable in an area like Pavone. I'm not really sure why he needed to shoot anybody . . . The police officer is shooting him from an upstairs window. I wanted to know how he could feel his life was being threatened. What was the reason for the shooting? People were getting angry. Nobody who was watching saw Maben with a gun."

The only thing they found on Maben was the set of keys.

8.

THE PROSECUTOR

On the morning of February 8, three weeks after Marv Fiedler killed Norris Maben, Johnson and five other black leaders, including ministers and local NAACP officials, gathered in the office of the county prosecutor, Dennis Wiley. They sat, like schoolchildren, in a semicircle around the cluttered desk as Wiley, looking tired and taut, stood facing them, his hands on the back of his chair, his eyes riveted to the nineteen-page report lying before him. Johnson listened, his mind drifting momentarily as he admired the postcard-like scene behind Wiley. From where he sat, the Reverend Johnson could see the river and, out beyond the lighthouse, ice floes bobbing like corks on the lake. He and the Benton Harbor community had waited, at first patiently and then with irritation, for the prosecutor's determination in the case. And waited. And waited. The days turned to weeks. And in that time, a local radio station reported death threats against Benton Harbor police officers. Angry citizens demanded Fiedler's firing. "It was a vicious act of racism," declared one resident at a city commission meeting. Indeed, just a few days after the shooting, recognizing that his reclusiveness and slow pace had only further agitated people, Wiley met with residents at Johnson's church. While promising a thorough and speedy investigation, he said little about the shooting itself. All that was reported was that Norris Maben had been wanted for driving with a suspended license and with improper registration plates. And that he was not the murder suspect Fiedler thought he was pursuing.

So the Reverend Johnson hurried Wiley through the formalities. He wanted to know whether Wiley intended to prosecute Marv Fiedler—though he figured he already knew the answer.

Wiley had been an assistant prosecutor for eight years, until he was appointed prosecutor in 1989, when his predecessor became a U.S. Attorney. A St. Joseph resident, Wiley is of slight build; his floppy blond hair, drooping eyes, and bushy mustache give him a kind of hangdog look, as if he had been up all night, night after night. He does work long hours, rarely breaking for lunch. I often saw him jogging in the evenings through downtown St. Joseph and by Silver Beach. "He always looks like he's on the last mile of the marathon," said a local attorney. Wiley is, according to admirers and detractors alike, an unusually private, humorless man, uncomfortable among strangers or in crowds, a somewhat puzzling character trait given that he holds elective office. In the courtroom, at early morning Rotary Club breakfasts, and at county Republican gatherings, he can be found standing off to the side, as if he were an uninvited guest. Even with people he knows, he stands at the edge of the group, unwilling to make much eye contact, his mind, it seems, somewhere else.

Wiley, friends say, is fanatically committed to his job and, in particular, is passionate about prosecuting any crime in which a child is the victim. He has six children of his own, and can often be seen in his van picking them up or dropping them off at the high school or church. He has also been an avid booster of the LOFT, a teen center in Benton Harbor, and has on occasion sat in the dunk tank for their annual fundraiser. And one of his first jobs out of Notre Dame Law School was with Berrien County Legal Aid.

"He's not strong. He can't make a decision to save his ass." That view by a local law enforcement officer is shared by many. The common complaint is that he agonizes over decisions, taking too long and often working in near-total seclusion from other community leaders. "To his credit and his detriment, Dennis does not consider public perception," says Dan Levy, the former assistant prosecutor. "He does what he believes to be correct. I never saw anything that I'd consider an impropriety, but there were times the appearance was never addressed. In the sense that he doesn't worry what people will think, I admire him. Dennis doesn't have much contact with the Benton Harbor community; that's true. But I don't think most people have contact with the opposing community. I don't think it's by design; it's just the way it is. It takes effort to have contact with the other community. He doesn't consider that people with a different mindset might see an incident differently."

Such was the case, in the eyes of Johnson and others, in the shooting death of Norris Maben. "I don't think the community is satisfied with the way Wiley handled it. I think they're more upset by the time he took, like it might be more of a coverup," the Reverend Don Adkins told the local paper. Added the Reverend Walter Brown, "Fiedler was a nice guy. I think he was a good cop. How the race thing came in, Wiley held back information, 'cause he always thinks black folks are going to riot. I think Feidler should have been charged. I think what got people hurt, though, was the coverup. He shot and killed a man. Too many mistakes were made. Wiley, to me, tried to cover it up by saying it was justifiable homicide."

Not only did the investigation stretch out over three weeks, in part because Wiley insisted on interviewing some of the witnesses himself, but by most assessments Wiley should have taken himself off the case and turned it over to an outside agency: either the attorney general's office or a prosecutor from another county. The prosecutor in any county is friend and ally of local police officers; it is the nature of the job. He or she relies on cops to do the legwork, to excavate and compile all the evidence—interviews, crime lab work, interpretation of autopsy reports. The police are like archaeologists, digging and uncovering the unknown, while the prosecutor is the historian, synthesizing and presenting—ultimately to judge or jury—the dig's artifacts. Prosecutors cannot afford to have an adversarial relationship with the local police, nor the police with the prosecutor. It is a relationship defined by its symbiosis. And so Wiley should have excused himself from this case, if for no other reason than to preclude the perception that he might be trying to protect the reputation of a cop. Which is how it appeared to the Reverend Johnson.

Wiley had invited Johnson and the others to his office so that he could share with them his findings before releasing them to the press. He lifted the report from his desk, barely glancing at his visitors, and stiffly read it from beginning to end. He explained to the ministers why he had remained mum about the investigation: "Otherwise it would be impossible for investigators to distinguish between 'hearsay' or 'street rumor' accounts from actual eyewitness observations." He then recounted the events of the afternoon, beginning with the suggestion that Maben's clothing—a dark jacket, dark pants, and dark brimmed hat—"closely fit the description of the murder suspect given Lieutenant Fiedler." He said that Fiedler "fired because the suspect turned suddenly, reaching to his side and looking up at him," and that he feared for his safety as well as the safety of the apartment's resident and the young boy downstairs. Wiley quoted an eyewitness as saying that Maben was shot in the chest, and told them that the medical examiner, Dr. E. Arthur Robertson, confirmed that, finding the entrance wound in the upper chest and the exit wound in the lower back. Wiley also mentioned that the Michigan State Police tests on Maben's body indicated traces of cocaine and marijuana in his system.

What did all this mean? Johnson and the others demanded. Would charges be filed against Fiedler? No, Wiley replied. During Fiedler's more than two decades on the force, there had been no citizen complaints regarding any use of excessive force or aggressive behavior. "He had probable cause to believe that Norris Maben was the person named in a valid murder warrant, that he was armed and dangerous to the officer and the community if not immediately apprehended, and was therefore justified in the use of deadly force to prevent his escape," Wiley said. "Thus," he concluded, still reading from the report, "no criminal charges will be filed against Lieutenant Marvin Fiedler at this time."

He looked up from his script and told the leaders that, in his estimation, the shooting of Norris Maben, who by his decision to jump head-first through a second-floor window gave Fiedler reason to believe that he was the murder suspect, was justifiable homicide. The words hung in the air. Justifiable homicide. Johnson, not one for histrionics, was the first to speak. He rose from his chair, again taking in the full view of the river and the lake, and, in an even, almost matter-of-fact voice, said to Wiley, "If that's the case, there's no reason for us to stay here."

"I'm willing to discuss any part of it," Wiley responded.

"You're making the statement that it was justifiable. There's nothing to talk about. I'm leaving."

Johnson thanked Wiley for his time, though he refused to shake hands, and left the office, the others in tow. "That galvanized a lot of the thinking among individuals in the community," said the Reverend Johnson. "If whites and blacks are involved, whites want to win."

At a press conference later that day, Wiley defended the length of the investigation, saying that he had had to wait for results from the Michigan State Police crime lab. "You're dealing with the life of a person that, by all means, did not deserve to die," he told reporters. "He was a victim of circumstances, some of which he created himself."

Two weeks later. Under a hard, cold winter shower, three dozen protesters paraded in circles outside the courthouse in St. Joseph, their umbrellas aloft and their water-soaked placards hanging from their necks. In the downpour, the white posterboard curled and the black ink ran, the dripping letters becoming abstract designs. And as the morning progressed, the signs—WHITE COPS DON'T UNDERSTAND BLACKS!!! and WHOSE FAMILY WILL BE NEXT?—became harder to read. Chilled and wet, Johnson and the other ministers who had organized the rally cut it short and gathered the marchers on the courthouse steps. Courthouse personnel pressed their white faces against the steamed glass doors to assess the scene outside. The Reverend Walter Brown, pastor of Benton Harbor's Ebenezer Baptist Church, spoke first, directing his remarks as much to the onlookers as to the demonstrators.

"There's no justice in Benton Harbor," he thundered. "Blacks are tried by white trial lawyers. They're found guilty by white juries. They're sentenced by white judges. There's no justice, just us. The prosecutor don't care. He's only interested in prosecuting people from Benton Harbor . . . He runs the county like he wants to. It's Wiley rules."

People shook their umbrellas in support. Brown's remarks seemed mild compared with comments made immediately after Wiley's decision. One minister, Milton McAfee, of the Bethel Baptist Church, suggested that Fiedler "should be tried for murder."

Johnson, always the conciliator, then asked the protesters to gather in a circle and to take one another's hands. They laid their umbrellas aside, the rain now soft but steady. As the water cascaded off the brim of his felt hat and seeped through his trench coat and through his suit, Johnson shook from the cold. His head bowed, he tightened his muscles to ward off the chill and offered a closing prayer. "I pray that the agents of justice in this building will see the light and be fair in their findings. We have a higher court we're making an appeal to. And we know in that court color won't be a factor, because the God we serve doesn't know about color. We assemble ourselves to show that we won't go away. No matter what forces come up against us, we'll stand for blacks and for Benton Harbor. We're praying for the prosecutor. Lord help him."

9.

THE DENTIST

Burton Weisberg, a local dentist, believed he was doing the right thing by helping his friend Marv Fiedler. But the Reverend Johnson and the other ministers wanted to know why people like Weisberg felt compelled to get involved in their town's affairs when the matter at hand had to do with a white cop killing a black boy.

When I first met Weisberg, at his dental office on the periphery of Benton Harbor, he had only a week earlier decided to close his practice. For two years, he'd had it up for sale and could not find a buyer, in part, he suspects, because of its location. "It's the picture in a lot of people's mind," he said. "My office isn't in Benton Harbor. It's in St. Joseph Township, but it has a Benton Harbor address, since it's on this side of the river. It's not a matter of race, but Benton Harbor has one of the highest crime rates in the state."

After thirty-one years of practicing dentistry, he had tired of his work. He no longer enjoyed maneuvering his fingers inside squirming mouths. He couldn't keep pace with the paperwork necessitated by the numerous health and safety regulations; moreover, the fear of contacting HIV added to his worries. Only recently, he had pricked his finger while giving a patient an injection. The patient, who went for testing at the dentist's expense, proved negative. "Why subject myself to that kind of thing?" he asked. "It was one more straw." He had become so depressed at the lack of interest in buying his practice that he chose simply to shut down, even if it meant taking a financial hit.

In the meantime, he and his wife, Carol, had purchased four acres in the Blue Ridge Mountains on the outskirts of Asheville, North Carolina, where they planned to build a home. Too young for retirement—he's fifty-six—Weisberg expected to find other work. He and Carol had recently signed up as Amway distributors, and he figured they might open a small house-cleaning operation.

The dentist, who still retains traces of his Bronx accent, is, even by his standards, a compulsive and tense man. His blue jeans are creased and ironed; he carries two pens in the breast pocket of his navy blue polo shirt and wears a computerized watch, which keeps addresses as well as time. He wears four rings: his wedding band, a marble-size sapphire stone that once belonged to his father, and two bulky bands presented by the Masons. This supremely self-confident man does not have much patience with the disorderly progression of ordinary conversation, so on my first visit, before I could ask a question, he launched into a description of a four-day course he took in the late 1980s on how and when to use lethal force.

"I give you this information as background so that you know where my interpretation is coming from in regard to the Marv Fiedler situation . . . Had I been the police officer, I would have drawn my weapon and fired under the same circumstances, thinking the kid had a weapon and was about to draw it and was about to use it . . . A sane individual with nothing to hide doesn't leap out of a second-floor window, never having been in the apartment before, not knowing there was a roof just below."

Weisberg and Fiedler knew each other because their wives were colleagues at a homecare agency: Carol Weisberg was business manager; Nancy Fiedler, the head nurse. They had dined together a number of times, and they lived in the same neighborhood, an area roughly ten by twenty blocks, on the same side of the river as Benton Harbor, called Fairplain. It is the one truly integrated community in the vicinity. Weisberg bought his single-story ranch home in 1968, when he moved here with his first wife, who was from the area and who in 1987 died of cancer. They couldn't afford a home in St. Joseph.

The two passions in his life are Jewish causes and guns. He contributes to the Simon Wiesenthal Center (he lost family members in the Holocaust) and to the B'nai B'rith Anti-Defamation League, as well as to the National Rifle Association. He owns a rifle, a shotgun, and "several" (he won't say how many) pistols of different calibers. When Michigan's senior senator, Carl Levin, visited Temple B'Nai Shalom, the area's one remaining synagogue, Weisberg rose during the question-and-answer session and challenged Levin on what he considered his anti-NRA stance. Levin, who is Jewish, joked that he got these questions every day but didn't expect to be assailed among his own on his position on gun control.

"I've basically become a one-subject voter," said Weisberg. "A candidate's stand on the Second Amendment will determine whether I vote for him." He pegged his fascination with guns to his time in the army, in the mid-1960s when he went deer hunting with the supply sergeant. Later he bought his first gun, a .22-caliber handgun, for target practice. More recently, he started carrying a pistol for protection. "I'm not saying people should be vigilantes and take justice into their own hands," he insisted, "but if you're under lethal threat and the police are not available, who's going to protect you?"

He tells the story of an evening in February 1987, when he had visited his first wife in the hospital. As he left the building, he was followed by a man in a trench coat. "I stopped. He stopped. Alarm bells went off. I caught him in midstride. At that point I put my briefcase down and reached under my shirt. Now, he can't see the weapon. I did not present it. But if he's street smart, he's got to know what I'm doing. I put the gun in my coat pocket, kept my hand on it, picked up my briefcase, and started to walk . . . He changed his mind and did a hundred-and-eighty-degree turn and disappeared into the night. There's absolutely no question that that was a mugging about to happen. If nothing else, he was well aware that I was aware of his presence."

The day after Weisberg learned of the shooting, he and his wife visited Fiedler at home. Fiedler sat glued to his rocking chair, his good humor and energy gone. When they asked how he was doing, he managed a half-smile. But he insisted he'd be okay; the justice system in its fairness would exonerate him. No one talked of the incident; in fact, Weisberg tried to engage Fiedler in other conversation, hoping, naïvely, to take his mind off it. He suggested that Fiedler might want police protection at his home, and a visiting police officer agreed. Fiedler declined. He couldn't imagine anyone wanting to do him harm.

During the weeks after this visit, the Weisbergs regularly joined Fiedler and his wife for dinner, often going to the movies or renting a video at home. Anything, they thought, to get Fiedler's mind off the events of that afternoon. On occasion, Fiedler would refer to the shooting, saying that he felt he had done the right thing, that he'd thought the young man was reaching for a gun. If he had any regrets, it was that the police department, because of its shortage of officers, had put him in a potentially dangerous situation by himself.

"We got to be good friends," Weisberg told me. "Two or three times a week we would be with them so that he wouldn't feel he'd been abandoned. Because at that point his police department turned on him [he was first suspended, then dismissed], and there were members in the community who started raising a ruckus about this being a racial shooting . . . In my mind, I seriously doubt that had this been a black officer who had shot a black child, a ruckus would have been raised. But this was a white officer in a predominantly black town who shot a black child who wasn't armed at the time. Ergo, it must be a racial shooting."

After Wiley released his findings, he passed the case along to the state's attorney general. It was a perplexing act. He had already cleared Fiedler of any wrongdoing, so when an assistant attorney general, Richard Koenigschnect, visited St. Joseph and Benton Harbor to interview police and others, he was greeted with derision. "I felt like the Lone Ranger out there surrounded by Indians," noted Koenigschnect. "The police and local civic leaders wished it would go away." The attorney general overruled Wiley and charged Fiedler with involuntary manslaughter and reckless discharge of a firearm. If found guilty, he could be sent to prison for fifteen years. There was a mistaken belief in St. Joseph that the attorney general had intervened at the behest of the Reverend Johnson and the other ministers.

Weisberg was enraged. Who was the attorney general to meddle? Who was the attorney general to overrule their prosecutor? Who was the attorney general to suggest that Marv Fiedler was a common criminal? Who was the attorney general to imply that the shooting was at all racial? Weisberg, his wife, other friends of the Fiedlers', and fellow police officers formed an organization called Citizens Organized for Public Safety—COPS. They held events at local bars to raise money for Fiedler's defense; they placed collection jars in local stores; they set up a booth at the Venetian Festival, the annual summer event that attracts tens of thousands of visitors to St. Joseph. In all, they raised nearly $25,000 and collected over five thousand signatures of support. And they made their presence known, passing out twelve thousand blue ribbons that people tied to their car antennas, so that on any given day you were bound to see parades of motorists with blue strips defiantly flapping in the wind.

COPS made the decision to go about their work without being

confrontational. They chose not to hold a counterdemonstration when the ministers picketed the courthouse. When the Michigan Civil Rights Commission came to town to hold a hearing on the shooting, Weisberg was the only COPS representative to testify. And neither he nor other COPS leaders made an effort to talk with Johnson and the other ministers. "I thought it would be a waste of time. It'd be like me trying to argue politics with Saddam Hussein. I steered clear of them. Right away, they start yelling it's a racial thing, it's a racial thing. I'm sorry, but it's not . . . I think it's a socioeconomic situation," he said.

"The city of Benton Harbor is almost entirely black and it's socioeconomically on the low end of things, and they look across the road, they look across the river, and see how prosperous St. Joe is. And since the people in St. Joe are predominantly white, it's very quick to pop up . . . I mean, I live in Fairplain and have blacks all around me. They don't bother me. And I don't bother them. They do a better job of keeping up their property than I do. If anything, they should be picketing, trying to get out of the neighborhood because of my living there. Not the other way around. I'm going to put my house up for sale soon, but only because we're moving out of state. Otherwise, I'd have no reason to leave that house."

The barbs flew back and forth like cannon fire, and black leaders accused COPS of inflaming racial tensions. Its leaders, they noted, were all white. "What really made it a race issue, the white community went and raised thousands of dollars for this cop's defense," said the Reverend Brown. "To me it looked as if they were trying to incite a riot. We weren't walking around with black ribbons on our cars 'cause of Maben." Almost all the COPS supporters were, indeed, white; in the minds of Brown and others, the blue ribbon flying on a car antenna came to signify not only the driver's loyalty to Fiedler, but also the driver's loyalty to his or her race.

Weisberg told a local reporter, "I thought there would be people who'd think that, but they're wrong. I know where I stand. I truly believe I'd be here today if this had been a black officer."

Four years later, I reminded Weisberg of this comment and told him that the ministers wondered why he and other white leaders hadn't taken a stand to protest undeniable racial slights in the past. "That's their problem," he told me. "Why should the black ministers get upset about not getting support? If they can't get their act together, why should that be my problem?"

And so when a Coast Guardsman spotted Eric's body a year and some months later, the lines had been drawn, the sandbags piled high. People retreated into the familiar. It was neighbors among neighbors, workers among co-workers, worshipers among fellow worshipers. Or, more simply, whites among whites and blacks among blacks. Now, while both sides of the river waited for the trial of Marv Fiedler, they had to wrestle with the mysterious death of yet one more young black man, Eric McGinnis.

10.

A BREAK IN THE CASE

Jim Reeves keeps the file on a shelf behind his chair. It's an arm's reach away at all times: over three hundred pages of interviews, medical reports, FBI and state police analyses, polygraph results, anonymous letters and phone calls, photos of Eric, and photos of a girl taken in Reeves's office (he no longer remembers who she is or why he took the Polaroid), even train schedules showing when the railroad bridge was open. The entire package—a bulging, brown cardboard accordion filer—is labeled *Complaint #1906–91*. Reeves has written across the front in black Magic Marker: "Microfilm but DO NOT DESTROY!" Every once in a while, he flips through the report, hoping he'll spot a clue he's missed. Sometimes the filer sits unopened for months, until something reminds him of the case. Maybe a call from Ruth. Or from her brother Bennie, the state trooper. Or, as once happened, a report that a jailhouse informant says he was present at Eric's death. Or, as is more likely, during one of my visits, when he turns to the report to refresh his memory.

I too have a copy of the report now. Reeves made it for me after

I filed a Freedom of Information Act request. I've placed it in a black looseleaf binder and, like Reeves, reread it, not always in its entirety, but rather in fits and starts, as one might read from a collection of short stories. The tales told in its pages, while hardly elaborate or fully detailed, remind me of Sherwood Anderson's Winesburg, Ohio, stripped to the bare essentials—stories of small-town America, of love, of hate, of confusion, and of loss. White girls who prided themselves for dating black boys. White boys who blacklisted those "nigger-loving" white girls. A derelict, arrogant sheriff's deputy. An inebriated white man chasing a frightened black teen. A girl so hungry for attention that she invented stories about the night Eric disappeared. And black teens so frightened at the thought of being stranded in St. Joseph that they asked a cop for a ride home. Each story by itself means little, but together, stroke after stroke, they form a definite—if at times confounding—portrait of relations between the two towns, and a picture, though sketchy, and ambiguous in places, of the last moments Eric was seen alive.

June 27, 1994. A few days before this date Reeves finished his testimony in a highly publicized trial. Two black teens, Terrance Dawson and Willie Hurse, had tried to carjack the van of a white nursing instructor at the local hospital. The hospital sits in St. Joseph, beside the river, upstream a mile or so from the courthouse and county jail. For many in St. Joseph the incident underscored precisely what they most feared: that the location of the hospital on their side of the river would attract an unsavory element. When, two years earlier, the hospital had announced plans to move some financial services, as well as its outpatient dialysis and physical therapy units, to a vacant St. Joseph school, neighbors complained that the move would attract blacks into their neighborhood. Said one resident, "I work at the mall, and I like to know that when I leave

Benton Township I'm safe in my little St. Joe house in my St. Joe neighborhood."

So the attempted carjacking and the resulting trial received extensive press coverage. Portions of the proceedings were broadcast over a local radio station; the *Herald-Palladium* ran a series of front-page stories. During the trial it came out that the boys, who were sixteen and fifteen at the time of the crime, had trailed Shelley Hennen from the hospital to her van in the parking lot. It was nine-fifteen at night, and Hennen, forty, was leaving a pizza party for some nursing students, when Dawson allegedly body-slammed her from behind, forcing her into the front seat of the van. Hennen put up a fierce struggle, yanking at Dawson's genitals, screaming, and blowing the van's horn. When some nurses heard the commotion and approached the van, the two boys fled, leaving Hennen cut on the face and on the back of the head. She was not seriously injured. But the emotional damage of course was immeasurable.

Reeves, the lead detective on the case, botched parts of the investigation. Early one morning during the trial, he gathered the three nurses who had witnessed the assault and talked with them about their upcoming testimony. The meeting potentially tainted their memories, so the judge instructed the jury to keep that in mind when assessing the credibility of the witnesses. The defense attorney, Jack Banyon, also got Reeves to admit on the stand that "it was a bad call" to wait until a week before the trial to send Dawson's blood-stained coat and knife to the crime lab. And Reeves, in a moment of candor, conceded that he made "an error" in not recording one co-defendant's statement that the other had held a knife on the victim.

Reeves left the witness stand, beleaguered and dizzied by the cross-examination, and headed directly for the double doors, looking at neither the jurors nor attorneys nor those in the gallery; rather, his gaze was fixed straight ahead, toward the relief that awaited him. In the hallway outside the courtroom, he gave an ironic laugh and shook his head from side to side. "I feel like the town idiot," he told me as he walked to the elevator.

Dennis Wiley personally tried the case, as he does many of the high-profile ones, and in his zeal he charged Dawson (the other defendant reached a plea agreement) with five offenses, including conspiracy to murder and attempted kidnaping. Some felt he over-reached—by a lot. The jury found Dawson guilty of only two lesser assault charges. It was not a good moment—either for Wiley or Reeves.

Nor for St. Joseph residents. The judge, Casper Grathwohl, received over seven hundred letters urging him to send Dawson to prison for as long as he could. One correspondent suggested building a fence between Benton Harbor and St. Joseph. Grathwohl sentenced Dawson to ten to fifteen years in prison.

So when I met Reeves a few days later for lunch at Schu's Grill and Bar, a local eatery, he was not in the best of spirits. He asked me how he'd come across at the trial, and trying to be polite and supportive, I said that I respected his candor and humility. Which I did. Though I still wondered how there could have been such lapses in the handling of the investigation. After we finished our sandwiches and I had reassured him once again, he agreed to walk me through the route Eric McGinnis had taken the night he vanished. He suggested we start next door, at the beginning, outside what used to be the Club, the basement hangout on Pleasant Street, just half a block from the bluff overlooking the lake.

We stood in front of a glass-enclosed vestibule as a stiff breeze blew in from the lake. A jacketless Reeves slapped at his tie, decorated with golf tees, and pointed out the stairs descending into what is now Czar's 505, a music club for adults. Here, for precisely one year, from June 1990 to June 1991, Chris Adams, a twenty-something local entrepreneur, had run a juice bar for local teenagers. It had attracted nearly three hundred kids to its opening and, according to Adams, a hundred teens on average every night afterward; it was open on Friday and Saturday nights—and Sunday nights during the summer. There were some slow periods, however, and then the Club would offer a special discount on its usual $5 entry fee. On occasion, it allowed couples in for the price of one. One summer night, girls in bikinis were admitted for free. "The Club was basically the only place for kids to go in St. Joe," says Colleen Milnikel, a St. Joseph teen. Moreover, the kids liked Chris Adams, who on occasion would waive the entrance fee completely or take an IOU if the patron was without cash.

The Club's deejay played mostly rap and house music, even though the majority of those in attendance were from St. Joseph and the surrounding predominantly white bedroom communities. Only a handful came from Benton Harbor. Only a handful were black. But even that commingling was unusual for the two towns. There were few places where black and white teens interacted. Some played basketball together at the YMCA, and some attended a teen dance on Sunday nights at the Pebblewood golf course, in nearby Bridgman, but there had been trouble there, in part because teens and young adults would drive up from South Bend and sometimes get into tussles with Benton Harbor youth. One Sunday night, well before Eric's death, four hundred to five hundred young people got into a series of fights that spilled over to a nearby Burger King. The police arrested ten teens. (Pebblewood's owners claimed the fight didn't start at their club.) The Pebblewood crowd was rowdy on such a regular basis that Chris Adams's brother would close his gas station across the street every Sunday night.

Adams wanted a place where kids could feel safe, so he not only prohibited alcohol and smoking, but also required that everyone check coat and hat at the door. Such a requirement, Adams hoped, would keep anyone from sneaking in beer or wine and would discourage the flaunting of gang affiliation. When the Club first opened, some St. Joseph parents referred to it as "the Devil's Den."

"Some of the reaction," recalls Adams, "was: 'You're going to start a club that close to Benton Harbor? What are you going to do about the blacks coming over?' . . . You grow up around here learning that bad things happen in Benton Harbor. You grow up afraid to go across the river."

The Club was pretty much free of trouble, though there were occasional scuffles outside; it was mostly teenage stuff, Adams says, arguments and occasional fisticuffs over small things—money owed, girls taken, and playful dissing turned nasty. The only serious incident occurred that winter, when a black teen from outside the area got into an exchange with Adams and threatened to shoot him with a shotgun he claimed was in the trunk of his car. The quarrel became a fistfight, and Adams, with help from his bouncer, pushed the offender outside and called the cops. Probably the one thing that would have most upset parents, if they'd known, was that Adams began dating a high school girl from a wealthy St. Joseph family, and, according to friends, they would often slow-dance together and neck at the Club.

The place attracted a younger crowd than Pebblewood. Some patrons were as young as thirteen. Virtually all the kids I talked to— black and white—spoke of the Club with fondness. It gave them an evening away from nagging parents, an evening among friends, an evening when they could test their independence, within bounds. They would dress in their finest. Girls would don skirts and pants suits; the boys from Benton Harbor paraded around in silk shirts and pants, mimicking the attire of the popular rap star MC Hammer. "It was their night out," says Adams.

The Club itself was spacious: two dimly lit rooms, 3300 square feet in all. In the front room were video games and a pool table; the back room had a bar where the kids could buy nonalcoholic drinks with exotic names like Blue Velvet and White Kangaroo. The DJ and an occasional live band played on a wooden platform as the teens danced in front of the full-length mirrors. On one wall, Adams let the kids scrawl their names and messages in chalk, which he could easily erase if there were profanities or gang signs.

It was here where Excell dropped off his son, Eric. Reeves tells me that, according to interviews with Club employees and patrons, Eric did not go into the Club that night. Because it was near graduation for the area high schools, many kids were attending private parties or going on dates, so it was a particularly slow night at the Club. So slow that Eric, who had apparently gone down to the entranceway and seen only a handful of kids inside, made his way back up the stairs, unhurriedly, one suspects, to allow time for his father to drive away.

Reeves beckoned me to follow him down a short alleyway directly across the street from the Club's former location. The alley cut between Tosi's, a quaint pasta and sandwich lunch spot, and the YWCA, and opened into a small city parking lot. "Here," Reeves told me. "Eric came here; at least that's what the others say."

In the days immediately following the discovery of Eric's body, Reeves put together and headed a task force, inviting detectives from both the Benton Harbor and Benton Township police departments as well as Eric's uncle Bennie Bowers, the state trooper, and the county prosecutor, Dennis Wiley. The group—it eventually expanded to include officers from the sheriff's department and St. Joseph Township—met daily, first in the basement of the Boulevard Hotel and then at the city council chambers to discuss the previous day's interviews. The members pursued promising leads and stumbled after false ones, among them a claim by a Benton Harbor girl that she had spotted Eric the night after he disappeared at Meijer's, a discount store, and another claim, this by a St. Joseph girl, that she had viewed Eric's body in the coffin and saw definite rope marks dug into his neck. It was, Reeves informed her, a closed-casket funeral.

They were frustrating days, scattered and unfocused. With so many officers—eleven in all—chasing tips and possible witnesses and friends of Eric, it was hard to keep track of every lead and difficult to ask the right probing follow-up questions. When I showed the write-ups of the ninety-one interviews to an experienced Chicago criminal defense attorney, Jed Stone, he commented, "It just seems all over the place."

Reeves made his first real inroad the day the body was discovered, when, shortly after meeting with Ruth and then with Chris Adams, he vaguely remembered a car burglary that had occurred in downtown St. Joseph the same Friday night Eric was dropped off at the Club. He went back to the police logs. There had been seven reports of lawbreaking that day, from a hit-and-run accident (an eighty-two-year-old woman backing into another car), to an assault (one girl slapping another at a bus stop), to six calls for general assistance. One of the entries was for a larceny reported at around nine-thirty that night. Reeves retrieved the police report; it was incomplete at best. He called the patrol officer who had filed the report.

Dale Easton, a tall, trim man with a crooked, warm smile and a small silver stud in his left ear, had been a Benton Harbor patrolman for twelve years before leaving to take a job with the St. Joseph police department. Easton likes to think of himself as wise to the activity on the street, often boasting of his numerous informants; and in some ways he is plugged in, though his zeal has on occasion got him into trouble. He once whacked a St. Joseph teenager in the testicles with his flashlight. "I think Dale read too many Wambaugh books," said Reeves. But Easton had rapport with a lot of the kids, particularly those from Benton Harbor. Yes, he told Reeves, he remembered the larceny Friday night. The dispatcher had received a call of a black youth being chased down Main Street; the boy, according to the caller, had just broken into someone's car. In the report, Easton had some names wrong, but, perhaps more critically, had not written down all the details of the evening. Moreover, Easton had misplaced notes he'd made that night after talking with three or four black teens he'd encountered outside the Club, and whom he had driven back to Benton Harbor.

"I felt kind of bad," says Easton about his lack of follow-through. Reeves felt that Easton's work was often sloppy, so he was not surprised. He asked Easton to come in and write up a report, even though five days had elapsed since the incident. The report read in part as follows:

> Theodore Thomas Warmbein; owns Great Lakes Office Supply; born 8/7/49.
> Warmbein caught Eric in his car; tried to tackle Eric. Eric ran south on State St. Car was unlocked. $44 missing . . .
> Warmbein said that he parked the car in lot across the street from the Elks Club. When he got back to the car, front passenger door was open; Warmbein yelled at Eric; Warmbein knocked Eric down before he could grab hold of him; ran after Eric but was outdistanced . . .

"My first thought was: it's Warmbein," recalled Reeves. He was, it seemed, one of the last people to see Eric alive.

II.

THE ELK

Warmbein's lawyer said he stopped chasing Eric when he found his checkbook . . . I can't believe that. I don't stop just 'cause I found the checkbook. I keep pursuing. It doesn't make sense. You pursue for your money.

—Jim Turner, Benton Harbor city commissioner

If this guy [Warmbein] caught the kid, it's hard to say what happened.
—Bill Elliott, Benton Harbor detective
who served on the task force

I first met Ted Warmbein in September 1992, a little over a year after Eric's death. I sought him out at his office equipment–repair store on Niles Avenue, a fastfood-studded drag that leads from the expressway into downtown St. Joseph. It's a small, unadorned storefront with used bulky electric typewriters, clunky-looking calculators, fax machines, and copiers lined up in the window, an homage to the precomputer era. Though the store was devoid of customers when I visited, Warmbein asked whether we could meet at another time, somewhere more private. I understood. I had heard that Eric's death was hard on him, that he had early on feared for his safety. He was so sure there'd be reprisals, he had suggested to the cousin who lived with him that she prepare to move out of town for a while. Moreover, I'm sure he didn't want to raise suspicions among his customers that he was in any way connected to Eric's death. We agreed to meet on his boat that evening after work.

He'd given me directions to the Pier 33 marina, which provides 227 slips for a magnificent collection of ships—handcrafted sailboats, house-size yachts, charter fishing vessels, and sleek speedboats—all neatly lined up like soldiers in formation. I wandered down the recently washed dock until I spotted Warmbein, resting on the deck of his thirty-foot cruiser with a can of Pepsi, his feet propped up on the railing. He had christened the ship *The Mirage*. Warmbein, forty-three, was not in the best physical shape. He regularly downed so much Pepsi and coffee that it was a wonder he could come down off the caffeine long enough to sleep, and he smoked two packs of Marlboros a day. His belly protruded from his otherwise slim frame like a defect on the inner tube of a bicycle tire; his face was weathered, with deep folds around the eyes, perhaps from his time in the sun as he cruised the lake on summer afternoons. His neatly trimmed gray beard and strong Germanic features gave him a hardened look, but he was actually a pleasant and reserved man. A lifelong bachelor, Warmbein by his own measure was something of a recluse; when he wasn't running his business, which was most of the time, he'd fish or tend to his vegetable and rose gardens.

Warmbein had by now recounted the events of that Friday evening numerous times—both to Reeves and Detective Dennis Soucek. He relived it often as he lay in bed, unable to sleep. "I'll be thinking why couldn't I have shown up five minutes earlier or five minutes later," he told me, and repeated this regret numerous times.

"All of a sudden my life wasn't so simple." It so troubled him—both the events that evening as well as the suspicion that he had had something to do with Eric's death—that he told an intermediary he would welcome a meeting with the local branch of the NAACP so that he could explain the sequence of that evening's events, at least as he knew them. The meeting, though, never took place. "I wanted to clear up any questions they had," he told me. "It's a hotbed over there."

This is what he would have told them. On Friday nights, the St. Joseph Elks and their friends would gather for drinks and end-of-the-week ribbing downtown at the semicircular bar on the second floor of Lodge No. 541. Lawyers—both defense attorneys and pros-ecutors—swapped trial tales. Shopkeepers compared notes. And husbands and wives danced to the CDs spun by a deejay or, on every fourth Friday night, a crooner belting out oldies accompanied by an accordion player. Warmbein was a regular; he sat on the board of directors. That night, May 17, Warmbein and his friend, Dee Cun-neen, a secretary at a local law firm, walked out of the Elks bar past the photo gallery of the lodge's former Exalted Rulers and the two elk heads down the staircase into the cool breeze coming off the lake. They strolled around the corner to the Silver Dollar Cafe, affectionately known around here as "the buck," to say hello to Cunneen's daughter, who was there with some friends. After fifteen minutes at the Silver Dollar, they walked to Cunneen's car, parked along the bluff by the Curious Kids' Museum, and she drove Warmbein to his car, a 1977 Buick, parked in the lot directly across the street from the Elks Club, adjacent to the YWCA.

"We pulled up and I could see a young man in the passenger side of my car," says Warmbein. "I ran up there and I attempted to tackle him and I said, 'What the fuck are you doing in my car?' He rolled under the open door and started running. I gave chase. We went down State Street . . . By the end of the first block he was so far ahead of me that I knew I couldn't catch him. It pissed me off. What the hell is somebody doing breaking into my car in downtown St. Joe?"

A few things should be noted here. When Warmbein began his pursuit, gasping for air with each stride, he yelled at the boy, "If I catch you, you're dead." That, according to Gordon Ford, who, like Warmbein, had just come out of the Elks Club. Ford was about to join in the chase, but his mother begged him not to, because he had his young child with him.

As Warmbein ran down the town's outdoor mall—directly away from the river—past the Landis Clothing store, past Uniformly Yours, past First Choice Pantry, past Lauren-Marino Galleries, past the State Street Hair Depot, and past Shade Tree Tees, he nearly knocked over a man getting out of his car. "I've been robbed," Warmbein yelled between gulps of air. "Call the police."

Warmbein, by his own estimate, had had three or four gin-and-tonics that night (enough so that the police who responded to the call could clearly smell the alcohol on his breath). By this point, the young man had long outdistanced Warmbein, who was slowed down by liquor, smoking, and age. A young couple driving by told Warmbein to get in their car. The three of them then drove in the direction the fleeing burglar had gone, and though they didn't find him, they did locate Warmbein's checkbook, which had been dropped on the cobblestone street.

The couple drove Warmbein back to his car, where he found his glove compartment door hanging on its hinges, apparently having been jimmied open with a screw driver. The car doors had not been locked. (This is, after all, St. Joe.) Warmbein discovered that he was missing $44 in cash, which he had collected by selling raffle tickets for the Venetian Festival, the summer event that draws thousands of visitors. Agitated and shaking, Warmbein spotted a carload of teenage boys moving slowly along the street, and, thinking that they may have had something to do with the break-in, stormed up to the car window and swore at its occupants, demanding that they return his money or at least tell him who'd broken into his car.

The day after Eric's body was discovered, Reeves became convinced that the person Warmbein chased down State Street was, indeed, Eric. The police had found $49 when they fished Eric's body out of the river, presumably the $5 his mother had given him and the $44 from Warmbein's car. When the St. Joseph police asked Warmbein to come in for an interview, Soucek had him recount what had happened that Friday night, so Warmbein went through the sequence of events. He told Soucek that the young man, whom he pegged to be between eighteen and twenty-two years old, had on a jacket, dark pants, and white tennis shoes, and was at least five feet, eight inches tall.

"Dennis, this is more than just someone breaking into a car. What's going on?" Warmbein asked.

"I think we may have an idea who did it," Soucek told him.

When Warmbein learned why he'd been brought in for questioning, he pleaded with Soucek, he says, "to bring in every single detective. I wanted everyone in on this because of implications that would have been there . . . I didn't like what was happening."

Soucek later wrote in his report:

[Warmbein] was initially upset over the incident, however since he lives in Benton Harbor [actually Benton Township] he felt that making a big issue out of finding the subject might cause him later problems and he felt that it wasn't worth getting overly upset about it.

So much seemed to point to Warmbein. "In my mind, he had motive and opportunity," says Reeves. "Motive was somebody had broken into his car. He was angry. He'd been drinking. I thought that maybe whoever broke into his car got away from him and then Ted came back after giving the police report and drove around until he found Eric and then approached Eric. There was a scuffle, and Eric slipped out of his coat and fell into the river. And Warmbein left."

Eight days into the investigation, Reeves asked Warmbein whether he'd take a polygraph. He agreed. When he showed up at the local state police post, accompanied by his attorney, Jim Ford, Reeves took Ford aside. "Maybe," he suggested, "we ought to make a deal right now."

12

THE GIRLFRIEND

Larina Robbins is what most parents would consider "a catch." She was a high school track star and a Miss Benton Harbor candidate. So Ruth McGinnis was pleased to learn that Larina was dating her son.

Larina remembers the exact day she met Eric. It was February 1, 1991, her eighteenth birthday. "A friend of mine, LaToya, took me out to this place, the Club. We were downstairs, dancing, and Eric just came up to me. He said 'Hi, how are you?' He was very talkative. Very friendly. He knew a lot of people in the Club. He was a flirt. We danced that night and exchanged phone numbers."

Eric, ever the fashion plate, had his hair styled in what was called a high-top fade, cut at an angle so that it rose in a slight incline like a ramp used for car jumps. He was wearing baggy jeans and his white turtleneck. Larina thought him cute and began to date him, despite being two and a half years his senior.

Larina tells me all this over tall glasses of cappuccino at an outdoor café in Ann Arbor, where she's studying electrical engineering, a field in which she is in the distinct minority both as a woman and as an African American. She has a warm, quick smile that, from under the shadow of her University of Michigan baseball cap, disarms me. As does her soft voice, which is so swallowed up by the boisterous student activity on the street (it's the day before graduation) that I have to lean far over the table to hear her. She's hard to read as well, and I find myself wondering, as we sit there in the late afternoon sun, whether, beneath that sunny yet reticent disposition, something is bothering her. Maybe it's Eric's death. Or some other loss. But whatever it is, it has to do with her time in Benton Harbor, for when I mention the town where she grew up and ask if she'll ever return, I receive a firm and unequivocal *no*. It is the only time I see her agitated.

Larina had had a somewhat unusual childhood; like Eric, she had a foot on each side of the river. The daughter of Raymond Robbins, owner of Benton Harbor's only black-owned funeral home, and Barbara Robbins, Larina had been sent to Lake Michigan Catholic, a parochial school. (With its acronym, LMC, it's frequently confused with Lake Michigan College, a community college.) Lake Michigan Catholic sits at the foot of the Bicentennial Bridge in St. Joseph, directly across the street from the sheriff's department and the jail. While most of its students are white—many are from the Benton Harbor School District, which includes surrounding towns, and their parents prefer they not attend the troubled Benton Harbor High School—there is a handful of blacks. Larina was one of two blacks in her senior class of fifty-six, and she often felt her loyalties divided.

Like most of Eric's friends, Larina remembers him as a spirited and sometimes mischievous boy who loved playing practical jokes. Larina laughs at her recollections of a couple of late-night visits from Eric. Filled with adolescent pride, he would pull up in his mother's red Ford Probe and, leaning on the car door, preen for Larina as she stood smiling in the doorway. He told Larina that he took the keys after his mother went to bed. "He seemed so carefree," Larina says.

The two would often go skating at a rink in Stevensville, a bedroom community south of St. Joseph, where Eric would whip by friends, scaring them enough to make them fall. Or they would hang out at Eric's house in Benton Manor, talking in his room, which was adorned with Detroit Pistons and Chicago Bulls basketball posters, nearly a dozen gym shoes lined up against one wall, and "a closet full of clothes.

"He just had a lot of stuff," she says. "I don't want to say spoiled, but he had a lot of things."

One of his friends, Derrick Burton, says that Eric would come to pickup football games at Benton Manor dressed in new outfits, bragging about all the items his mother had bought him. He always had $20 to $30 on him, Larina recalls, given him by his parents. After her birthday visit, though, Larina never returned to the Club. "I wasn't too much of a party person," she says.

It was during the four or five weeks the two dated that Larina entered the competition to become Miss Benton Harbor. The winner would represent the town in the annual Blossomtime Parade on the first Saturday in May. At the contest, held at Benton Harbor High School, Eric pulled Larina aside. "He told me I was going to win, but I didn't believe him," says Larina. Each of the seventeen girls represented a country; Larina was assigned Scotland, so she appeared in black beret, plaid kilts, knee-high green socks, and penny loafers. She made it through the first two rounds of evening gown competition and, above the hoots and hollers, could hear Eric's high-pitched cheers rooting her on. Each of the five finalists was asked what she would do to improve her community and why. Larina said she'd try to eliminate the distribution of drugs by increasing the police force. Drugs, she argued, were ruining the community. The judges announced Miss Congeniality, Miss Entrepreneur, the third, second, and first finalists, and then Miss Benton Harbor. "Eric was jumping up and down. He kept on saying, 'I told you you'd win. I told you you'd win.' And gave me a hug."

Larina was soon caught up in the swirl of the county Miss Blossomtime competition; the winner would be chosen from twenty-nine girls representing the surrounding towns. In the weeks preceding that contest and the parade, the girls were chaperoned from a children's hospital to a radio station to a pig farm, and they participated in an elegant fashion show. Though Larina wasn't chosen Miss Blossomtime, the period was a heady experience, even for someone with Larina's aplomb.

Then she met someone else, a boy closer to her in age and maturity. "I drove out to Eric's house. He mentioned that he hadn't seen me and I hadn't returned his phone calls. 'How can you do me like that? You're breaking my heart.' He was sad and melodramatic. And then he told me he was going to bug me, 'cause I broke up with him." The two remained friends, though, and talked on the phone every other week or so. The last time Larina saw Eric was at the Blossomtime Parade.

It is *the* event of the spring. Originally a celebration of the area's bountiful fruit harvest, the annual parade is an old-fashioned hodgepodge of high school marching bands, a motorcycle drill team, Shriners riding miniature bikes, Lions tooting around in child-size wooden airplanes, the Coast Guard towing its Boston Whaler, National Guard trucks, antique cars, and a succession of floats carrying each town's queen, a teenage beauty in evening gown, elbow-length gloves, and of course, a glittering crown. A full four days before the parade, families reserve spots along the route, setting out blankets, plastic tarps and tablecloths, lawn chairs, two-by-fours, wooden benches, even ladders, so that by parade morning the town's Main Street resembles a quilt of various colors and objects. This year, 1991, the quilt came apart at the seams.

The parade traditionally begins in St. Joseph, near City Hall, wending its way down Main Street to the Bicentennial Bridge and into Benton Harbor. The towns, each wary of the other long before race defined the divide, had long ago agreed that the marchers would cover roughly the same distance in St. Joseph and Benton Harbor. But this year the Blossomtime officials, concerned about the safety of the marchers, wanted to shorten the route in Benton Harbor. They also demanded that Benton Harbor deploy thirty officers along the route. In the previous two years, twenty-one people had been killed in the town, an astronomically high rate for a community with a population no bigger than two Manhattan blocks; it was more than triple the per capita homicide rate in New York and Chicago for that same period. The parade organizers worried that marchers might be the targets of rocks and bottles, tossed by the town's youth.

Benton Harbor's leaders took offense at the suggestion that their town's teens were likely to assault parade participants. "Rocks can be thrown anywhere in Berrien County," noted a miffed Benton Harbor commissioner. "Let's stop playing games." In the end a compromise was reached. The parade route would extend into Benton Harbor farther than the Blossomtime board of directors wanted, but shorter than proposed by the Benton Harbor city commission. Nonetheless, come parade day, seventy police officers, several from outlying agencies, lined Benton Harbor's Main Street.

In her black evening gown and red velvet cape, Larina looked like a medieval queen borne on Benton Harbor's float, CREATIONS GLORY, whose theme was international unity. The flatbed, enshrouded in pink crepe paper, carried a large globe bordered by the flags of various countries. In front of the globe, made to resemble an apple, sat Benton Harbor's three runners-up. Larina was on a pedestal at the back of the float, its white crepe paper waving, along with Larina, in the chilly lake breeze. Ronald McDonald, clowning from the back seat of a convertible, preceded Larina; the Lawn Rangers, a drill team of potbellied men pushing lawn mowers, followed her.

Larina felt deeply uncomfortable that day. She, like others, were worried about their reception once the parade made it over the bridge. Would they be greeted with catcalls and boos? Or worse? St.

Joseph's mayor, Bill Gillespie, a drug-store owner whose business card pictured a friendly drunk on a park bench, rode in the back of a convertible, attired in a straw derby. (He later used a photo of himself in the parade on his business card.) As the car rolled into Benton Harbor, a group of young people yelled, "Honky, go home!" Larina says, "There was a lot of tension. A lot of people from my school band were concerned about going into Benton Harbor."

I'd been told once that if I really wanted to visualize the divide between Benton Harbor and St. Joseph, I should attend a Blossom-time Parade. So I did. And it was just as it had been described. Whites lined the parade route in St. Joseph; blacks lined the route in Benton Harbor. In St. Joseph, I could purchase Confederate flags; in Benton Harbor, I could buy barbecued ribs and chicken. The television crews and radio stations set up their booths in St. Joseph; the police patrolled on bikes and all-terrain vehicles in Benton Harbor.

As Larina reached the crest of the bridge, she could feel her stomach tighten. She didn't know what to expect. "A lot of people didn't like me in Benton Harbor, 'cause I didn't go to the high school," she says. "But then I saw Eric. He was dressed in a new shorts outfit and was waving at me." Eric stood with some friends on the curb, bouncing up and down, his arm frantically slicing the air to get Larina's attention. "It was so nice to see him," she remembers. A familiar face. A friend. A fan. There was comfort in that. There were no incidents that day.

Two weeks later, Larina heard from a friend that Eric was missing, that he'd gone to the Club and never returned home. Then, early that next Wednesday evening, Larina was returning to Lake Michigan Catholic from a track meet. "I was just getting into my car, and LaToya's mom, who was there to pick up LaToya, told her they'd just found Eric's body. LaToya came and told me. I got hysterical. I was shaking and crying." So much so that she couldn't drive. She left her car at the school, and LaToya's mom drove her home.

She attended the funeral and remembers being awed by the size of the crowd, several hundred people, and surprised by the presence of white mourners, Ruth's colleagues and a handful of girls from St. Joseph. Ruth, she recalls, became so hysterical that at one point she tried to pry open the casket. The days following, though, were the worst. Larina, who had to go into St. Joseph every day for school, felt caught in the middle. "That was the worst feeling in the world. Friends in Benton Harbor said, 'Well, you go to St. Joseph; who did it?' And I was afraid that if this could happen to Eric, it could happen to me."

Larina looks away. A breeze blows her dangling earrings against her neck, and she shifts in her seat, restless. The memories aren't easy for her. I pull myself upright and begin to collect my notes. What are your plans after you graduate? I ask, making small talk as I prepare to leave. Do you want to move back to Benton Harbor? She, too, sits up. The warmth fades. She looks directly at me. "I would not go back to Benton Harbor if my life depended on it," she says firmly. "After Eric's death it made me real wary. My grandparents told me not to go over to St. Joseph at night. My grandfather had heard Eric was going with a white girl and that his death was a message to people. They don't want coloreds over there."

I do not have to lean forward. I can hear her now. Her voice is stronger, fuller. There's something more.

"My grandfather got killed at Rap's Fish House in 1994. They say it was a hold-up attempt. I haven't really been back since."

Her grandfather, Moses Walker, sixty-seven, had come in to work on his day off because another clerk hadn't shown up. At 8 P.M. on May 18, a man walked up to the register, pulled out a handgun, and announced a hold-up. He then shot Walker in the chest. The shooting received much press coverage, in part because Walker was the brother of Chet Walker, a former Benton Harbor

High School basketball star who had gone on to play for the Philadelphia 76ers and the Chicago Bulls. But the slaying, like so many
others, faded into the next and the next and the next, until they all
begin to run together, and only the extraordinary or sensational
were remembered.

"I still think to this day if it had been a white man, they would
have found out who did it. It was eight in the evening. People were
outside. People were in Rap's Fish House. That same month, a
white man was killed at a trucking company in Benton Harbor.
Somebody put up reward money, and they caught the people within
a week. Here it is 1996, and we still don't know who killed my
grandfather." Larina pauses. Her smile has not returned. I feel now
as if she's angry with me. "They would have found out what happened if he was white," she says again. And with that our time
together is through.

13.

THE OTHER GIRLFRIEND

Larry Lavalley mothered a family of ducks.

Lavalley, the terminal manager at Lafarge Cement just upriver of the Coast Guard station, supervises the loading and unloading of cement from the behemoth freighters, which, like seafaring Gullivers to the river's Lilliputian pleasure craft and sailboats, clumsily pull into harbor here. Lavalley is no small man himself; his stout belly rests comfortably on his thick frame, which in turn rests on his rusting metal desk chair, from which each small movement elicits an ear-piercing squeak. He waves his hand toward the river—*squeeee*—and tells me the story of a mother duck who four years earlier had abandoned her three ducklings; just took off one night and never returned. Lavalley cared for the baby ducks, feeding them and placing them in a cage at night for their protection. As they got older, though, they became rebellious, testing their independence. One night, as they frolicked in the river maybe twenty feet offshore, Lavalley couldn't coax them back. They wouldn't respond to his pleadings or to his amateur duck calls. So he began to throw stones, pebbles really, over their heads, hoping to herd them back in. As this potbellied gent was heaving rocks and talking gently to the three intransigent and now agitated waterfowl, a St. Joseph police cruiser pulled up. "Wants to know what I'm doing," he recalls. "Got a complaint that I'm out there trying to kill these birds." The officer told him that an elderly resident of the Lakeview Apartments, a fourteen-story high-rise on the other side of the river near the old Whitcomb Hotel, had called the cops. "There's nothing that happens in this river that someone in Lakeview doesn't see," Lavalley says. So he reasons that if someone had tussled with Eric by the water, those bored seniors would have seen it, even though Eric presumably entered the river at night.

I came to see Lavalley hoping he would have a record of freighters that had entered or exited the harbor on May 22, the day Eric's body was found. If I could pinpoint a freighter that was in the river at the time, maybe I could find a crew member who spotted the body bobbing to the surface and get some clue as to where Eric entered the water. But as I soon learned, the firm's records don't go back that far.

Lavalley, a friendly sort who seems to want company, asks me about my book. His office, a square room roughly twenty by twenty feet, contains little; the only objects I can recall are a snack machine and Lavalley's desk, which has become a resting place for his feet. I tell him the story of Eric's death, at least what I know to be fact, and he remembers the incident. "Logically, if it were race-related he would have been killed and then dumped into the river," Lavalley says. "There had to be marks on his body. Did they find alcohol or drugs on him? . . . If someone chased him and he fell in, you can't say they're responsible for his death."

Do you see race as a problem around here? I ask him. "Not really. Not on a daily basis."

I then tell him that the police suspect Eric broke into a car that night. "Ooooh," he exclaims, as he lifts and slowly recrosses his feet, landing them in almost exactly the same spot. *Squeeeee.* "Extenuating circumstances. Well, I want to ask you something. What would be your feelings if you came and found somebody breaking into your car?"

"It would piss me off," I reply.

"It would piss me off, too. Not enough to kill him. But enough not to care what happened to him."

Behind me I hear two coins dropped into the snack machine. I turn around and see a pony-tailed man, his muscular arms bulging from his white sleeveless T-shirt. "This is Jeff," Lavalley says by way of introduction. "Jeff, this guy's writing a book about that kid they found in the river a few years back. Remember? They found him at the Coast Guard station." *Squeeeee.*

Jeff, who has acknowledged my presence with a barely perceptible nod, rips open a bag of pretzels and turns to leave. Then he pauses for a moment, looks over his shoulder, and between bites says, in a tone so matter-of-fact that it's as if he's talking about one of the freighter's having made a wrong turn, "That nigger came on the wrong side of the bridge." Lavalley turns in his seat. *Squeeeee.* "He should have stayed on his side of the river."

It's not that people don't want blacks crossing the bridge. It happens all the time. There is in St. Joseph a tacit understanding that almost anything goes—working with blacks, golfing with blacks, drinking with blacks, even occasionally voting for blacks—but not bedding down with them. When Betsy Miller, an attractive court clerk, danced with a black friend at an end-of-the-year party given by a group of lawyers, she was teased and scorned. People called her "Nicole," as in Nicole Simpson. One attorney told another, "Boy, I hate some big black guy dancing with a white girl. She should be with me. I can't stand the idea of it." When Amy Johnson, a St. Joseph dentist's wife who works at a Benton Harbor afterschool center, suggested to St. Joseph school officials a pen pal program across the river, she was turned down. She was told by a high school official, "Well, if they start writing, they might start talking on the phone."

"Eric's death reminded me of Emmett Till," says Tony Mitchell, Benton Harbor's director of economic development, referring to the fourteen-year-old Chicagoan who, on a visit to Mississippi relatives in 1955, was accused of whistling at a white woman and was lynched. "That was the first thing I thought of. It wasn't shocking or surprising. I just wondered who and when. Who was going to be foolish enough to cross that river. It was like who was going to be the one. It was understood that growing up, there were certain things you didn't do."

Like date white girls.

They called themselves wiggers.

Their classmates called them nigger lovers.

Around the time Eric died, there was a group of St. Joseph High School girls, a loose-knit collection of friends, who in their adolescent rebelliousness dated only black guys. It was a source of great pride to them and of great shame to their friends and parents. One girl told me that her parents grounded her for six weeks when they learned she had hitched a ride home from the Pebblewood dance club with some blacks. A black teen, after dropping off his white date, was followed into Benton Harbor by the girl's uncle and told to keep away.

"Once the white girls dated black guys, the white guys wanted to have nothing to do with them," says one St. Joseph teenage boy who attended the Club. "That's one thing not accepted around here. I've seen fights break out over that." Says another, "The Bible says your own kind should stay with your own kind."

These same boys saw Benton Harbor as a challenge, and on

Friday or Saturday nights would drive across the river and play a version of the game of chicken. Their car packed, they'd slowly motor past the high school to the corner of Empire and Broadway, a bustling spot where teens hang out by Roy's Party Store and the Rib Shack. A block from where Marv Fiedler killed Norris Maben, this notorious intersection is the site of fistfights, knifings, and shootings. An elderly woman who lives in a neighboring house has seen three killings: one in front, one in back, and one on the side of her home. These white teens, perspiring and chattering nervously, would lean out their windows and holler, "Hey, nigger," or "Booty lips," and then, just as heads turned, would squeal their tires and squeal in triumph as they headed for the bridge. One woman, now in her thirties, told me that her male St. Joseph High School classmates would not only taunt the black residents but would throw bricks, getting scores for hitting either cars or people. The kicker for this game called "brick" was that if you missed your target, you had to retrieve the brick.

The daring white girls incurred the wrath of the daring white boys not only for dating boys from across the river, but also for imitating their ways. They dressed in the hip-hop fashion made popular by MC Hammer and other rap artists, wearing blue jeans big enough for two, the crotch down to their knees. They hung braided gold necklaces around their necks and styled their hair with finger waves or braids. A few guys, too, fashioned themselves after their counterparts in Benton Harbor, dressing "wiggerish," wearing the same sagging jeans.

"The whites tried to be cool with us, but we stuck to ourselves," recalls Mark Miller, a friend of Eric's. "There were a lot of stereotypes, you know, mimicking our speech," says David Jones. "Real high-pitched greetings. There was this one dude who'd try to act black. He'd say things like 'I'm hanging out with my homies.' " A few white teens even identified themselves with one of the Benton Harbor gangs, and one small band was caught carrying out holdups with a BB gun. At St. Joseph High School, the wiggers greeted each other in the hallways with a high-five or a twitch of the head. "Hey, nigger, whas up?" they'd inquire. "Man, jus chillin'." Jim Reeves laughingly called them wannabes.

The Club and Pebblewood were the only places where black and white teens socialized, though a few met while working at the St. Joseph Burger King. But it was a group of Benton Harbor boys who loved to dance that made the white girls swoon. The group included Eric. They called themselves the Untouchables, and attended the Club on Friday and Saturday nights, often dressed in matching outfits: silk pants that billowed between the tight fit at the waist and at the ankles, black and polka-dot silk shirts, polished patent leather shoes ("tux shoes," the girls called them), and haircuts styled in a fade. Under the Club's strobe lights, the four or five boys would run through their routines, their legs and arms splaying about in sync with the accompanying rap. They admired themselves in the full-length mirrors. The girls admired them from the edge of the dance floor.

"We'd just sit there and drool," recalls Colleen Milnikel. "They'd tell us they danced with MC Hammer and Vanilla Ice. We didn't believe them, but we wanted to." Why the lure of black guys? "I respect black people," says Colleen, now in her early twenties. She sits on a picnic table by her house with her current boyfriend, a truck driver who is black. "White people, you know, they try to put on a front for everybody. Black people, everybody's family. You walk down the street and they say, 'Whas up, bro? Whas up, cous?' . . . All my friends don't look at me as white. They consider I'm black . . . I don't know what it is. In high school the white guys wouldn't give us the time of day. This is how I see it: black guys, one thing about them, a lot of them will use people but they don't let their girlfriends walk over them. They don't take no shit from no one. You can get a white guy, and girls can treat them like crap.

Look, it's this way. My white friends who date white guys, they could talk to them like they want, disrespect them. But you see black men with women, they don't let their women disrespect them or cheat on them. My mom thinks the reason I go with people who disrespect me, the man who raised me was an alcoholic and he verbally abused me, so she thinks I'm attracted to men like him. I've had some boyfriends who treat me real rudely, but I've had some who treat me real nice . . . Oh, I just think they're sexy. Their voice, their body, the way they dance. It might be a phase I'm going through. That's what I often think. My aunt has a theory, though, that in my past life I must have been Harriet Tubman or Aunt Jemima."

Donnie Allen, who briefly dated Colleen, says, "I was surprised that all those white girls wanted to date black guys, I think 'cause of the dancing. We came clean all the time. We'd tear up the floor. I think they liked it. White girls were different from the black girls. The black girls were so bossy. 'Oh, you can't do this or can't do that.' Not the white girls."

But to hear Colleen and her peers talk, interracial dating was, for at least a while, simply a fad, made more acceptable when it became publicly known that one of the more popular girls in the school, a pretty, pony-tailed blonde, was seeing a black. "All of a sudden one year everyone had to date a black guy," recalls Jennifer Bowerfind. "Suddenly rap music got popular. The girls our age didn't see anything wrong with it."

One of these girls was Lisa Liedke. Her yearbook photo for that year shows a slim eleventh-grader with shoulder-length light brown hair teased into a cascade of curls. Her silver-dollar-size glasses and buttoned-at-the-neck blouse made her look prissy, like a budding librarian. Unlike the other students on the yearbook page, all of whom seem genuinely happy, a few caught in midlaughter, Lisa looks subdued, her smile almost forced. She was, by most accounts, not a happy kid. According to the book's index, that is the only picture of Lisa; she did not have a senior portrait in the next year's yearbook.

During her junior year Lisa began to change. Still softspoken and sweet-natured, she cut her hair short and first dyed it auburn (though it looked more rust-colored or orange), and then jet black, a color she quickly adopted. Black fingernails. Black jeans and shirts. Black shoes. She also, like some of the others, began talking jive and using idioms like "I be . . ." all in an effort to sound black. "If she was just with me, she wouldn't talk like that," says Bowerfind, who had been a friend of Lisa's since fifth grade. "But if she was around other people, she would. She did it for attention. She just wanted to pretend she was someone else. A while later she acted like she was a punk. Lisa needed attention from somewhere . . . She always had to do things to impress people. If I went to buy new pants, she'd go out and buy new pants *and* a new shirt. She always had to outdo you. I don't think she felt very good about herself . . . I never thought of her as wild, but she did things to get attention."

She got attention from Eric. The two dated for maybe a month or two—the length of time is unclear—shortly after he broke up with Larina, though their relationship, like that of many teens, was ambiguous and hardly emotionally intimate. Friends say the two met at the Club, where they could always be found dancing together, Lisa often smothering Eric's face and neck with kisses. "That's all Eric did was talk about Lisa," says Donnie Allen, one of the Untouchables. "He'd say, 'I don't know what I'm going to do with this girl, she's too wild.' They were kicking it in the bathroom. People'd be walking by. They were becoming really obsessed with each other." Apparently, Lisa and Eric saw each other only at the Club, though they regularly talked by phone. And when Eric called her house and her parents answered, Lisa later told Reeves, "He'd change his voice so he'd sound white."

Why did Eric date white girls? I posed the question to a number of his friends. " 'Cause he liked it," one told me with a slight roll of his shoulder, as if to say, "Man, why are you asking such a silly question?" But a number of girls I spoke with had clearly given it some thought. They suggested that Eric was not all that popular among the girls at Benton Harbor High School. Not that he wasn't well liked. It was hard not to like him. Always joking. Always playing. Always clowning. But he lacked self-confidence. "He couldn't get any play at the high school, so I knew he had to go somewhere," says Gia Graves. "I asked him why did he date white girls," recalls Leona Gonzales, who knew Eric from church. "And he said, 'Girls are girls,' and that was the end of the conversation. You had to know Eric in order to like him. He wasn't real mature. He wasn't one of these guys all the girls wanted. He was fun to be around, but he could be annoying at times. Maybe white girls liked him better."

His self-doubt ultimately got him into trouble with Lisa. She found out that he boasted to friends about their bathroom exploits. Lisa met another boy, a white boy, and stopped seeing Eric shortly before his death. She told Reeves, "People were telling me that he was telling people stuff that we did, and it upset me so I just told him to leave me alone . . . I was kind of mad. I told him what they were saying, and he said that he wasn't saying nothing. He goes, 'You can believe them or you can believe me,' and I said, 'Bye.' That's the last time I saw him."

On Wednesday, May 15, two nights before his disappearance, Eric phoned Larina. Though they had split up, they still talked by phone.

"Larina, I need to talk to you," he told her curtly.

"He sounded anxious," recalls Larina. "He didn't sound like his normal self. He sounded like he really needed to talk to me. It was sort of unusual, because he was so happy-go-lucky. I told him I was

14.

ANOTHER VIEW

"You're not going to use my name, are you?" Bobbie Nadus asks. "I'm scared."

Of what? I wonder. Revenge?

Nadus (not her real name) taught mathematics for five years at Benton Harbor High School, not a place for the weak and timid. Half of the teachers, including Nadus, are white, though many students insist the percentage is much higher. Nadus taught physical education at a nearby junior high school, but because of a financial squeeze, her position was cut. So she transferred to the high school in September 1990 to teach math, and three months into the school year, before she had a chance to settle in and memorize the names of all her students, one of them, Tamika Swanson, was killed.

On December 10, Tamika, along with three girlfriends and her brother, was leaving an evening youth basketball game at the King Preparatory Center, when three young men, all members of a local street gang, jumped out of the bushes. Each had a pistol. Each started shooting. One of them hollered, "Now, who's shooting at who." The police later speculated that Tamika's brother had belonged to a rival gang.

Four months later, a neighbor was killed, a shooting that confirmed the worst of many whites' fears.

On April 13, 1991, shortly before 2 A.M., the Benton Harbor police found Michael James Klutts, a thirty-two-year-old dry-waller from Stevensville, slumped against the steering wheel of his black Chevy pickup in an alley. Klutts had been shot in the head. The police immediately suspected a drug deal gone awry; Klutts had been known to frequent Benton Harbor to buy cocaine. "They'll shoot you for a pair of tennis shoes, or for five dollars, or over an argument," Klutts's neighbor and former employer, Donald P. Lewis, a construction contractor, told a reporter from the *South Bend Tribune*. The police, though, began to suspect that Klutts had been in Benton Harbor with a friend from Stevensville; his mother said that he'd left home with a neighborhood pal. The police had two theories: Klutts was killed by drug dealers he had cheated out of money, or Klutts was killed by a friend but was left in a Benton Harbor alley to make it look as if he had been murdered by blacks.

It was enough to wear out the strongest of souls. But Nadus, at forty-five years, was not worn down easily. A short, muscular woman, Nadus has a handsome, rugged face that makes her look stern and judgmental, and if it wasn't for an easy smile, she might appear downright mean. Although she was tough with her students, she took an interest in them, so much so that some of the kids complained that she was a busybody, nosing around to find out why they came to class upset or tired or depressed. "She got too involved sometimes," one of the school administrators said.

Despite the violence in the community, Nadus remained upbeat about the 1990–1991 school year, her first at the high school. "It was a great year. I worked really hard, and it was fun. I love math as a subject, and the kids were real receptive."

She met Eric in the second semester; he was transferred to her applied math class from first-year algebra, where he'd been having trouble. "When I first had Eric," recalled Nadus, "he was somewhat undisciplined and not very interested in school. And generally talking a lot. He did a lot of fooling around, throwing stuff. At first he slept some in class. That's a common thing for kids who want to cop out and not do the class work."

As an exercise to get her students thinking about the future, Nadus had each one find an occupation that interested him and then do research on how much education—specifically, how much math—would be required for that vocation. Eric, as he was apt to do, didn't take the assignment seriously and wrote with a silliness, bordering on the self-conscious, that he wanted to be "a love doctor" who would help people through their love and sexual problems. "I told him I don't think you'll find this in a career book," Nadus recalls. "Now, maybe a psychologist."

Eric might have been just one more indifferent student passing through Nadus's class had he not expressed an interest in gymnastics. After school and in the evenings, Nadus ran a gymnastics club in Stevensville. Located in a cavernous building carpeted with blue mats, the club served mostly girls, mostly white. It was here, Nadus explained, that she really got to know Eric.

Nadus's math students knew that she coached aspiring tumblers, and one morning after class in the late winter Eric and another student, Dwan Hall, asked Nadus what it would take to join. Nadus outlined the costs, but told the two students that if they did their homework and assigned chores before gymnastics classes, she would waive the fee. So the two began to come. Eric, who had troubles with the body-bending routines, seemed to enjoy the atmosphere, and, in particular, reveled in being one of the few males in the place. He spent much of his time flirting with the leotard-clothed gymnasts.

"He was happy here and he liked being here and he was out of trouble here and he knew it . . . He went from D-to-F work to

C-to-B work, doing his homework every day. He'd do it here at the gym. And I was real proud of him.

"I felt he was a loner in a crowd. I'm like that. I think that's why he took to me. We were similar: we liked being around a lot of people but basically keeping to ourselves . . . I also thought that he could make it at school, that he had the intelligence, and that he had steady parents. I think in a lot of ways Eric didn't fit in that community [Benton Harbor]. He asked if he could come live with me, 'cause he felt he'd do better in this environment. But I told him no. I said, 'Eric, you have a mom who takes good care of you and you have a nice place to live . . .' "

Nadus was troubled that Eric at times could be manipulative. He would boast that he had got $20 from his mom and from his dad by telling each that the other had refused to give him any money. It confirmed Nadus's general impressions of Benton Harbor's youth; it reinforced her own stereotypes.

"He didn't think he should have to do any work. I guess he was bitter about the idea of having to work or having anybody see him work. They all get that way. Every kid I've ever brought out here on a work-study. Evidently they don't realize that all the rest of us work. I don't know, but the community is used to a lot of handouts. And that's why an awful lot of them are happy living with seven people in a two-bedroom tenement. And the ones who aren't happy, they aren't happy but they still don't seem like they want to get out and work and change it. All this stuff probably isn't going to help me out in that community.

"I had a problem with Eric here. With things missing while he was here. Things that according to him it didn't matter because nobody used them anyway. He took a pair of grips . . . They were in his school bag. And the boy who lost them came in to talk to me about them. He says, 'Well, I let Eric use them in practice but told him to put them back in my locker.' And I said to Eric, 'What's the deal here?' He goes, 'Well, he told me I could have them.' I said,

'No, he told you you could use them.' I know he also took a couple of T-shirts at a competition that we went to, and one of the other kids caught him, and he lied and said, 'No, they were given to me,' and the other kids just stood there and shook their heads and said, 'No one gave those to him.' "

Nonetheless, Nadus liked Eric, and though she chastised him for stealing, she continued to let him attend class. He wasn't particularly talented as a gymnast and often despaired that he couldn't bend like the others, but he seemed especially comfortable with the younger children, so Nadus thought maybe she could help him become a coach.

Three weeks before he died, Eric came down with the chicken-pox, which for an adolescent is tantamount to coming down with leprosy. The itching and fever aside, the disfiguring, though tempo-rary, can be traumatic. And, if you're not self-disciplined enough to keep from scratching, the resulting infections can lead to permanent scars.

Eric returned to school on the Monday before he disappeared, and Nadus winced at the teasing he took. His face was still covered with pockmarks, dime-sized scabs that discolored his dark complex-ion. It looked as if someone had taken a razor and scraped away small circles of his skin and then stained it ghost white.

"The kids gave him a real hard time about how he looked," Nadus recalled. "He had a lot of pocks on his face and on his arms, and they still bothered him. He'd rub his stomach, and he was ornery and uncomfortable. The kids called him 'leper,' 'cheetah,' and 'ogre.' They told him he should have stayed home. I told him in time the scabs would ease up. They usually fade. But I knew he didn't feel well, still."

Eric stayed home from school on Tuesday and Wednesday, and when he returned on Thursday, Nadus remembers, there was a noticeable change in his attitude. He fell asleep in class, so she pulled him aside afterward, but before she could say anything, Eric, seething with hostility, barked, "What I do with my life is my business. STAY—OUT—OF—MY—LIFE." His voice softened for a moment. "Things are a mess anyways and they're not getting any better. Just leave me alone. You hear me; leave me alone. You don't care anyways. Nobody cares." He turned and stormed out of the classroom.

The next day, Nadus tried to reassure Eric. The scars will clear up, she told him. Ignore the teasing. Just because you've been out of school for a while doesn't mean you're going to fail. After class, Eric approached Nadus, his lanky frame towering over hers. "You don't have to worry about me anymore," he said. "Because I'll never be right again."

That night he disappeared.

15.

SUSPICIONS

Saturday, the day after Eric hadn't returned to his mother's home, his father, Excell, a compact, robust man who had long ago remarried, stepped out into the chilly breeze and got into his gray four-door Mercedes, parked beside his white wood-frame house on Benton Harbor's Pipestone Road, an avenue that boasts what once were the most majestic of homes. The hundred-year-old Victorians with detailed woodwork, and the Colonials with massive white columns, used to belong to white doctors, lawyers, and industrialists; now they look worn and tired, porches leaning, columns crumbling, paint peeling. Many have been divided into apartments and have taken the abuse that comes of accommodating five or six families. Excell drove past these small estates, through the town's downtown, and over the Bicentennial Bridge into St. Joseph. There, he followed the road past the jail and the courthouse toward the lake. At the Holiday Inn, he turned right and motored back across the river, this time over the Blossomland Bridge, a hundred yards downstream from the Bicentennial. As Excell crossed the bridge—still in St.

Joseph, mind you, since the town somewhat inexplicably includes a sliver of beachfront property on the Benton Harbor side of the river—he slowed down, motoring along at maybe twenty miles an hour.

Thickets and trees sandwich this stretch of country highway, which runs north of the bridge along Lake Michigan, eventually leading to Whirlpool's corporate headquarters and a string of small resort towns. This is the route, Excell speculated, that Eric would have taken to his mother's if he'd been on foot. It is the most direct route from St. Joseph to the Benton Manor Apartments, about two miles down the road. So Excell, his hands loosely holding the car's steering wheel, slowly drove along that stretch of road until he reached the exit for Benton Manor; then he made a U-turn and headed back to St. Joseph. And then he did it again. And again. And again. By early evening, he had driven the route five times over, from south to north, north to south. With one hand on the steering wheel, he leaned out the driver's window or stretched across the passenger seat, surveying the brush along the road, stopping on occasion to inspect a log or a bush, anything that held the slightest resemblance to a body.

"I don't know what made me do it," he told me. "I just thought, I don't know why, I might find him dead in a ditch along the road. I know St. Joe. I grew up here." He paused. "I was wrong, though," he said matter-of-factly. "He was in the river."

In my five years in and out of St. Joseph, I would, as a matter of course, ask people whether they went into Benton Harbor. With only a few exceptions, they would tell me that they purposely avoided the city, not because they had anything against the people there, but because they feared for their safety. In 1994, the city held the dubious distinction of having the highest murder rate in the country.

What I didn't expect was the equally strong response from the people in Benton Harbor when I asked whether they ever visited St. Joseph. Almost everybody assured me they crossed the bridge only when they had to, primarily for visits to their doctor and dentist or to pay utility bills. They didn't feel welcome. Indeed, there was a period of thirty to forty years when St. Joseph quietly discouraged blacks from settling in the town. Elisha Gray, the former head of Whirlpool and a progressive man, had on a number of occasions told friends that, when he first came to the area, he was assured by a St. Joseph city official that blacks weren't allowed to live there. (Quietly indignant, Gray bought a home in Benton Harbor.) According to a 1965 *Herald-Palladium* article, not one black family had been sold a St. Joseph home since World War II. Most settled in Benton Harbor, which built the bulk of the county's public housing. St. Joseph was, at one point, denied federal funds because it refused to build subsidized housing. In 1965, when Shannon Madison, a black engineer hired by Whirlpool, was able to purchase a home in St. Joseph (after being turned away by real estate agents and then filing a complaint with the Michigan Civil Rights Commission), the *Herald-Palladium* editorialized:

> St. Joseph is a city of nice homes and nice people. Anyone who holds up his end will get a fair shake, regardless of color.
>
> And who knows?—a few of those agile colored youngsters might do a lot for the [St. Joseph High School] Bears' basketball fortunes.

Today, many Benton Harbor women won't shop in St. Joseph. They say they're followed by store clerks. Dan Levy, the white former assistant prosecutor, would often jest, "If you ever wanted to make money committing a crime in St. Joe, the sure way was to have a black friend walk into a store in front of you. The shopkeeper would be so focused on the black person, you could walk out with whatever you wanted." Men, particularly the younger ones, would enter St. Joseph with caution. Virtually every young man I met had a story of being stopped by the police while driving—or of being taunted while visiting their neighbors. Geoffrey Morrow, a reporter for WFHB, was tending the radio station's booth at the Venetian Festival when he heard one man say to a friend, "I didn't know WFHB hired spooks." Another Benton Harbor resident, who worked at the Venetian Festival as a security guard, was called "a nigger rent-a-cop." David Burton, returning one evening from St. Joseph's Pizza Hut, was pulled over by a state trooper because one of his headlights was out. "He slammed me against the hood," says Burton. "I asked him what the problem was, and he told me to be quiet. He went through my pockets and threw my wallet and keys on the hood. He cuffed me and threw me in the back of the car and ran a check on me. Then he released me." Burton filed a complaint with the state police. Drew Pearson, a Benton Harbor teacher who occasionally shops in St. Joseph, told me, "I pull up in parking lots and hear car door locks clicking. It gets to me." When Western Michigan University opened an extension office at the St. Joseph High School building, it attracted a number of Benton Harbor residents. A St. Joseph police officer stopped by the offices to find out who these people were. "This is a residential neighborhood," the officer told the center's director. "We have to be careful."

Many blacks disapproved of interracial dating because, in part, they feared the repercussions. And many, after Eric's death, quietly expressed disbelief that the teen had frequented a club on the other side of the river.

Such was the case with Excell. He had never liked the idea of his son going into St. Joseph. Particularly at night. It wasn't safe.

One of the first stories Excell told me was this. When he was seventeen years old, he found a job washing dishes at a St. Joseph restaurant called the Tip-Top. Sometime during his first week, he decided during his lunch break to eat his meal at the restaurant. As he sat at the counter perusing the menu, the restaurant's manager came over and told him that this would not work; he had to eat in the kitchen. He didn't say why. He didn't need to. Excell was black. The restaurant's clientele was white. Excell, humiliated, says he quit on the spot. He told me this tale by way of explaining his earlier statement: "I know St. Joe. I grew up here."

"I don't like crossing that bridge. I know how they is," he said. He passed on the somewhat conspiratorial theory, which I've heard from others, that in 1972 St. Joseph tore down the Silver Beach amusement park "because they didn't want blacks coming over there."

We sat at his kitchen table, tightly tucked into a corner by the back door. Excell, who worked in construction most of his life, was still, at the age of sixty, a vigorous, solidly built man. His hands, thick and sturdy, rested on the Formica tabletop. They clearly were the instruments of someone who earned his livelihood through manual labor, someone who could power a hammer and finesse a wrench. When I arrived, Excell was in the shed behind the house, repairing a lawn mower. As he came out to greet me, he rubbed his grease-streaked hands up and down on his gray trousers. He also had on a blue workshirt and ankle-high work boots, and mentioned to me, as we walked into the house, that these workclothes had become popular among Eric and his friends and that Eric, shortly before he died, had requested a similar outfit.

Once we got inside, he motioned me to sit on one of two wooden benches pressed close to the kitchen table; I placed my notebook and tape recorder on the Formica top.

"I'm not sure I want to be doing this," he said as he sat facing me, one leg extended along the bench. "What's in it for me?"

"Nothing," I told him, assuming—correctly, it turns out—that he was speaking of money. I explained that I couldn't, as a matter of principle, pay for interviews, but I hoped that I would help him get closer to the truth of what happened to Eric. Maybe, just maybe, I said, not sounding too confident, I could actually find out for certain how Eric died.

"But you can't promise me that," he said.

"I can't, but I can promise you that I'll work my butt off trying." What I didn't tell him was that I already had, yet wasn't sure I had made much progress. At one point, I was so frustrated that I'd sent a copy of the police report to an experienced criminal defense attorney. He came back, equally lost, and suggested that I hire a private investigator.

Excell told me that off and on he'd thought about hiring a private investigator, but the cost was prohibitive. "Well, consider me a kind of free private investigator," I said, knowing that I fell short of a true gumshoe. He replied that he wasn't sure he wanted to talk with me about Eric. It didn't feel right—someone making money off the death of his son. His reluctance didn't make sense to me at the time. I was, after all, his best chance to find out what had happened to Eric. But I came to realize over time that maybe he didn't want to know. He could imagine different possibilities, each more macabre than the next, but his not knowing for certain allowed him to concentrate less on Eric's last moments than on the good times, which were more clear and certainly more rooted. Images of Eric dancing or riding his bike or intently wiring his stereo were cherished—and far more comforting.

We did, nonetheless, spend the next three hours at the kitchen table talking about Eric. Having someone to share his suspicions with was clearly of comfort, at least for the moment.

Although Eric lived with Ruth, he spent a good deal of time with Excell, and from his father he learned the intricacies of electric circuitry. He would often accompany Excell when he rewired the apartments he owned. Eric particularly liked to rebuild stereos, so on occasion the two would venture to flea markets, where Eric would buy used tuners and speakers. He earned the money for these purchases from his dad, who regularly paid him $4.50 an hour for chores around the house. Excell was firm with Eric and recalls the time when Eric, at fourteen, pleaded for a motorized bike. Excell, uncharacteristically, consented, but told Eric he would have to earn the money to pay him back for the moped. Eric agreed, but he defied his father's order not to drive the bike on the street. That indiscretion, coupled with his slowness in paying for the bike, led Excell to reclaim and then sell it.

Excell told me that a few weeks before Eric's death, Eric moved in with him and his wife. He told his father that he'd had an argument with his mother. Teenage stuff, Excell speculates. He didn't ask, though he mentioned that Eric was upset that his mom had yanked him out of Nadus's gymnastics club. Ruth didn't like the tenor of Eric's relationship with his teacher, and was suspicious that it was something more than a friendship. To me, Ruth never directly referred to Eric's moving out, though she occasionally alluded to it. Nor did she talk about her discomfort with Nadus, though she asked me once whether I thought anything untoward had gone on between the two. I told her no, though I'm not sure that alleviated her concerns.

Excell's account of Eric's last night—driving him to his mom's to drop off the hamburger and then to the Club—did not differ from Ruth's, though, unlike Ruth, Excell said he had serious misgivings about Eric's attending the Club. "I asked him whether any other black kids went there. I know how the Twin Cities do not get along. Especially blacks over there. I wanted to make him stop going but I didn't know how . . . He never did say he was dating any white girls, 'cause if he had I would have stopped him. I know what happens. You're asking for trouble then."

Excell felt uncomfortable enough about dropping off Eric in St. Joseph after dusk that, once Eric descended the stairs to the Club, Excell waited a few minutes before driving away—and then he drove slowly, peering into his rearview mirror, looking for his son, fearful that if for some reason he wasn't admitted to the Club, he'd be stranded on the wrong side of the river. But while idling at the STOP sign, his eyes riveted to the mirrored view of Broad Street and, in the distance, Lake Michigan, he didn't spot his son, so he continued his drive home.

Excell shifted uncomfortably now on the bench. He sat up and leaned forward, stiff and alert. "I never told this to the police," he said, "but that night, sometime between midnight and two A.M., the phone rang. No one was on the line." Excell didn't know whether the caller hung up or remained mute. Shortly after the phone call, a four-door sedan pulled into the vacant lot next door and then pulled back out.

He also confided that Troy, a son by another marriage, seemed unusually troubled by his half-brother's death. Troy, who lived in Benton Manor near Eric, was five years older—a difference that matters at that age, he quickly added. Yet Troy took Eric's death harder than just about anyone else, Excell said. He lent Troy a suit for Eric's funeral, which he wore for five days running. "I always thought that was a little strange."

Without answers, Excell was looking, at the very least, for the right questions to ask. The phone call may have been the wrong number or one of Eric's friends expecting to get Eric, not his dad. Troy, whom I later met, explained to me that he was so griefstricken that for a short time afterward he was in a haze. Excell was groping, clawing for possible clues.

Excell regretted not having viewed Eric's body; Coburn had urged him not to. It was not the way to remember a loved one. Swollen. Bloody. Discolored. And fetid. Also, an untrained eye would be unable to tell whether there were any unusual marks or lacerations on the body. Nonetheless, Excell said to me with a moan, "I'm not sure I did the right thing."

But more than anything, Excell believed that Reeves did not take the case seriously. Maybe, he once suggested to Reeves, Eric had been drowned in a bathtub and then thrown in the river.

Reeves pooh-poohed the idea, and since then their relationship became virtually nonexistent. "I don't talk to Lieutenant Reeves anymore," Excell said, " 'cause every time I talk to him, it makes me sick to my stomach."

Feeling that I may have overstayed my welcome, I got up to leave. But Excell, who rose, too, didn't seem eager to lose the company. He told me that he had continued working, even though he was eligible for retirement, because he wanted money to help Eric go to college. "I think he would have gone," he said, and beckoned me into the living room, where, opposite the television, was a row of framed photographs, mostly of family. One was of Eric at the age of seven. Excell took it from the shelf and handed it to me. Eric, tall and gangly, was wearing a red-checked shirt buttoned at the collar and the most charming and mischievous of smiles. That was how Excell should remember his son. I saw the autopsy photos, and there was no resemblance. Not the least. I handed the photo to Excell, who caressed it before placing it back among family. "If I keep praying, I think he'll answer me."

After work one evening shortly after Eric's death, Ruth drove to Broad Street in St. Joseph. She got out of her car and stood in front of the site where the Club had been, positioned as if she were walking south, away from the river, just as she imagined Eric did the night he disappeared. She looked to the right and could see the rippling surface of Lake Michigan; to the left, she saw the string of boutiques. She walked through the narrow alley beside the YWCA, just as Eric had done, and just as Jim Reeves and I had done. Again, she tried to imagine what was on Eric's mind. Did he expect to meet someone? Did he have a destination in mind? She stopped in the parking lot, where he had allegedly broken into a car, and then followed his route to State Street, where she stopped. How afraid was he? Was it really Eric who'd broken into the car, or was it someone else? She turned to go back to her car, and as she did she considered walking straight ahead to the river, to the place where Reeves thought Eric may have entered the water. But she couldn't bring herself to go down there. It was too hard, particularly trying to piece together the last moments of his life. She had had dreams, dreadful dreams, in which she found herself in the St. Joseph River, fully clothed, choking, gasping for air—before she woke up in a sweat, batting her arms about as if she were still in the river. There was nothing mysterious about the meaning, Ruth said. "I wanted to take his place."

Had Ruth continued the three blocks to the river, she would, after walking down a steep slope, have first passed a bronze statue of two children building a sand castle. She would then have strolled onto the manicured grass of the Margaret Upton Arboretum and from there to the water's edge. I've stood there many times, one foot on the grass, the other on top of the steel retaining wall that holds the water at bay—and drops precipitously. It is clear to me that had Eric gone into the river here, it would have been difficult if not impossible for him to get out. The surface of the river is five to six feet below me. Even a strong swimmer would have great difficulty lifting himself over that barrier, and though there is a steel ladder leading out of the river, it would be tough for a person to locate it at night. If Eric had made it across the river, he would have had to contend with another retaining wall or, just upstream of that, tomb-stone-size slabs of stone that line the shore; at night a tired swimmer would have trouble finding his footing.

A forgiving woman, Ruth has a hard time believing that some-one threw her son into these waters, particularly because the person might have been upset over something as seemingly insignificant as Eric's dating a white girl. She, after all, has many white friends at work, a number of whom attended Eric's funeral. Many knew Eric from company picnics, and he had given informal dance lessons to some of their children. "I didn't raise my son to be prejudiced," she says, "and if he danced with a white girl, that's okay. But whatever happened, it was not enough to take his life. He would never think someone would do something to him because of who he danced with."

Ruth, ever trusting, had chosen the Florin Funeral Service to arrange Eric's burial; they were the first morticians to call. Many in Benton Harbor, including family members, wondered why Ruth had allowed a white-owned funeral home to do the arrangements. Did the service have a closed-casket funeral so that mourners wouldn't see the bruises? Did it rush the burial so that the body could not be further examined? "Those are family choices," says Ruth's pastor, the Reverend Johnson. "For whatever reason, they chose Florin. But that was their determination; I had nothing to do with it. I just said 'Hey.' " People's suspicions were unfounded. Besides Ruth was trusting. But she, like Excell, didn't trust Jim Reeves.

"I think there's a certain amount of coverup," Ruth says. "And I think, because of the type of boy Eric was, it would have blown the two cities apart. There's no doubt in my mind on that."

One particular matter tugs at Ruth, nags at her incessantly. Playing out the events over and over again, toying with the details so that the plot played itself out each time with slight differences, she tries to understand what could have been going through the mind of Stephen Marschke, a detective with the sheriff's department. In December 1992, eighteen months after Eric's death, Ruth called Reeves.

"Jim, I want to know if anything else came up on my son, or did you guys drop it, or exactly what's going on?" she asked. "I'd like to ask a question. I'd like to know, on that particular night, a police officer, Marschke, why didn't he do his job? . . . Why, even though he's a fellow officer, why can't you ask him these things? Is it such an exclusive club that he's beyond being touched?"

"Ask Steve why he didn't do something?" Reeves repeated.

"Why? Give me some satisfaction."

"Steve *was* asked why," Reeves insisted.

"But I never knew why. This is what's important. Now Eric, I can't do anything about him, but since I'm left here, I am the one in my family and his father; we're the ones who need to know."

"Whether or not I agree with what Steve did, I took the information from him that he called the police after he was told to by Warmbein. Why he chose not to go back outside, he says . . ."

Ruth interrupted. "And to make a statement like it's not uncommon to see a black kid running through St. Joe. Do I look like I'm stupid? It is about as uncommon as you want to find. That's like saying I see a green person running through Benton Harbor every day. That's bull, and you know it."

"Ruth, I can't tell you what goes through another person's mind."

"I realize that. I'm just telling you that people are not stupid. They are not stupid . . . Everybody's not going to be whitewashed all the time . . . We just want some answers. We want something that sounds like it makes sense. Is that asking too much?"

16

THE ASPIRING SHERIFF

This thing with McGinnis never would have gotten this far if
[Marschke] had given chase. What blows my mind is when you have a
black kid hot-footing it down the street in an all-white town, you know
something's wrong. I can't understand why he didn't follow.

—A local FBI official

Ruth was not the only one nettled by Stephen Marschke. Nor was she the only one who believed Marschke knew more than he was saying.

"The general population feels he's got to know something about what happened," insisted Jim Turner, a Benton Harbor city council member.

Added Carolyn Graves, a bus dispatcher for the Benton Harbor Schools, "Steve to me is an okay guy. But he knows what happened to Eric." Maybe. Maybe not.

But what can be said with certainty is that Marschke, then a detective with the Berrien County sheriff's department, could have prevented Eric's death. It could also be asserted that Marschke had a singular ambition to be elected sheriff—and that his chance encounter with Eric got in his way.

When Ted Warmbein pursued Eric down St. Joseph's State Street, we know that he nearly collided with someone. It was Marschke, headed for the Silver Dollar Cafe to meet a friend for dinner. He was off duty, out of uniform.

When Warmbein yelled, "I've been robbed; call the police," he was directing his plea toward Marschke. By Marschke's own account, he had just seen Eric whiz past. Marschke marched into the Silver Dollar and, from the pay phone just inside the front door, called the St. Joseph police. "There's been a robbery," he told the dispatcher. "The suspect's a black male. He's running south down State Street." Marschke then stepped outside under the tavern's red-and-white awning and waited for a couple of minutes, until he glimpsed one of the town's three squad cars turn the corner onto State Street; the police department is situated just a block away. He then went back into the Silver Dollar to join his friend for dinner.

The question asked by almost everyone, from Ruth to Reeves, was why Marschke didn't give chase—or at the very least why he didn't wait to steer the police in the direction of the fleeing youth. Surely, the sight of a white man chasing a sprinting black teen through the heart of St. Joseph's downtown must have screamed out: Something's terribly wrong. Yes, Marschke was off duty—and there are no hard-and-fast rules governing off-duty police. But I think it's safe to say that most citizens expect off-duty cops to be ready and willing to jump into the fray.

When I first arrived in the Twin Cities, in the summer of 1992, a year after Eric's death, I stumbled into one of the nastiest elections in Berrien County's history. It was the race for sheriff, pitting Marschke against the former undersheriff, Bob Kimmerly. Marschke was viewed as the upstart, the outsider, despite his twelve years in the department. At thirty-five, he retained a boyish look. His soft features and curly brown hair (which he grew long and unruly when he worked under cover) disguised his resolute, ambitious nature. He had risen unusually quickly—some felt too quickly—in the ranks, becoming field supervisor of the narcotics unit when he was twenty-eight. As head of that unit, Marschke orchestrated massive drug busts, sometimes arresting as many as a hundred people at a time. The raids received front-page coverage in the *Herald-Palladium,* with mug shots of those cuffed.

"Whenever they got pot, it was Colombian Gold or Sinsemilla, whatever was hot at the time," recalls Steve Pepple, a police reporter who went on to become the *Palladium*'s managing editor. "One time I challenged him on it, and he pulled out a copy of the magazine *High Times,* with the prices. It became a joke . . . He had a goal in mind, and he would do whatever he could to get there, to be sheriff."

Kimmerly, however, was viewed by many as the rightful heir to the post. At fifty-five, he had been with the department for twenty-seven years, nearly half his lifetime, and had served as undersheriff for eleven of those years. He was especially popular among other officers for his modesty and intelligence. A reader of Keats and Byron, Kimmerly went about his work quietly. In 1970, while driving by Lake Michigan, he spied a six-year-old boy struggling against a powerful undertow. Fully clothed, he dived in after the child and helped to rescue him. Assured that the boy was all right, Kimmerly drove off. When a reporter caught up with him later, he said, "Don't give me any credit. It was all the work of the lifeguard," who had also jumped in after the boy.

Despite all this, Marschke had the inside track for a particular reason: he was loyal to the party, which in Berrien County means only one thing: the Republican Party. Berrien County is, with the exception of a few small liberal-leaning pockets like Benton Harbor, firmly Republican. Since 1936, its top officeholders—prosecutor, treasurer, clerk, and state and national legislators—have been members of the Grand Old Party. David Stockman, who went on to become director of President Reagan's Office of Management and Budget, represented this district in Congress. So it came as no surprise to those around Marschke that, given his political designs, he would ingratiate himself with the county's political movers and shakers. He organized a chapter of Young Republicans in Berrien Township and also chaired the annual Lincoln Day Dinner. And he served on the party's executive committee. "You've got to carry the water to the elephant," Marschke would tell those around him.

Among those in the party to whom he was closest was Dennis Wiley, the prosecutor. They shared conservative views and, perhaps as important, were contemporaries, each in his thirties. The friendship—and Marschke's service to the party—paid off. "Basically, I've been positioning myself careerwise for at least ten years," Marschke unabashedly told the *Herald-Palladium* during the campaign.

The previous fall, Nick Jewell, who had been sheriff for twenty-three years, retired. It was his expectation, as well as that of others in the department, that his successor would be Kimmerly. By statute, three county officials—the prosecutor, the clerk, and the chief probate judge—were to appoint Jewell's successor, who would hold the post until next August's election. By a vote of two to one, they selected Marschke.

By the time the election rolled around, six months later, most sheriff deputies and area police officers were pretty riled up. Although the county's Republican leaders—including the national representative, the local state legislators, and, of course, the prosecutor—endorsed Marschke, a substantial majority of those in the law enforcement community thought Kimmerly, who had resigned rather than serve under Marschke, deserved the job just by virtue of his long years on the force.

Marschke became the object of derision during the campaign.

Some sheriff deputies defiantly drove to work with Kimmerly posters on their cars; one balanced a billboard-size Kimmerly sign on the flatbed of his pickup. But the deepest and perhaps most cruel dig came with the circulation of what became known as the "Run, Stevie, Run" videotape. Local bars played the one-minute tape, like a popular porno flick, on their big screens. Copies were made and passed around.

The video recorded a presentencing hearing for Butch Davis, who had been convicted of killing his girlfriend, Mandy Spears; she had allegedly threatened to squeal about Davis's forging money orders. Marschke had been key in building the case against Davis.

The videotape, taken by a courtroom camera, opens with Davis, in dress shirt and tie, listening intently to the judge set a sentencing date. When the judge finishes, Davis slowly rises from his chair, his hands clutching the armrests. He freezes momentarily, and his deep-set eyes lock on to Marschke, who sits a few feet away. It all seems to happen in slow motion. Like a tiger preparing to pounce, Davis rolls his tongue against one cheek and then the other, flares his nostrils, and bites down on his lower lip. Then, before the guards can restrain him, he lunges at his prey. Marschke pivots and bolts from the courtroom.

While five sheriff deputies tackle the muscular Davis to the carpeted floor, Marschke peers from behind the doorway, a safe distance from his attacker. Two deputies have planted themselves on Davis's back, another grapples with his kicking right leg, and another calls on his radio for ankle shackles.

"Bring your arm back, bring your arm back," one of the deputies barks.

"You fuck'n broke it, you son of a bitch," Davis snarls.

The handcuffs get snapped on his wrists. Still face down, Davis arches his back, raises his head, and once again locks eyes with his intended target, who has one foot tentatively in the courtroom, the other safely out. Marschke again disappears behind the doorway.

Davis later apologized to the guards who had wrestled him to the ground. It was Marschke he wanted, not them.

To those in the law enforcement community, the tape captured what they already believed: Marschke was weak-kneed or, at least, unvaliant. To others, it helped explain why Marschke had not chased Eric.

"He leaves a little bit to be desired when it comes to backbone," says a former St. Joseph detective. "I'd say for ninety-nine percent of police officers, young and old, bells and whistles would have gone off if they saw a black kid being chased by a white guy down the streets of St. Joe."

"It doesn't surprise me that he didn't give chase," says Bobby Simmons, a St. Joseph Township officer. "That's him. He's just not a physically aggressive person."

"I've always liked Steve," the *Herald-Palladium*'s Steve Pepple says, "but I think that his political ambitions were for him all that mattered . . . It didn't surprise me, knowing his personality, that he didn't join in the chase . . . I'm not sure in this case it was so much cowardice as that he had a meeting to go to. That was much more important than chasing this kid down."

Questions about Marschke's inaction might have ended there had there not been strong suspicions within the Benton Harbor community that Marschke did not take kindly to blacks. A few days before the election, Marschke ran an advertisement in the *Herald-Palladium* that offended residents—of both towns. The ad, a black-and-white photograph, depicted Marschke, dressed in jacket and tie, prodding a young black man, his Chicago Bulls jacket slipping off his shoulders, his hands cuffed behind his back, into a squad car. The headline read: IN THE WAR ON DRUGS WHO KNOWS THE ENEMY BEST? SHERIFF MARSCHKE! And below the photo was a tagline: " 'It's about time,'—A Berrien County Citizen." Two days later, twenty-five Benton Harbor civic and religious leaders held a press conference denouncing the political spot. But Marschke stubbornly refused to acknowledge that equating blacks with the enemy might be seen as abusive, particularly to a people who were once legally considered chattel and who barely thirty years earlier were viewed in some Southern towns as the adversary. He told a local reporter, "I make no apology for arresting drug dealers and helping the citizens of this community take back their streets." The ad ran again in the next day's paper.

Reeves, who had placed a *Vote for Marschke* sign in his front yard, was dismayed by the ad. "Maybe his ambitions got out of hand," he said. "I think Steve could have done some positive things in Benton Harbor. If it's true, the campaign advertisements, that those were put in at Steve's initiative . . ." Reeves drifted off, muttering, "It was arrogance."

Marschke lost the election, garnering only 42 percent of the vote. Although Benton Harbor, which experienced an unusually large voter turnout, took credit for the loss, the truth of the matter is that he lost in every precinct in St. Joseph as well.

17.

OFF THE RECORD

Immediately before the sheriff's campaign—and precisely one year after Eric's death, long after the incident had fallen out of the daily consciousness of the two towns—residents picked up their afternoon copy of the *Herald-Palladium* to find a front-page story headlined: TEEN'S DEATH STILL BAFFLING. In the accompanying photograph, Ruth McGinnis, sitting on her living room couch, clutched the framed photo of Eric dressed in his white turtleneck, the same picture that had been on his coffin. Ruth wasn't looking at the newspaper photographer. Instead, she was gazing at the photograph of her son, her eyes half shut, as if she were trying to protect him—and her memories. Ruth is a very private woman; agreeing to talk with a newspaper reporter was not an easy decision. The story read, in part:

> Ruth McGinnis believes in her heart that someone knows what happened to her son . . .
> "I'm pleading as a mother, if anybody knows anything I hope they come forward," Mrs. McGinnis said.

Clouded in mystery from the start, the circumstances surrounding McGinnis' death are no clearer now than they were a year ago.

"He has a fine family," Berrien Prosecutor Dennis Wiley said. "They'd like to know what happened to him. I'd like to know."

Not everyone believed that. Most people in Benton Harbor, including Ruth, were convinced that Wiley—along with Reeves—had conspired to cover up parts of the case, that they had conspired to protect fellow citizens of St. Joseph. James Rutter, the school superintendent, who had been mistreated by a local police officer, was quoted in the same article: "Murders are not supposed to go unresolved." Murder. That is how nearly everyone in Benton Harbor refers to Eric's death.

As it turns out, Wiley, along with Reeves and Marschke, had indeed hidden elements of the case from the public. And that only reinforced the belief among the citizens of Benton Harbor that someone had killed their fellow villager.

In May 1991, when the Coast Guardsmen had plucked Eric's body from the river, Dennis Wiley was still taking heat for his handling of the police shooting of Norris Maben. When the attorney general overturned Wiley's finding in the case, he did so because he learned that Fiedler, just a few months before the shooting, had attended a two-day trial in which Maben faced charges of assault. (Maben was acquitted.) Consequently, the attorney general argued, Fiedler should have known that Maben was not the murder suspect he was looking for. The attorney general's decision infuriated Fiedler's supporters and buttressed the belief of Benton Harbor leaders that Wiley had willfully ignored the law to protect a white police officer.

That summer of 1991 both communities waited anxiously for Fiedler's trial (which, it turned out, wouldn't take place for two years), so Wiley, concerned about possible eruptions in the Benton Harbor community, stepped in to act as the spokesperson in the investigation of Eric's death. He would deal with the public and the press. He would, he hoped, defuse tensions.

It was an odd fit for Wiley. A cautious man by nature, he distrusted the Third Estate. Reporters complained that he didn't return phone calls and that his office wouldn't release information unless served with a Freedom of Information Act request. He had been so restrained in talking publicly about the Maben shooting that the cautious *Herald-Palladium,* usually a friend to the powers-that-be, editorialized:

> [Wiley's] silence on this matter—while well-intentioned—has only contributed to community fear and tensions . . . Officials had a potentially volatile situation on their hands last week and they knew it. But instead of easing community concerns, they contributed to the general aura of uncertainty by clamming up and letting the rumor mill run wild . . . legitimate questions about an issue of public concern—particularly one of this magnitude—warrant more than cold strong silence.

Acting in character, Wiley was close-mouthed about the details of Eric's death, one detail in particular: that Eric had broken into Ted Warmbein's car.

A week into the investigation, Wiley and Reeves had gone to Benton Manor to visit Ruth. Wiley had yet to face local reporters, who were pressing him for at least a snippet of news on the case's progress. He knew that he had to give them something, even if no more than an acknowledgment that the inquiry was proceeding. He was reluctant, though, to release the fact that Eric had stolen money from a car. He and others in St. Joseph worried that black youth were looking for any excuse to rampage. They believed the evidence was there for anyone to see: the threats against whites, the beating of white students at the Benton Harbor High School, and the open speculation that Eric had been murdered. Moreover, shortly after Maben was shot, three to four hundred young people had gathered at a busy intersection in Benton Harbor, taunting passersby and hurling bottles and rocks at police decked out in riot gear. Announcing that Eric was a thief, Wiley believed, would only disparage the dead boy and further enrage the Benton Harbor community. What purpose would it serve? he asked other civic leaders rhetorically.

Some disagreed. "We told him he had to come forward," says Bill Wolf, Benton Harbor's mayor at the time. "We told Wiley the best way to handle this was to be straightforward, because that would defuse the situation. One thing about Wiley: he needs to test the political winds. We were sitting on a tinderbox, but Wiley didn't want to be accused of trying to defame a black kid who was last seen in St. Joe."

So Wiley and Reeves looked to Ruth for guidance—or maybe all they really wanted was her consent. Reeves's recollection is that on the drive out Wiley was uncertain about what to do. "I introduced Dennis to Ruth," recalls Reeves, "and we sat in the living room and Dennis offered his condolences. He told her there was going to be this press conference. Ruth asked, 'What good is it going to do? If it's true [that he broke into the car], what good is it going to do to release it publicly?' " Ruth later deeply regretted giving her nod to the deceit.

"We were there for half an hour. And when Dennis left, he was sure he wasn't going to say anything about the theft. Eric was dead. Eric couldn't defend himself. What good would it do? Dennis said he appreciated that and was glad that he'd taken the opportunity to visit Ruth . . . Looking back on it, emotionally I still believe that was right. Maybe it should have come out right away."

But it didn't. Wiley pulled aside the newspaper's managing editor, Steve Pepple, and told him off the record about the incident. Pepple felt obliged to keep his word and was unable to confirm it through other sources—though in hindsight he wishes he had pursued it more vigorously. Bob Dewitt, the news director of WSJM, had uncovered the story through sources of his own, but without prodding from Wiley chose not to broadcast it because, he said, "It would have further polarized the two communities." And so St. Joseph's leaders, who had little reason to deal with their black neighbors, certainly little reason to deal with them as peers or as colleagues, operated in a climate of misconstrued overtures and false assumptions.

"Everybody's gotten so paranoid about one another, they're worried even about telling someone the truth," observed one public official new to the area. "It's just crazy. It wasn't malicious. It was just like 'oh, my God, if we say this, they won't believe us.' Even if your intentions are absolutely pure, once you do something like that it comes back to kick you in the ass." It did. During the sheriff's race.

July 23, 1992. In the last week of the campaign, Marschke faced Kimmerly in a public debate. Four hundred people attended. No one could remember such keen interest in a local election. The candidates spent nearly ten times the amount spent in that year's prosecutor's election (which Wiley won). Kimmerly attacked Marschke for being too political. "I may be a candidate for political office, but I assure you I am not a politician," Kimmerly told the crowd in his opening comments. Marschke seemed on the defensive. He explained why he'd once been fired from the Benton

Township police department. He was a clerk at the time, he recounted, and only eighteen. He'd made a foolish choice, calling in sick so that he could attend a high school prom.

A young man in the audience challenged Marschke about Eric's death. There were rumors that he'd seen Eric chased through St. Joseph's downtown. What happened? he demanded. Marschke revealed that yes, he had seen Eric sprint down State Street. The boy had just broken into a car.

Benton Harbor leaders couldn't believe it. For one year and two months, Marschke and Wiley and Reeves had kept this fact from them. They had hidden the truth. And now everyone wanted to know, quite simply, what else they were hiding.

The *Michigan Citizen,* the statewide black newspaper, ran a cartoon in which a black boy, presumably Eric, is racing to the river, yelling, "Help!"; he's being chased by three white boys wielding clubs. Front and center is a floppy-haired, wild-eyed Wiley, leaning against a signpost that reads: "Welcome to Berrien County 'Little So' Africa." Wiley is pictured scratching his rear. Below, the cartoonist has written: "I'm scratching my head, I don't know how the body got in the water."

But if anyone wanted evidence of the disbelief in Benton Harbor, one needed to look no further than Michael Green, a softspoken New York Life Insurance agent who worked closely with white business leaders to bring together the two communities. He headed an organization whose acronym NISE (Neighborhood Information Sharing Exchange) seemed more suited as a description of his personality. People thought of him as someone who didn't want to make waves. So when he wrote a guest editorial for the *Herald-Palladium,* questioning the circumstances surrounding Eric's death, people on both sides of the river were rattled.

> Why haven't local law enforcement officials pushed to give
> answers to the public about this case and why haven't St. Joseph

residents demanded answers either? After all, the mystery involves their police department and occurred within their city limits . . .

In this case, after 15 months, there are still no answers to the mystery of how Eric died. Only more questions. Could someone possibly be dragging their feet and why? . . . Someone knows what happened to Eric McGinnis. He didn't just jump into the St. Joseph River and drown.

18.

THE SEPARATIST

It was, I thought, the phone call I'd been waiting for. And it had nothing to do with Eric's death. At least not directly.

As a teller of stories, real stories, I'm both confined and liberated by the unpredictability and sometimes the unbelievability of real events, so when I look for yarns to spin I purposely look for heroes and villains, perpetrators and victims, conflict and, I hope, resolution. The combination of those elements, after all, produces the most compelling tale. And I was particularly looking for them in this story about race. Where were the heroes? The villains? The resolution? I wasn't finding them in the matter of Eric's death. The deeper I got, the harder it was to find my way out. The more people I spoke to, the more, not less, confused I felt. Race relations in the last days of this century, I came to realize, was a tale short of victors.

Heroes? Shoot, every time I drove over that bridge, I'd let out a sigh of relief, eager to get away from the innuendoes and gossip of whichever town I was leaving. In Benton Harbor, civic leaders pulled me aside to inform me that St. Joseph once tore down an empty junior high school building to avoid the slightest possibility of their having to take Benton Harbor students. In St. Joseph, a former mayor confided to me in a conspiratorial tone that shortly after the death of Martin Luther King, Jr., in 1968, four to five hundred blacks massed by the Bicentennial Bridge, preparing to assault their white oppressors across the way. Luckily, he added, the police had the foresight to barricade the bridge with their patrol cars and prevent the bloodletting. Neither of these events, I discovered, had occurred.

In April 1995, I received a call from Sherwin Allen, the superintendent of the Benton Harbor schools. "I've been trying to reach you," he said in his high-pitched voice, which makes him seem in a constant state of agitation. "I read your story in the *Wall Street Journal* about that Eric McGinnis case. That's nothing compared to what's going on now. Nothing. Man, you got to come up and talk with me. We need national press."

I explained that I was no longer at the *Journal* but that I was working on a book about race relations and the two towns.

"Oh, man, you really need to come up here. When can we get together? You want to talk about race? You should hear what they're trying to do to me and the Benton Harbor schools. This is the story. This is your book. Race?" He chuckled. Then he described the graffiti recently found on the school administration building. On the side door to his office someone had scrawled, in red Magic Marker: NIGGER ALLEN *This is your one warning KKK*. A few feet away, on the building's brick wall, the defacer had written: KKK LIVES. He went on to tell me that the white power structure of the county was trying to oust him from his job and were intimidating black residents from voting in a school board recall election.

"Welcome to the plantation," he offered. "When can we get together?"

The seven members of the Benton Harbor school board had hired Sherwin Allen two springs earlier, in 1993, inspired by his grandiose plans, his indefatigable gusto, and his affability. He seemed assiduously prepared in his effort to get the job. When he came to Benton Harbor for his first interview, he visited schools incognito, dressed in overalls and work boots, telling the principals he was a prospective parent. He was one of two finalists for the job, so three board members—the Reverend Johnson of the Union Memorial A.M.E. Church, George Barfield, an educator, and Dan Ertman, a child welfare worker—flew out to Phoenix to conduct a final appraisal of the candidate. Allen at the time was acting superintendent of one of the city's school districts.

He had them picked up in a limousine and taken to one of Phoenix's swankier resorts, where he played golf with Johnson and arranged for the others to attend a Seattle Mariners exhibition baseball game. He invited them to a breakfast with a group of parents and gave them a tour of two schools. But the high point was a visit to his house. In the living room, empty of any furniture except for golf balls and a putter, Allen had laid out on the floor sheets of paper charting the grade levels of Benton Harbor students. He went through the test scores school by school, recalls Dan Ertman, who sat with the others on the floor and studied the impressive graphs. "He was a straight shooter," Ertman recalls. "I was pretty impressed." Barfield says, simply, "It was magical." They were so taken with Allen, they offered him the job on the spot.

Allen was coming to a troubled school district. It had begun to deteriorate, at first almost imperceptibly, back in the 1950s, when white families quietly and then clumsily attempted to create two school systems, separate and unequal. In 1955, the NAACP's Thurgood Marshall attacked the predominantly white Benton Harbor school system for building a new elementary school in an effort to draw black students away from a neighboring school. Ten years later, black leaders protested efforts to build a second high school, which they believed was intended as a way to provide separate schools for the races. It was never built. Nonetheless, in 1968 the NAACP and black parents sued the school district, arguing that because of past practices, the district had been segregated by fact, if not by law. The predominantly black schools were rundown and had inferior facilities, the NAACP charged. The arbitrary boundaries drawn for elementary school districts only perpetuated segregation. Black teachers were assigned to black schools; white teachers to white schools. And in the junior high and high schools, which were more integrated than the elementary schools, students were tracked, with most black students, the NAACP argued, placed in the slower sections. In a court battle that stretched over fifteen years, the NAACP eventually won, and the court drew up a desegregation plan that called for voluntary busing between two heavily white rural school districts and Benton Harbor. (They were included because they had taken tuition students, most of them white, from Benton Harbor.) During all this, though, voters, angry with the desegregation suit, turned down a series of property-tax increases that would have provided needed school funding. As a result, the Benton Harbor schools suffered more. By the early 1990s, the schools were in such bad shape that an estimated $30 million was needed for repairs. And the students performed so miserably on proficiency tests that the governor threatened to take over the town's schools.

Enter Sherwin Allen. A wisp of a man, Allen resembles a stick puppet; it looks as if a strong wind might not only knock him over but separate his torso from his arms and legs. His watch hangs loosely on his slender wrist; when he waves his arms, it slides up and down on his forearm. His head, small even for his narrow frame, seems precariously perched on his shoulders. But looks, as they say, can be deceiving. He is, in fact, a determined—some might say obstinate—administrator who, with a goal in mind, runs over, around, and through any hurdles that get in his way. As an elementary school principal in Dallas, Allen resigned from one post when, he claimed, administrators reneged on their promise to let him pick his own staff. In the same city, he so improved the performance of students at T. L. Marsalis Elementary School that it was honored by Phi Delta Kappa, a professional educators' organization, as one of the top three elementaries in the country. In Phoenix, despite protests from parents, he extended school hours in the district he oversaw and also offered Saturday morning classes.

When Allen came to Benton Harbor, the school board endorsed his announced mission: to raise test scores, specifically the Michigan Education Assessment Program, known as MEAP. The scores were abysmally low, and, as Allen pointed out early on, tests are "the measuring stick of the employment world." Not only had the dropout rate shot up from 27 percent in 1988 to 50 percent by the time Allen arrived, but only a few years earlier the high school's seniors tested on average at an eighth-grade reading level.

Allen set out to make changes. He introduced evening prep classes in the town's seven subsidized housing developments. Banners went up in classrooms: MCCORD [SCHOOL] CAN HANDLE THE MEAP, and YARD BY YARD, INCH BY INCH, IT'S A CINCH. BEAT THE MEAP, and IT'S MEAP SEASON! KICK IT! The Hull Elementary School held a MEAPS rally, as did one of the housing complexes. The staff served hot dogs and pop, and Allen spoke to the kids, exhorting them to excel. On the day of the tests, Allen personally passed out caramel apples and bubble gum to the students.

"They had those kids so psyched. They put those kids on top of the world," recalls Danethel Whitfield, director of the town's public housing. "Kids would be out of school at three-thirty and on our doorstep at four or four-fifteen for afterschool classes. Not only kids from the housing development. Kids would walk from other neighborhoods. Darndest thing I ever saw. Yeah, I was addicted. To me he was a man who was really committed. He worked long and hard. He was a workaholic. He wasn't a selfish person. He wasn't a person who carried his degree on his shoulder. He'd introduce himself as Sherwin Allen, not Dr. Allen. And he would always say that he accomplished things only because God wanted him to. He was a humble person."

Whatever you can say about Dr. Allen, which is how he introduced himself to me, he was not reticent about his accomplishments. The first time we met, he said, "I have a schedule that a lesser person would not be able to keep." In that busy schedule, the test scores rose dramatically. In two years, the percentage of fourth-grade students testing at their reading level soared from 11 percent to 38 percent. The results in math were even more astonishing: from 12 percent to 53 percent. In the wake of this success, Allen reintroduced Advanced Placement classes into the high school, and talked grandly of providing a laptop computer for every student from kindergarten to twelfth grade.

Allen also prided himself on the formation of what came to be known as Superpac (Superintendent's Parent Advisory Council), an organization made up mostly of mothers who had not been active before, either in local politics or in their children's schools. A few years earlier, a Whirlpool-sponsored study concluded that the system's two greatest ailments were low self-esteem among students and minimal parental involvement. Allen addressed both.

In the first year, the monthly meetings were held at Stump Elementary School over a free hot breakfast. As many as two hundred parents would attend. Allen exhorted and preached. He'd quote from the Bible, which he held at his side, often comparing the persecution of Job with his situation. He'd tell the parents they deserved better for their children, that the schools were their dominion, not the administrators' or the board's. Some mothers felt so empowered that they showed up at schools unannounced, in one case demanding the firing of a teacher who, they felt, mistreated their sons and daughters.

The meetings always ended with the women gathered in a circle, holding hands. Allen would offer a prayer and lead them in a rendition of Whitney Houston's "The Greatest Love of All."

I believe the children are our future . . .
Let the children's laughter remind us how we used to be
Everybody searching for a hero
People need someone to look up to.

It became their anthem; Allen, their hero.

For that first year, it was a love fest between Allen, the parents, and the school board. Test scores rose. Parents became involved. And the board members, celebrating the progress, handed more and more control to Allen. It was as if Robert Moses had arrived in Benton Harbor to repair its roads, or as if General Douglas MacArthur had paraded into the city to lead its citizens to battle. Some even compared the new superintendent to Jesus.

Barfield said it best: it was magical. Or so it seemed.

19.

THE POWERS
THAT BE

The meeting at the Union Memorial A.M.E. Church was called for noon, but the dozen or so local ministers arrived early. It was May 24, 1995, two years after Sherwin Allen had been hired.

On Wednesdays, women from the Reverend Alfred Johnson's congregation cooked and sold weigh-me-down, gotta-have-seconds lunches, so the ministers arrived in time to make sure there was plenty of food still around.

They took their seats at two long tables, plates heaped with yams, greens, crispy and succulent fried chicken, and cornbread so sweet, it was more like dessert. All of them had long been active in the Benton Harbor community; many played prominent roles in the protests over Eric's death as well as over the shooting of Norris Maben. Johnson welcomed his colleagues and opened with a short prayer. "We have one priority," he told them. "Getting people out to the polls."

Sherwin Allen, who stood by Johnson's side, had spearheaded a campaign to recall two board members, both of whom were white, both of whom were trying to fire him. Allen hoped to remove them before they removed him.

When I first came to talk with Allen, I was surprised to learn that the seven-member Benton Harbor school board had three white members. That's because the school district included, in addition to Benton Harbor proper, the six mostly white bedroom communities and rural hamlets immediately surrounding the town, and even though most of the families in them either sent their kids to parochial schools or no longer had school-age children, they voted in considerably larger percentages than the people of Benton Harbor.

So, while blacks made up the majority of seats on the school board, it was a bare majority; moreover, there tended to be more feuding among the black board members than there was among the white board members, leading one Benton Harbor resident to pull me aside and ask, "How do you know how to do this? Do you take lessons? How do you all stick together the way you do?" Indeed, one black school board member had joined in the attempt to oust Allen.

Allen thanked Johnson and, as the ministers feasted, assured them that "this is not about Sherwin Allen," though of course it was. He made a point early on to let these men of the cloth know that he was not in it for the money. "This is my only suit," he said of the blue ensemble hanging loosely on his thin frame. "I have no jewelry," he vouched, holding up both hands, fingers stretched wide, so that the ministers could view the evidence, or lack thereof. Allen started to pace. His head bobbed, like that of a figurine in a car rear window.

"There's a conspiracy against people of color in Benton Harbor," he told them, and he included in that cabal Wiley, the prosecutor, and the three white school board members.

"In southwestern Michigan, it's been decided that the children in Benton Harbor will not be educated," he continued. "When they get finished with me, they're coming after one of you. America is built on haves and have-nots, on slaves and slave masters. This whole thing's about educating our children in America. In America, it's un-American to talk about taking out two white men. There's a group of parents. They've gone out and got twenty-six hundred signatures for the recall petitions . . .

"I know that on Tuesday, we're either going to make it or break it. They're daring us to do something with this election. If you tell people to vote *yes* on recall, they'll vote *yes*. If you tell them to vote *no,* they'll vote *no* . . . They can have my body. But they're not getting our soul. Here's a chance for Benton Harbor to get in charge of its destiny. I've seen people living in places here where the flies don't go. People like you and me, dark-skinned, nappy-haired. We don't even have don't speed signs by our schools, no signs to tell cars to slow down—and we profess to love our children.

"In Berrien County, it's going to be Jim Crow. You know what I mean by Jim Crow. Whatever a black person do, a white person's going to find him guilty. They're going to get me in the morning and get you at night. Once they get a taste of blood, they'll keep on biting. I've got them surrounded. I've got all seven angels around me. This issue's not about me. It's about your children, your city, the people in your congregation."

The ministers seemed energized by the talk, though the food kept them in their seats. They nodded in assent and brainstormed among themselves about how to get people to the polls—or, as the case might be, get the polls to the people. The easiest way, they figured, to encourage people to vote was to distribute absentee ballots—even to people who had no plans to be out of town.

Maybe it was the craziness of the O. J. Simpson trial, but 1995 in the Twin Cities was a time of brittle, raw nerves. Sensibilities were knocked around. When a local tourist organization touted the area up and down Lake Michigan as the White Coast, some blacks objected. The use of the word *white,* they felt, was intended to brag not only of the pristine beaches but also of the beach towns' racial makeup. And when David Walker, the black chief of the Benton Harbor police department, moved to hire more black officers—only four of the twenty-four officers were black when he became chief in 1993—whites in the area denounced him as racist. This despite the fact that St. Joseph's police force had been uniformly white until that same year, when it hired its first black officer—ever. And a rumor circulated through St. Joseph that Louis Farrakhan, who had purchased seventy-seven acres in the southern part of the county, did so because of his connections to Walker and Allen. He knew neither man.

But nothing compared with the fracas over Benton Harbor's schools. It was as if people had lost their footing. Blacks wanted desperately to believe that someone—in this instance, Allen—had stepped up to rescue their community. In Allen, many saw someone unafraid to face down the powers that be, who in their arrogance and hubris appeared to want nothing more than to put an outspoken, popular black man in his place.

Whites, on the other hand, felt vindicated. Here was proof—in the form of Allen—that blacks could be just as hateful, if not more so, than the most wicked of white bigots. There it was, in black and white.

But the truth was less certain than either side was willing to concede, and one needed to look objectively no further than the sad facts—deteriorating school conditions and the alarmingly high dropout rate—to recognize the origins of the anger in the black community or the frustration among whites. Although it was Allen who introduced race into the battle, the white board members—and their friends in high places—took the bait, in the end acting with the imperiousness that Allen and his flock had accused them of all along.

While the Reverend Johnson chaired the school board, the two members who wielded the most clout were Dan Ertman and Ken Woltman, the two now targeted for recall.

Ertman, his body twisted and hunched, has been deformed from birth. His left arm hangs limply by his side. His right hand is turned away from his body at an impossible angle. Often I would hear comments like that of Mamie Yarbrough, a fellow school board member and wife of a city commissioner: "You'd think Ertman would have more compassion. He thinks if he can make it, anyone can make it." Other times, as in the hearing on Allen's future, residents cruelly referred to him as "the cripple" or "that crooked man." But people's main beef with Ertman was that he sent his stepdaughter to a parochial school, which in their minds meant he stood on hollow ground when talking of his commitment to the city's public schools.

Ken Woltman, an insurance agent, is considerably more affable than his colleague. He's chummy, a jester who revels in off-color jokes about women, ethnics, and blacks. He likes to boast that his son married a black woman and that blacks make up half of his business. He'd say that he knew the meaning of CPT: "It's colored people time. I learned that. If you have a banquet that begins at six, it really doesn't begin until six forty-five. They'd joke about it." The time I visited Woltman in his small storefront office in St. Joseph, a middle-aged white man walked in to buy insurance for his new motorcycle. It was in the midst of all the Allen turbulence, and the man proceeded to go off on a riff about "the jerks" running the Benton Harbor schools. "You got to stop the free handouts," he told Woltman, who, clearly uncomfortable, shifted his gaze back and forth between the customer and me. When the man left, his insurance forms filled out, Woltman confided that "that guy refers to 'them goddamn niggers this, goddamn niggers that.'" I couldn't help wondering whether Woltman challenged him when he used such language or, as he had done this time, said nothing.

By the time I walked into this mess, the campaign to oust Ertman and Woltman was in full bloom. Allen publicly said they were "out to lynch him." They did want to fire Allen, the underlying reason being that he had misappropriated school funds. Some of the charges were petty—like allegations that he'd spent $5.01 for a package of Class Act condoms and sixty-eight cents for a Snickers bar—but others bore more weight, like the charge that he spent $9,644.50 to move barely four rooms of furniture and that he bought $386 worth of golf equipment for personal use.

But at the core of the dispute was the issue of power: who wielded it and for what purposes. Ertman, Woltman, and two other board members believed that Allen intended to usurp their role in running the schools, if he hadn't done so already. When Allen's Superpac applied for a $300,000 state grant for student health screening, these board members objected vigorously. How could a group of mothers administer that kind of money? "It was almost like a religious cult," said Jane Strand, the third white school board member. She had attended Superpac meetings for the first year. "He stood up and preached from the Bible. He called Benton Harbor 'a godforsaken hellhole,' and people clapped. He told people it didn't matter what the newspaper said, because you can't read anyway. And people clapped. He said, 'Has anyone told you they love you today? Well, let me be the first.' And they clapped . . . I still think there are five or ten women who would drink that Kool-Aid for him."

When a local preacher complained that Benton Harbor High School students had been taken to see Spike Lee's *Malcolm X,* "an un-Christian movie," these board members demanded that Allen respond. They also demanded that he respond to a letter from a secretary he had dismissed. Allen told the board that he wouldn't be their "public whipping boy" and taunted them by suggesting that they "buy out my contract," a ploy he would use on more than one occasion. And some felt that Allen's emphasis on raising test scores was done at the expense of real learning. There were accusations that some principals had students take old MEAP tests as a way to prepare, a practice that some considered out-and-out cheating, though supporters argued that this was no different from what was done to prepare middle-class students for tests like the SATs.

There were personal clashes, as well. These three board members complained that Allen was late for meetings and for ceremonies, and sometimes didn't show up at all. Jane Strand reeled off half a dozen events, among them a banquet to honor teachers of the year and the performing arts banquet. One principal recalled his walking in forty-five minutes late for a sixth-grade graduation, and offering no apology. They accused Allen of sometimes not showing up for work; instead, they asserted, he could be found on the golf course. Allen did love golf, and he and the Reverend Johnson would, they said, discuss school matters during rounds.

The allegations flew back and forth. It was a footrace to see who could unseat whom first.

On the Friday before the recall election, roughly three hundred parents and students filed into the Benton Harbor High School auditorium, a cavernous hall that, in contrast to the rest of the school, is not only in good repair but boasts some of the best acoustics in southwestern Michigan.

Three television crews, their satellite trucks parked outside, and half a dozen radio and newspaper reporters milled about near the front of the hall. School security guards and police officers paced the hallway outside. I could feel the friction. Outside the school, I had been accosted by a young man who, on spotting me taking notes, half-jokingly suggested to his friends that they hang me from a nearby oak tree. It was like altitude sickness: people seemed short of breath and light-headed. Ertman had asked the sheriff's department for personal protection, which he received. (People wanted to know why he wasn't comfortable asking the Benton Harbor police to carry out the job.) By the school's front door, two young men quietly handed out green fliers, one of which depicted Ertman and Woltman, dressed in Ku Klux Klan garb, about to lower a guillotine on Allen. The blade in the cartoon was nicknamed Wiley.

The seven board members sat far back on the stage behind vel-vet-draped metal lunchroom tables, Ertman and Woltman off to the right by themselves. Each sat stone-faced, without affect. Ertman twiddled a pencil. Woltman crossed his arms against his chest. It was as if they wanted to make a point of appearing calm, quietly confi-dent, almost indifferent to the turbulence around them. Allen, alone with his attorney, sat at a table to the right of them.

After Johnson gaveled the proceedings to order and asked for public comment, speaker after speaker—preachers, teachers, moth-ers, students—rose to denounce the white trio and to praise Allen.

Pastor James Wilkins, of the Peter's Rock Missionary Baptist Church, was the first to approach the microphone set in the aisle, and he brought with him his cloth Bible. "Weep not for me but weep for yourselves and your children," he read, to the accompani-ment of hearty *amens* from the audience. "This is the attitude that this superintendent has taken," he warned. "If they do these things to a well-educated man who has come into our community to help us and our children, what will happen to those less educated?"

Accusations were leveled. "One of the board members roots for the [St. Joseph High School] Bears," asserted Reverend Brown, shaking his head in disbelief. "This is racial. If we get these kids educated, you won't be able to fill up your jails. You won't have people on welfare. You won't be able to print in your newspaper that this is the worst place to live . . . Pitiful. Just pitiful."

A young girl, a student at the high school, pleaded with the board. "I don't understand why you'd want to fire someone who's been an inspiration to us. I understand that some of you don't care, 'cause you don't have children in the Benton Harbor schools. And at some of your businesses you have Bear signs. Go there, then."

"We're ready to die for you, Dr. Allen, 'cause we're not going back," declared the parent Belinda Brown.

And on it went, declaration after declaration, gauntlet after gauntlet thrown down, until a police officer strode down one aisle and ordered people to evacuate the building. "We have a bomb threat," he bellowed. "Please, we need everyone to leave. Quietly and orderly." Everyone obeyed, and when they began to return, twenty minutes later, after the auditorium had been searched, a stinging odor greeted them. Someone had sprayed a canister of mace, so once again parents, students, and reporters, now covering their faces with their hands or kerchiefs, straggled out of the auditorium.

When the meeting finally reconvened after no incendiary device had been found and the mace had dispersed, Strand, the third white board member, a self-proclaimed liberal who had four adopted children, some of whom were full or part African American, introduced a motion to move the meeting to St. Joseph, where presumably they would feel safer. In truth, St. Joseph had nothing to do with this struggle over Benton Harbor's schools, but blacks equated the powerful (in this case, the white board members) with St. Joseph, and the powerful equated St. Joseph with order and security.

The suggestion was met with derision. The Reverend Brown rose from his seat, his body shaking. "You can't control what's not yours! St. Joe can't solve nothing here!" he shouted at Strand. "If Benton Harbor's got a problem, we'll solve it here." Some in the audience stood to applaud.

Allen, meanwhile, had sneaked off the stage and, like an apparition floating among his believers, appeared at one of the microphones. "If this meeting goes to St. Joseph, I won't be there," he declared in his warbling voice. The crowd erupted in applause; then, with a wave from Allen, grew quiet. "I feel a need to talk to these parents and students," he explained to the board members, who seemed bemused by, if not indifferent to, this theatrical display. "A lesser man you might have run off that curb, but not me. You can't pick our heroes . . . I was brought to this district to deal with school achievement, and I feel I've done a good job at it. In fact, I feel that I'm the best in the country at it. Whatever my epitaph reads, I want it to read, 'I came to improve students, and I did.' " Then he pointed to a group of teens sitting nearby. "And you students have made me so proud. Willie here is going to audition for a band scholarship at Grambling."

The Reverend Johnson, uncertain and tentative, looked at his watch, a deliberate motion intended to get Allen's attention. When it didn't slow Allen down, he said, "Your five minutes is up. Dr. Allen. Your five minutes is up."

Allen, with similar dramatic flair, looked at his watch, which he had to retrieve from his forearm. "Is there anybody who will give me their time?" he asked, craning his neck as he surveyed the auditorium. Tens of hands went up. People hollered, "You got my five minutes . . . And my five minutes." Allen continued, while his ally and friend, Johnson, drew back in his chair, clearly bewildered about how far or how hard to push.

"Let me sum up, then," Allen went on. "I can tell you I never stole any money. I'm not going to sit down until I talk about this. The condoms. I don't know where that came from. I don't use them . . . I only have a minute to finish. I might not have this job when I leave here today. The next time you ask for a superintendent, you need to be careful what you ask for. My first two months, I went to every big white person here and said, 'Massuh, do I have your permission to educate these children?' They said yes."

He was rambling now. The board members, including his allies, all got up to leave. Johnson pounded the gavel on the table. "We'll

break for lunch," he shouted over Allen. "We'll break for lunch."
And they did.

Early that afternoon, the hearings resumed.

People continued their march to the microphone, championing
their leader. Allen was beckoned offstage. A minute passed; then
two. The crowd stirred. Allen emerged and informed the school
board that he had been subpoenaed by the state police. The stakes
had been raised. A criminal investigation was now under way; they
had a warrant to search his car and apartment. So Allen and a hundred of his followers headed for his home at the Napier Manor
Apartments, a modest row of three-story apartment buildings.

While state troopers rummaged through Allen's apartment and
car, the parents and ministers gathered by the stairwell, praying and
chanting. What particularly infuriated them that afternoon was the
discovery that Dan Ertman's name appeared on the subpoenas, suggesting that he had initiated the investigation. He denied it. He said
the state police had got in touch with him, wanting to know where
Allen kept his expense receipts.

20.

FISSURES

May 30, 1995. Four days after the search warrant. A week before the recall.

The charges against Allen appeared to have some merit, although they would hardly rate alongside big-city corruption. Allen defended his purchase of golf equipment, because he eventually donated it to the high school. He said the incidental expenses—the condoms, the cigarettes, the dry cleaning—were an error, that he had mistakenly given the receipts to his secretary. He admitted that he spent $98.13 for Georgio Red perfume as a gift to the women school board members, but he argued that it was a legitimate expense. He said it was probably his secretary's mistake that he had submitted receipts for both a rental car and mileage costs, when he should have been reimbursed only for one or the other. But the moving costs, the largest single expense, were the most irksome. A local mover testified that Allen had paid more than three times what other movers would have charged for comparable work. What's more, Allen didn't pay for the move until twenty-two months after his appointment.

The facts aside, the dispute disintegrated into just plain nonsense—on both sides. Ken Woltman complained that Allen drove an old, beat-up car and lived in "a crappy apartment complex" when he should have been setting a better example. And he described the Superpac members, Allen's supporters, as "the dregs." Allen, in his effort to win the recall, had handed out over eight hundred absentee ballot applications, some of them to Benton Harbor High students who had turned voting age. And the fliers not only equated Ertman and Woltman with the Ku Klux Klan, but depicted Allen hanging from a tree limb. The flier read:

STOP THE LYNCHING
VOTE TO RECALL
MAY 30

Wiley, the prosecutor, launched an investigation into the distribution of absentee ballots, and at one point seized records from the school administration building and sent his investigators into homes of residents, warning them of the possible penalties for voting as absentees when they had no plans to be out of town. A local judge issued an injunction against the further distribution of the ballots. Allen and his supporters, turning up the rhetoric a notch, compared these actions with efforts to deny blacks the right to vote in the Jim Crow South. As a protest, Allen refused to accept a Martin Luther King, Jr., award presented at the local community college.

So by the time the school board reconvened, the lines had been drawn. Sabers rattled. Accusations were hurled. And Allen's detractors appeared intent on unseating him. The board hired an accounting firm, at $80 to $115 an hour, to audit Allen's expenses; one of the accountants testified at the hearings. And they invited Gary Shaffer, a detective with the state police, to report on his criminal investigation into Allen. It was Shaffer who had conducted the search of Allen's apartment and car and headed the criminal inquiry into Allen's alleged malfeasance, which now included charges of evading state taxes.

At the next public hearing, Shaffer recounted in detail the results of a search, conducted after a warrant was served on the man who had moved Allen's furniture. He testified that there was no evidence that this was a professional mover or, for that matter, that he was a mover at all, suggesting that Allen had paid a friend generously to move his goods or that no move had taken place. Shaffer's testimony was damning. But people wanted to know how a detective could talk publicly about an ongoing investigation. And then, in what even the most casual of observers considered an arrogant display of power, Shaffer refused to respond to any questions posed to him by Allen's attorney, Roosevelt Thomas. An exasperated Thomas peppered the portly detective. Who, he wanted to know, had initiated the criminal complaint against Allen? Was it Ertman? Another board member? Shaffer refused to answer.

"Are these people [who filed the complaint] black or white?" Thomas asked, to the stifled giggles of the crowd.

"It doesn't matter," Shaffer replied.

"Are they short or tall?"

"It doesn't matter."

"Are they residents of Benton Harbor?"

"They are residents of the State of Michigan." ("Amen," someone hollered from the back of the room.)

"Are they residents of the Benton Harbor school district?"

"Yes."

"Are they members of the Benton Harbor school board?"

"I can't say."

"You can't say or you won't say?"

"I can't say."

"How many people filed a complaint?"

"Several."

"Several? Less than two?"

"No. Several."

"More than two?"

"No. Several."

"Several?"

And so went the exchange. The giggles turned to guffaws. And Roosevelt Thomas's prodding turned to taunting. Shaffer physically recoiled with each barrage. David Walker, the police chief, walked out of the assembly hall, shaking his head. "When they want to get someone, they lose their senses," he muttered.

For many, there was an uneasy familiarity about the proceedings. The powers that be were conspiring to topple yet another black leader—or so the thinking went. Ever since Benton Harbor had elected its first black mayor, Charles Freeman Joseph, in 1971, politics have been emotionally, and sometimes physically, fierce. Much of the wrangling has been between black politicians. But—and this is not forgotten—the county's white politicians have meddled as well.

Shortly after the start of Joseph's second term, political opponents, many of whom were black, initiated a recall campaign, alleging malfeasance, including charges that the city attorney had spent $39 to board his cat, Fluff, while taking the state bar exam. Voters recalled Joseph.

But the memory that lingers for many is the grand jury investigation into Joseph, the first of its kind in Berrien County, launched by the U.S. Attorney. It did not go unnoticed that the grand jury was all white, nor that the U.S. attorney, who was also white, said that he had launched the investigation out of "curiosity." After Joseph emerged from his appearance before the grand jury, he told supporters, "They asked me about my travel to Washington, about the sources of my money, about whether I was getting money from Muhammad Ali, Herbert Muhammad, Willie Mays, or some black national leader." Nothing came of the investigation.

Joseph's successor, Joel Patterson, who was also black, didn't fare much better. He too faced bitter opposition from others in his community. In 1979, he beat Wilce Cooke, another African American, by four votes, but Cooke had the election overturned when he learned that a bureaucratic snafu had kept three residents from voting.

Again, enter the powers that be. Two days after he was out of office, Patterson was indicted by a U.S. grand jury for allegedly defrauding the government. For months, fifteen FBI agents, investigating the charges, had scoured city records and interviewed city employees. In the end, Patterson was cleared of any wrongdoing. Nonetheless, the common perception in St. Joseph is that federal dollars poured into Benton Harbor and fattened the pockets of local politicians, and there is a parallel belief in Benton Harbor that its leaders have been singled out for prosecution.

Political civility has not improved much. One year, the city lost nine department heads, either through resignation or termination. Another year, the town went through three city managers. During my time there, two commissioners came to blows outside the council chambers, and Mayor Emma Hull faced a campaign to recall her from office.

Benton Harbor residents became so frustrated with their own that in 1988 they elected Bill Wolf, a white owner of a local boat supply store. Wolf is a West Point graduate and St. Joseph native who had moved his residence and business across the river and seemed committed to rebuilding the town. In his one term, he attracted developers into downtown, including his brother, who renovated the Vincent Hotel. Many were encouraged. But what embittered many blacks was that Wolf seemed to make such progress because he had strong connections to the county's business and civic leaders. And, of course, he had those connections because he was white.

As the elections approached, Allen's supporters were confident. They had the votes, they assured me, to recall Ertman and Woltman. They then could elect fellow travelers, and Allen would be assured of keeping his job. What they didn't take into account was the split within their own community.

"You got your whites in charge," Allen would say, "then the house neeeee-groes, and then the field niggers." He would draw out *Negroes* so that it sounded like a paragraph instead of a word and give his listeners time to snarl and snicker with him at the condescension in the term. Allen said it so often that his followers began to repeat it as if they had come up with it themselves. For them it helped make sense out of the sharp divisions over Allen within their own community. It was meant to imply that some blacks bowed and scraped to get into the good graces of the whites, who could dole out favors to those they liked, to those they trusted, to those who might do their dirty work. To Allen's flock, it helped explain why Gladys Peeples Burk, a black educator and school board member, joined her white colleagues in their efforts to fire Allen. It helped explain why someone like Sherry Collins, principal of the Gifted and Talented School, decried the emphasis on test scores and suggested that preparation for them bordered on cheating. It helped explain why five former black school board members signed a letter supporting Ertman and Woltman. And it helped explain why George Barfield, the former board member who had helped to hire Allen and who at one point was Allen's right-hand man, had turned on his boss and was chairing the campaign to fight the board members' recall. These people were, in their minds, beholden to those in power. Tomming, they would say. Oreos. Bourgeois Negroes. "They'll sell out the whole race," Allen warned. "The house neeeee-groes can kiss my ass."

If anyone needed evidence that the black community is not monolithic, here it was, crossing and crisscrossing like tracks in a railroad freight yard. All that some whites could see was this roaring steam engine of enmity directed at them, but the truth was, if they cared to look closer, that the black community, unlike its neighbors across the way, held heated and vigorous debates around the issue of race. Where someone like Allen saw salvation within the black community, where he saw the possibility of a separate but equal calculus, others had never lost sight of the prize, racial integration, a sharing of ideas and of resources. Allen believed "they" were after him because he was an outspoken black man. Others thought him a charlatan, who cared little for the district's students and, with no real defense against the embezzlement charges, could only cry racism.

"He was like the emperor without any clothes," said Collins, the principal. "It belittles the real issues. We do have a racial problem. When you conjure up and make up problems, it keeps the real issues buried." Friendships broke apart. Public housing's Danethel Whitfield stopped speaking to Gladys Burks, though they once were friends. Congregations split. The Reverend Donald Adkins, pastor of the Second Baptist Church and father of the comedian Sinbad, who grew up in Benton Harbor, made a point of never discussing Allen with his congregation; the issue was too divisive. And within the schools, principals and teachers split into pro-Allen and anti-Allen factions.

On Tuesday, May 30, voters by a two-to-one margin chose to retain Woltman and Ertman. Again, the predominantly white precincts in the school district far outvoted the heavily black precincts. Ultimately, only two hundred absentee ballots were cast, and they were equally divided between those for recall and those against.

One week later, after weeks of hearings, after the disclosure of a state police investigation, after the testimony of the accountant and the detective, the school board, by a vote of four to three, fired Sherwin Allen. Gladys Peeples Burks voted with the three white board members.

"Now listen," Allen told his supporters afterward; "they're going to have to get someone. Someone's going to have to get on the cross . . . Benton Harbor is a plantation. We have masters. And we have house neee-groes. Benton Harbor is just a bunch of field laborers. The Bourgeois Negroes will sell out the whole race."

The divisions ran deep.

Jared Graves, Benton Harbor police officer: "For them to issue search warrants and shit like that, that lets you know that whites rule, that their power is big."

Carolyn Graves, Jared's mother and former school board member: Gladys Peeples Burks "wakes up every morning and she's the same color as me but she doesn't know it."

Gladys Peeples Burks: "Dr. Allen stirred up racial fears. Had he done it for some purpose other than his self-aggrandizement, I might not have been so appalled."

George Barfield, chair of the antirecall campaign and former Allen ally: "Sherwin Allen is a bell ringer. They ring the bell: 'They're doing it to us again.' Bell ringers believe 'I can't succeed at life 'cause *they* won't let me . . .' You have people like Sherwin Allen who go around convincing people they're victims, when the irony is that Sherwin Allen worked his way to the top of the pile. He earned a Ph.D. How did he do it? I think the loving thing would be to say, 'This is how I did it. Come follow me.'"

Bill Wolf, the former white Benton Harbor mayor: "Blacks can publicly accuse whites of being racist, but whites can never do that to blacks. One thing we joke about is that there's a black Congressional Caucus, a black Conference of Mayors. What if we created a white Congressional Caucus, a white Conference of Mayors? We wouldn't tolerate it . . . there's a clear double standard, and it's infuriating."

Ken Woltman: "The guy was a thief right after he started . . . It's a smoke screen. If you're wrong and have no other defense, you use race. If Mr. Leader Man is a liar and a thief, what else are you going to say but 'racists'?"

David Walker, the Benton Harbor police chief: "Dr. Allen was before his time. He frightened the hell out of people. The progress in the school system, people say it wasn't real, but I doubt that. He moved too fast and the change was uncomfortable."

The Reverend Rodney Gulley, associate minister of the Hopewell Baptist Church: "If he had been more of a yes man, scratched his head, shuffled his feet, he would have made it . . . I thought it was just as well Dr. Allen got fired. I worried he'd turn up missing. Just like that McGinnis boy."

The state police never filed any charges against Sherwin Allen. Allen, who appealed his dismissal, left Benton Harbor and took work as a consultant with, among others, Chicago's public schools. Dan Ertman stepped down after his term ended. And two years after Allen's departure, the State of Michigan became so distressed at the continuing downward spiral of Benton Harbor's schools that it threatened to take them over.

But what lingered long afterward was a thought expressed many times both by Allen's supporters and by his detractors. It was whispered at the hearings—and shouted at a rally. It was hurled at a local

21.

A CONNECTION

On September 11, 1993, shortly after Allen had been hired and long before the skirmish over his tenure, the *Herald-Palladium* ran a front-page, above-the-fold, banner-headline story about allegations made by a Benton Harbor family that suggested Jim Reeves was a bigot.

Reeves picked up the paper that day and seethed. "I don't like this race card stuff," he told me, the color rising in his cheeks. He let out a long, low whistle, and vigorously shook his head from side to side. It would have been comical, had I not known how damn mad he was.

"It doesn't cut any water with me," he continued. "If you're blue, you'll get treated the same way as if you're red. I don't arrest people according to the color of their skin or where they live. I like to think I treat everyone fairly. That Austin case burns me up."

The incident in question had occurred a year and a half earlier, just a few months before Eric's death. Shortly after three in the afternoon of February 27, a Wednesday, a black man dressed in tan coveralls and a navy blue knit cap entered the Emporium, a St. Joseph downtown store that sold swim wear, skateboards, novelty T-shirts, and other assorted items, mostly for the younger set. According to the police reports, he thumbed through a display of greeting cards and then a rack of sunglasses, allegedly looking for Revos, a particular brand. His presence so unnerved the young clerk, Jackie Hill, that she called her boyfriend. The customer sauntered over to the counter and, grinning, told Hill, with an almost soothing calmness, "I'm going to rob you." Hill, taken aback by his smile and his relaxed demeanor, at first thought he was kidding. "I'm going to rob you," he stated again, almost chuckling, but this time thrusting his left hand underneath his sweatshirt so that it appeared as if he had a gun. Hill gently placed the phone receiver on the glass counter, opened the register, and handed the man all the cash, $145.

"That's it?" the man asked.

"Yeah, you can check." She paused. "Do you want the change?"

"No." He was still smiling.

The man placed the wad of bills in his sweatshirt pocket and strolled out of the store as if he had just made a purchase, though once he was on the street, he picked up his pace until he was running west toward the lake.

Hill ran to the front door, locked it, and then called the shop's owner, Connie Yore, who ran a second establishment downtown, an antique store. Hill breathlessly told her of the robbery, described the man, and hung up so that she could call the police. Meanwhile, Yore began the one-block walk to the Emporium; on the way, she spotted a black man in tan coveralls and a knit cap climb into the back seat of a white Honda; two black women sat in front. She memorized the license plate, 722–QCA, and ran to the Emporium as she watched the car make its way to Benton Harbor. She too called the police.

Reeves, who had been cruising the alleys and parking lots downtown looking for the robber, received the description of the Honda over his car radio and began to drive to Benton Harbor. He heard that squad cars from both towns had pulled over the suspects on Riverview Drive, just a short hop over the Bicentennial Bridge.

When he arrived, half a dozen police had surrounded the car, their guns pointed at the suspects, undertaking what in police parlance is known as a "felony stop." Reeves watched from a distance. His assistance at this point wasn't needed. A large black woman in her twenties had just been ordered out of the car. "Keep your hands up," said an officer. "On your neck. On the back of your neck. Don't turn around. Don't turn." The officers were shouting now as the woman walked backward from the car. Then the second woman, in her forties, did the same. "Okay, you, now you," an officer yelled at the man in the back seat. "D'you hear me? Keep those hands up. On the back of your neck. Any resistance and we'll shoot." Lloyd Austin, a housepainter, got out of the car, trembling. As he backed up to the police, his hands gripping the nape of his neck, he was ordered to get down. "On your knees. On your knees. D'you hear me?" Austin knelt down as one cop handcuffed him and, lifting him up, pushed him over the hood of the squad car and searched him for weapons.

Austin pleaded with the cops. Could they loosen the cuffs? What's going on? Why am I being arrested? Could you call Joan Stewart, a former St. Joseph commissioner? She'd tell them, Austin said, that they'd just been painting her house. Could you call the paint store? They'll tell you they were just there ordering paint. Please, what's going on?

A St. Joseph squad car, with Austin in the backseat, made its way back across the bridge to the Emporium. Reeves followed. In an alley alongside the boutique, Reeves ordered Austin out of the patrol car so that the clerk, Jackie Hill, could make an identification. Austin, his hands still cuffed behind his back, emerged and stood up in the alley, just off the street. An anxious Hill couldn't look directly at his face, at first, so she scanned him from the legs up. The paint-splattered tan overalls looked familiar. "That's the clothing," she mumbled. Then, continuing her inspection, she saw the face and, without hesitation, told Reeves, "That's not him. That's not him."

Reeves removed the handcuffs and asked Austin whether he would come back to the police station. He did, and there Reeves apologized to him, his stepdaughter, and his wife, who by this time was in tears. Reeves took mug shots of him, which, Reeves recalled, Austin consented to. Reeves said he took the photos because there had been two armed robberies in St. Joseph's downtown in recent weeks, and this way, if Austin was stopped again as a suspect, he could be quickly cleared. Austin was so cooperative, recalled Reeves, that he offered to be fingerprinted. Reeves said that wasn't necessary—and apologized again.

That was the end of it as far as Reeves was concerned. They had a suspect who, at least by his skin color and apparel, resembled the description of an armed robber. They had gone by the book. The felony stop was nothing out of the ordinary; the police were trained to stop and arrest someone they had reason to fear might be armed. The on-the-street, one-person line-up, while a bit unusual, had been okayed by the prosecutor's office. And when it was determined that they had the wrong man, they released him. And, Reeves would emphasize later, with apologies.

But Lloyd Austin and his family saw it differently. In a lawsuit brought against the St. Joseph police department, they alleged, as reported on the front page of the *Herald-Palladium,* that the police had falsely arrested them and had used excessive force—and, most notably, had violated their civil rights. The lawsuit pointed out that where the robber was wearing a navy blue knit cap, was clean shaven, and stood somewhere between six-two and six-four, Austin wore a brown knit cap, sported a mustache and full beard, and stood five-foot-eleven. Each man was in his midthirties.

The incident generated much buzz. St. Joseph residents I spoke to saw it at worst as a misunderstanding. "You saw a lawyer with a chance to make some bucks to sue the city," asserted Ben Butzbaugh, a city commissioner. "I think that was an honest mistake. That was communication on the fly. As soon as they knew they had the wrong person, boom, they let him go."

Those in Benton Harbor, though unsettled by the occurrence, saw it as confirmation of what they already knew: blacks in St. Joseph raised suspicion. Reeves received an unsigned postcard saying: "Is this how you treat blacks in St. Joe?" So resigned were blacks to what they considered unfair treatment by the authorities that the incident was, in some circles, even met with humor. "They think we all look alike," Carolyn Graves told me. "We all five-nine, hundred and eighty pounds, nappy hair with a beard. Male or female. They say we all look alike. Ohhh, I love doing this to them. Boy. When they say this is John and over here they say this is Pete. And when I get them together and I'll point to John and I'll say, 'Oh, so you're Pete.' He says, 'No, I'm John.' I'll say, 'You only prove my point y'all look alike.' " Carolyn guffawed. "I love doing that."

Not long after the newspaper article appeared, the city reached an out-of-court financial settlement with the Austins. It maddened Reeves. In his mind, the agreement was an admission that he had done something wrong, that he had acted in a mean-spirited, bigoted fashion.

"When somebody says, 'Well, you did this because I'm black,' I'm at the point where I get pissed," Reeves fumed. "That's ridiculous. Especially if they're going to talk about me . . . People are going to hang on to the race card. Well, maybe the black person was oppressed three hundred years ago [sic]. I had nothing to do with that. Nor because I'm a police officer did I have anything to do with the accidental death of Norris Maben. Don't hold me responsible for something somebody else did . . . I don't want to be a bigot. I don't want my children to be bigoted. That's why I'm so adamant about the Austin case. He played the race card. That burns me up."

Reeves had become a lightning rod for the rancor of Benton Harbor. That had much to do with his being a cop. Officer Friendly is not a familiar icon in the African-American community. On the contrary, law enforcement—embodied by a figure like Birmingham's public safety commissioner Eugene (Bull) Connor—has often been the enemy or has been viewed that way. In the South, early in the century, sheriffs often turned a blind eye to lynchings and on occasion participated in them. During many of the devastating urban riots in the 1960s, the police shot innocent bystanders. And, of course, more recently we witnessed on videotape four white Los Angeles police officers assaulting Rodney King, a black motorist they had pulled over for speeding. Only in recent years have police departments made a concerted effort to hire black officers, and when they do, as was the case in Benton Harbor, they are often accused of lowering their standards. Or, as was also the case in Benton Harbor, it is suggested that black officers may be reluctant to arrest their own. So, for many in Benton Harbor, Reeves was just one more apple in the cart, one more white cop insensitive to his neighbors across the river.

The McGinnis case, though, was his albatross. It was raised again and again—and if his name didn't come up directly, it was always "the St. Joe police," which, Reeves knew, meant him. During a friendly game of golf, a black acquaintance questioned Reeves about Eric's death; the doubts expressed so unsettled Reeves that he invited his friend back to his office to examine the case file. And when the Austins filed the lawsuit, a *Herald-Palladium* reporter inquired of Reeves, "What impact did the McGinnis case have on this one?"

Reeves would tell people he welcomed any leads or tips. He would ask them for their own theories—and then debunk them with whatever evidence he had. "I just want the facts," he'd say. But the accusations that Reeves had participated in a coverup stung particularly deep. He would tell me during our numerous visits that people could challenge his prowess if they wanted to. They could second-guess his police work. But, please, he'd implore, don't doubt his intentions.

"That's what infuriates me. Eric died. We could come up with every imaginable scenario, and you know what? We're never going to know until someone shows a videotape or they can tie everything together . . . I take being a police officer very, very seriously, but I take my integrity above everything else."

Reeves took the hits personally, especially those delivered by Ruth—or Ruthie, as he was apt to call her. A few months into the investigation, Reeves realized that he and Ruth, in addition to being parents, had other common ground. For Reeves, it made Eric's case all the more disquieting.

It was a Friday night in August, nearly three months after Eric's death, and Jim said good night to his five-year-old daughter, McKenna, as he left for his twenty-fifth high school reunion. Reeves had graduated from Benton Harbor High School in 1966, at a time when racial tensions were palpable. The complexion of the student body in Benton Harbor's schools had begun to change; in 1961, 10 percent of the graduating class was black; by 1966, the percentage had doubled.

After college, Reeves settled in Fairplain, where he'd grown up, and remained there until just three months before Eric's death, when he and Denise, concerned about where their children would attend school, purchased a home in St. Joseph. Nonetheless, he remained a loyal Benton Harbor High School booster and attended most of its home football games, even rooting for the Tigers when they played the St. Joseph Bears.

Reeves had enjoyed his high school years and eagerly anticipated the reunion. Dressed in a brightly striped Izod golf shirt and blue blazer, he was one of the first to arrive for the start of the weekend's festivities: a cocktail reception at the St. Joseph River Yacht Club. A two-story, prairie-style house that once belonged to a local industrial family, the yacht club is nestled among the plump sand dunes. While it is on the Benton Harbor side of the river, it sits on the strip of prime lakefront property that belongs to St. Joseph. The club still sponsors sailboat races and excursions, but it's primarily frequented for its large swimming pool and monthly summer parties. Its boiler has long since been removed, so it shuts down once the westerly autumn winds blow in. It also sits a hundred feet from the Coast Guard station where Eric's body was found.

On the yacht club's second floor, where picture windows overlook Lake Michigan, Reeves gathered with old friends, some of whom had traveled from as far away as California, Oklahoma, even Caracas, Venezuela. They played with time, drinking and jesting as if this were a pregraduation social. Under the photos and watercolors of beachfront cottages and sleek sailing craft, Reeves's friends spotted his high school sweetheart and mercilessly needled their buddy about the other girls he had secretly dated on the side. He and his boyhood friend Dan Shewman reminisced about their weekend treks to the Edgar Allan Poe Club to hear a friend's rock band. And they laughed uproariously about the time in Mrs. Maas's homeroom when a group of them wrapped shade cords around their necks and, to the gasps of Mrs. Maas, plummeted one by one out the second-floor window. (They landed on the library roof, a couple feet below.) Reeves downed another glass of Rhine wine.

As a friend recounted how Reeves's angora sweater caught fire from a chemistry lab's Bunsen burner, Reeves spotted a familiar face in the board room, a nearby alcove whose walls were decorated with paintings of nineteenth century schooners. Dressed in a purple nylon jogging suit, she sat in a captain's chair, one among many at a long conference table, her attention far away from the chatter about her. It was Ruth McGinnis.

Ruth, too, it turned out, had graduated with the Benton Harbor High School class of 1966. She had not planned to come to the reunion, but her mother, concerned that Ruth had become reclusive since Eric's death, insisted that she get out of the house. It would be good to see old friends. A needed distraction. Besides, her mother stressed, most of the people there wouldn't know about Eric's death. She could, for the first time this summer, talk about something else. So Ruth, reluctantly, had agreed to attend the reunion. Maybe it would get her mind off Eric, at least for a night.

Since Eric's death, she would on occasion buy a fifth of brandy on a Friday night, hoping it would fill the endless emptiness of the weekends. She hadn't had any this night, but by the time she arrived she desperately needed something to calm her jitters. The club's parking lot bordered a marina with sailing vessels and thirty-foot cruisers, with names like *Shalom, Eclipse,* and *Lady Z.* It was the first time since Eric's death that she'd been so close to a body of water. She felt then that she should return home, but, having promised her mother that she would make an effort to get out and meet people, she stayed. Inside the club, she snaked through the crowd past faces vaguely familiar, smiled and nodded, and got herself a brandy. Finding a cluster of old friends in the board room, Ruth pulled up a chair and began almost immediately to drift away.

A short mustached man, slightly tipsy, approached her. Ruth sat upright. "What are you doing here?" she asked accusingly, believing he had come to question her.

"I went to school with you." Reeves extended his hand in greeting.

Ruth looked at him with disbelief. Who are you kidding? she thought.

"Really," Reeves persisted.

He went off to find a copy of their yearbook and returned within minutes. There on page 195 was his senior picture, a smiling, much thinner, big-eared, greasy-haired Reeves. He showed it to Ruth.

"I'm doing everything I can," he said. "All I can. We're interviewing everybody. Everybody. I wish I had more. But, Ruth, I'm doing everything."

"I think you guys are covering something up," she said coldly. "That's what I heard."

"I'm not like that," Reeves insisted. "I'm not covering anything up. That's not how I work. I'm doing everything. Everything possible. Ruth, you know that. And if you hear anything, anything at all, call me. Please call me."

They exchanged a few pleasantries, and Reeves went back to his friends while Ruth wandered through the crowd, occasionally finding a familiar face through the emotional fog. Reeves doesn't remember the evening all that well, though he wonders whether he'd had too much to drink and seemed overbearing to Ruth, or had apologized too profusely for having nothing new to report. Ruth, who remembers the evening only slightly better, has the distinct memory of Reeves pursuing her that evening, like an adolescent boy after an uninterested girl, repeatedly reassuring her that "I'm doing everything. Everything I can." Reeves introduced Ruth to his friends, and though he said nothing about Eric's death, she felt, as she had the first day after his body was discovered, that everyone knew. Wherever she turned, people were whispering, she thought, "That's the mother of that boy who drowned. You know, Eric McGinnis. What was he doing in St. Joseph? He must have fallen in. It's so sad." The conversations, however imaginary, enveloped her.

She felt claustrophobic. Getting out had not helped after all. Without saying good-bye to anyone, she found her way downstairs and left.

But even then, as she walked to her car in a light rain, her umbrella raised, she remembers, Reeves trailed her, wanting to get in one last word. She turned on him, she recalls, and scolded, "If you spent as much time investigating my son's death as you've done following me, you'd find out what happened." Reeves doesn't remember that occurring. Maybe it's because he had drunk too much. Maybe it's because it's what Ruth wishes she had said.

Ruth went on by herself, leaving Reeves to return to the gathering. When she reached her car by the marina, she stood, hypnotized by the boats' rolling movements in the small swells, the rain at her feet washing through the narrow slats of the wooden boardwalk. It suddenly occurred to her, as she looked out over the water, that she was a stone's throw from the river that took her son—and as she turned to the right, she saw through the darkness and the gentle shower the Coast Guard station where her son's body had been discovered. Her remaining strength gave out. Her arm and the umbrella fell by her side. Her chin dropped to her chest, and dripping strands of hair clung to her neck and cheeks. A river of tears mixed with the rain. She pulled at her moist jogging suit, which stuck to her skin. All she could think of, all she could visualize, was what it must have been like to come upon her son's body, bobbing like the boats before her, water-logged and lifeless. "I was searching so hard for things that would make me feel better," she says. But going out on that Friday evening had only made her feel more alone. How could anyone possibly understand her loss?

And as for Reeves, though Ruth would never know this, the discovery of their connection, however tenuous, made the enigma of Eric's death that much harder for him to bear. He looked so grim when he returned to the festivities that his friend Shewman sug-

22.

THE GANGSTA'

Along Pipestone Road, once Benton Harbor's most majestic boulevard, sits a modest forest-green clapboard house. That is, it used to be a house. Now, it's trashed and scorched. The pillars, once white, that hold up the porch roof are charred black. But they're still standing, which is astonishing, given the gutted condition of the rest of the structure. I can only figure that as the flames licked at these posts, threatening to destroy the porch's underpinning, Benton Harbor's three fire trucks arrived. (They were soon assisted by two pumpers from St. Joseph.) The fire had already eaten away at the porch's floorboards, leaving them gnarled and misshapen, like logs after an evening campfire. The flames leaped with such fury and heat that the firemen not only removed the front door and knocked out all the windows, but had to punch a refrigerator-size hole in the roof. Even a couple of weeks after the blaze, passersby could still smell the harsh smoke. It lingered. A fire's ghost.

Passersby also took note of a sign stapled just to the right of where the front door once had been. The Michigan Arson Protec-

tion Committee offered $5000, the sign said, "for information lead-
ing to the arrest or conviction of anyone on arson-related charges." I
couldn't help smiling; almost everyone knew who did it.

It's here, in the story behind the housefire, that we get a hint of why
Ruth McGinnis was haunted by a desolating thought: that Eric had
died as a result of foul play—at the hands of another black. And she
had someone specific in mind. She felt it so strongly that she went to
Reeves, whom she did not at this point trust, and Reeves, perhaps
because of that wariness, vigorously pursued it.

To understand why Ruth believed that Eric may have been
killed by a black, it is necessary to keep in mind what the scholar and
author Cornel West calls "the monumental eclipse of hope, the
unprecedented collapse of meaning, the incredible disregard for human (especially black) life in much of black America." If one spends
time in Benton Harbor and St. Joseph, one can't help being aware of
the turbulence of one and the tranquillity of the other. For all the
fears of St. Joseph's residents that crime will spill over into their
neighborhoods, it hasn't. Most of the victims of Benton Harbor's
sometimes frenzied environment are blacks.

The root of such behavior, admittedly perpetrated by a small
minority but one with a disproportionate impact on the rest of the
community, undoubtedly lies in deep and layered soil. Poverty: 45
percent of Benton Harbor's households receive public assistance.
The breakdown of family: 62 percent of the town's families are
headed by single women. The unraveling of community: the major
institutions, including the newspaper, the hospital, the YMCA, and
the federal offices, have moved to St. Joseph. The loss of hope: an
estimated 29 percent of adults are unemployed. And, of course, just
plain foolish, self-destructive choices.

The whites of St. Joseph certainly had reason to fear for their
safety when visiting or passing through Benton Harbor. Two of the

more highly publicized murders during my visits were those of a white truck driver, who was shot by a nineteen-year-old over a few dollars, and that of the white assistant manager of the Red Lobster restaurant, on the outskirts of the town, who was brutally stabbed by an employee. But the blacks of Benton Harbor also had reason to fear for their safety—all the time. One long-time resident, L. Sonny Bowens, shut down his bar, Sonny's Place, because, he said, "I knew eventually in my business someone would kill me or I'd kill them 'cause of the drugs and crime . . . We create a lot of problems for ourselves."

So it was not a stretch for Ruth to believe that, in a town which in one year recorded twenty homicides, eighty shootings, fifty stabbings, and six hundred reports of shots fired, Eric had been the victim of a brother's frantic fury.

But before we meet the teenage gangster Ruth believed may have been responsible for her son's death, we should hear the story of Cleve Smith. It was Smith who lived in the green clapboard house on Pipestone, with his common-law wife and three children. Just a few weeks before the house was torched, they had fled to another state, to another region of the country. They got as far away as they could. Smith knew people would be coming after him. His tale will, I hope, help explain why Ruth, for a while at least, and quite confidently at one point, believed that the enemy lurked within.

Cleve Smith was living an uneventful life when he shot and killed eighteen-year-old Stanley Perry. And all because of a dispute among children.

Smith's days were consumed by his job as assistant manager at Eagle Super Saver, a Benton Harbor grocery store; in the summer, his evenings were spent with friends, drinking beer amid the five rusting junkers in his backyard. They'd sit on the hood of Smith's corroded black Buick or recline in his vintage lawn chairs under the shade of an oak tree, and talk mostly about the day's events, work, and family. At forty-six, Smith, just over six feet tall, was of slender build, with a thin face sporting sideburns and a scruffy goatee. He was a quiet man. Smith had worked at two jobs in his adult life: twelve years as a laborer at Superior Steel; then, after the factory shut down, thirteen years at Eagle, the last few in management. For nine years, he'd been living with Marion Bady, a spunky woman with doe-like eyes who was ten years his junior, and though they were not married, they had three children together, a girl of five and a set of eleven-month-old twins. Bady had an eighteen-year-old daughter from a previous relationship who also lived with them at 586 Pipestone. Bady worked at Eagle, too; it was where she and Cleve met.

Early in the evening of July 11, 1995, Bady's niece, Tiaisha Bell, ran breathlessly into Smith's backyard. Four girls pulled up in a van and ran after her, shouting at her, deriding her for not joining their street gang. Bady cautioned the girls; this was someone's home. Respect that. Respect her niece. They left. It didn't seem a big deal, though Bady and Smith were distressed by the girls' brazenness. They were sure the girls would have pursued the niece into the house if they hadn't been there.

The two, along with Bady's brother, Anthony Walker, who lived in the basement, and his girlfriend, Rochelle Buels, continued drinking and laughing in the backyard when suddenly brakes screeched and car doors slammed. Twenty to thirty teens, boys and girls, emerged from half a dozen cars lining Catalpa, the street behind the house. Smith and the others raced to the house's back entrance and placed their bodies square against the wooden door as a human barrier. The teens came rushing through the woods toward the house.

"Ain't nobody gonna mess with my Teka," Smith warned them, using the nickname of Bady's niece, Tiaisha. He later testified that then "the crowd got a little rowdy and started coming in on us a little bit. Anthony and me, you know, we stood right at the back door to keep them out of the house, and all of a sudden this guy run up and stop, and when he stop he took his hand right here"—Smith placed his hand under his shirt by his belt—"like he had a pistol and backed back off of me and told me, 'Don't push my brother.' I said, 'Man, I didn't push your brother. Who is your brother?' That's when he come back at me with his left hand. But he never did take his hand off of his pistol . . . So while he's swinging at me, I'm duck'n, duck'n his licks, and the fight broke out then."

Someone swung a broomstick at Bady, hitting her solidly in the thigh. Her brother, Anthony, was knocked out; he couldn't remember how. One of the teens—whom everyone called, with good reason, D-Day—then fired a pistol into the air three times. Either it was an arranged signal or the sounds inspired his friends, because at that point others in the crowd, no one knows how many, brandished their handguns and started firing. But not into the air.

A bullet struck Rochelle Buels in the upper back as she kneeled over her unconscious boyfriend, Anthony Walker, and lodged in her bladder. Another shell grazed Bady's forearm, leaving a trail along her skin. Luckily, no one else, including the infant twins, was injured. The teens retreated through the woods. Doors slammed. Tires screeched. Like a sandstorm, they were gone as quickly as they had appeared.

When the cops arrived, Smith, agitated and, according to one officer, "obnoxious," pleaded with them to give chase, but they insisted on a description first, which neither Smith nor the others, in all the commotion, could provide. "Well, don't worry about it," Smith told one of the officers. "Those motherfuckers come back over here, I'm gonna kill them all." The words would haunt him.

Later that night, another of Bady's brothers, concerned for his sister's safety, delivered a shotgun, a ninety-year-old one-shot pump Remington, so rusted and cracked that he had to fire one of its three shells to prove to Smith that the museum piece actually worked. Smith hadn't fired a gun since he was a young boy in Arkansas hunting snakes.

Now fast-forward to the following evening, a Wednesday. The adults and the children at 586 Pipestone were dreading a return assault. Smith, though, didn't want the gun in the house, where the children could get at it, so he had locked it in the trunk of the Buick out back. He and Walker leaned on the hood of the car, sipping on twelve-ounce-cans of Milwaukee's Best, which they'd taken from their cooler.

In the dusk, Smith heard, then saw, three figures trample and rush through the woods toward the house. One of them, Stanley Perry, his shorts hanging off his butt, his torso naked in the tropical summer air, his striped shirt balled in one hand, slowed down and sauntered up the driveway. He stopped a few feet from Bady, who was guarding the back door.

What Perry, whom everyone called Lang-Lang, then said is in some dispute. "I'm gonna kill you mothafuckers. I'm gonna kill all you mothafuckers," is what Bady and her brother Anthony Walker heard. Another witness contended Lang-Lang made no such threat. But everyone does agree that he asserted, "You gotta keep me outta this shit. I didn't have nothin' to do with yesterday." He shook his finger at Bady.

Bady called out for Smith, using his nickname, Danny. "Danny, Danny, they back! He got a gun. Shoot, Danny, shoot. He got a gun."

Smith, who had been leaning on the hood of the Buick, ran around to the trunk and grabbed the loaded shotgun. *Baaaam.* One shot. Perry took off, running. Smith stayed by the Buick. He knew the police would be by soon.

When Peter Gavalis, a Benton Harbor patrol officer, arrived, Smith turned over the gun. Gavalis then searched the driveway and in the beam of his flashlight found first a striped shirt, next, a few feet farther along, a .22-caliber Jennings semiautomatic pistol (which, it turned out, belonged to Perry), and then the body of Perry, lying on his side, his shorts down below his green underwear. His face was planted in the grass, exposing the words WEST SIDE G'S carved in his hair at the base of his scalp. The pellets from Smith's shot had peppered Perry's left side, leaving pencil point–size wounds, some oozing blood. The pellets had penetrated virtually all of Perry's organs, notably his heart and lungs. Smith hadn't known his shot had hit Perry until the officer found the body. He was cuffed and arrested and charged with first-degree murder.

Smith took the stand at his trial, where he admitted under cross-examination that he never saw Perry with a gun, though he assumed he had one because Bady had screamed, "He got a gun." His view of Perry was partly blocked by one of his junkers, a white Blazer rimmed with rust. "I was trying to protect my family," Smith haltingly told the jury, trying to hold back tears. "I didn't want him to shoot Marion or no one else, but he was up there with his gun. My thought was to shoot before he shoot."

It's sometimes said that each of us is connected to everyone else by six degrees of separation. This shooting, it might be said, was connected to eight other shootings by merely two degrees of separation. D-Day, whose proper name is Anthony Robinson, two weeks after this incident shot and killed Robert Hubbert, or Huggy, over $10. Huggy's brother Shawn, also known as Pop-a-Lot, shot a seventeen-year-old girl in the face who had, in his words, gotten on his nerves begging for dope. Antwan Armstrong, the lone witness to this shooting, killed himself because he had been accused by gang members of being a snitch. Cortez Atkins, who witnessed the suicide, shot and killed Robert Clark after an argument at a party. Perry himself was a suspect in the slaying of Donald Jenkins, a Benton Harbor High School ninth-grader. And Cleve Smith's brother Tommy was shot at in two separate hold-up attempts of his convenience store, Bumpy's.

All of this in a town of twelve thousand. All in a period of twelve months.

And this does not take measure of the retaliations against Smith and his family. Smith's mother had a rock thrown through her front window. Police were so worried about friction at the trial that they patted down everyone entering the courtroom. The day of the verdict, the Benton Harbor police brought in state troopers to help patrol the town; there had been threats by the gang against Smith's family. And a month later, according to the state fire marshal, the house on Pipestone had been set afire with gasoline poured over the front porch and in the entranceway. The police suspect it was set by members of Perry's gang.

After the three-day trial, the jury of eleven whites and one black deliberated for four hours, discussing how they might have done the same to protect their own families, yet lamenting the taking of a young life. In the end, the jurors, identifying with Smith, found him not guilty. Smith and his family immediately went into hiding and soon left town to start life anew.

"I guess what it shows is if you're there, it'll eventually come to you," said Janet Kilpatrick, one of the jurors. "He lived a decent life and yet he still became involved."

That is what Ruth had most feared: that even though Eric was a decent kid, he might be drawn into the anarchy of the town's gangster youth.

Kathy Miller, Ruth's friend and co-worker, gave me more background and history. "I was at Deer Forest Park. There's this girl there. She says, 'Everybody has said everything about Eric, but I know the truth.' And I said, 'Oh, do you?' I never let on who I was or anything like that, and she says, 'Yeah.' She says to me that some-body in the police force had said that Eric was at the Club and there was a girl there. She was a Caucasian. And Eric had got into a confrontation with some guys in the Club, and she said that the guys had chased Eric.

"And another version came up that Eric had stole some money out of a person's car, twenty-four dollars [sic]. Did you ever hear that one? And it's said one guy took off to chase him. And then another one chased him. And then Eric had got caught against a dead-end and he had a choice of getting killed or jumping . . .

"Another theory is that he was up there on the bridge on a challenge and then fell in, 'cause they say he was real daring and that he liked to bullshit around and stuff like that . . .

"I wouldn't rule out suicide. You'd be surprised how the young kids are troubled in their minds about different things in their life that you just don't know about.

"And then there's Ruth's theory: that some black guy killed him. Did she tell you that? She thinks that a black guy killed him because of something that happened out there at the [housing] com-plex . . . I think she blocks out that whites could have killed him, 'cause she's close to a lot of white people. And to believe that they would do something like that to her child is unperceivable."

Indeed, shortly after Eric's death Ruth told her boss, Dick Mil-ler, "I don't want this to be a racial issue. Eric got along with too many people. I have too many friends on both sides of the river." Miller was one. After Eric's death, he paid to have one of Ruth's brothers flown in from Seattle for the funeral. At company gather-ings, Eric had taught dance moves to the children of some of Ruth's white colleagues. Ruth purchased many of her clothes at Honeybee Fashions, a clothing boutique in St. Joseph. And after Eric's death, Ruth received her greatest comfort from a support group of parents who had also lost children. The group, which met in the basement of St. Joseph's First Congregational Church, was, with the exception of Ruth, all white. One long-time member, Harvey Johnson, a dentist who had lost his son in an auto accident, was especially important to Ruth. On her first visit to the group, she lost her nerve and turned to leave before entering. Johnson ran up behind her and called her name. Ruth started to cry.

"He said, 'You're gonna be okay,' " Ruth told me. "He just took me in his arms, held me so tight. I just busted out. Broke down. I couldn't figure out how I was crying and here are all these people who were crying. But I learned.

"It was very hard for me to cross that bridge and go over there, but I got to tell you it was the best thing I ever did."

Ruth got along. She had to. She lived in Benton Harbor. She worked mostly with men and women from St. Joseph. She trusted, so much so that she didn't hesitate to call on the white-owned funeral home to handle Eric's burial. And she was dismayed by the heightened abuse in her own community. "The more I saw what was going on on the news," she told me, "I could see something like that happening" to Eric.

One afternoon, a few weeks before his disappearance, Eric had come home from school sulking. He barely mumbled hello before going up to his room, his head pulled down into his shoulders. Ruth followed him.

"What's going on?" she asked. "Why aren't you outside playing basketball or something?"

"Ehh, I don't want to," Eric said as he flopped face down on his bed.

Eric told her that another boy from the apartment complex had been threatening to hurt him if he didn't stop dissing the guy. Eric loved to score on friends and could easily get carried away, though he told his mom that someone else had been egging the boy on, whispering that Eric was passing on rumors about him.

Eric was not particularly streetwise, though at times he crowed to others, particularly in St. Joseph, that he was "deep into it." In truth, he wasn't particularly savvy in the streets. He didn't smoke marijuana, according to friends. Nor did he run with the gangs. Nor did he like to fight. "I'm the fighter," Ruth told me. "He's not. He'd run from any type of conflict."

Ruth asked him who the boy was. "We looked out the back window and there he was. He was older than they were. He was like eighteen already. So I went out, because eight or nine months ago this kid'd been over to the house. He'd been down in the basement, playing records and stuff. And I'm just thinking about me being a teenager, this stuff happens, and then they're back friends again.

"I went out and told him, 'Hey, Dennis, what's going on? Why are you and Eric arguing like this? What'd he do to you?' And he says, in a bully tone of voice, 'Well, you know he had no business going back and saying so-and-so about me.' I says, 'Come on. You've been in my house. You've ate my food. You don't need to be doing this. Come on; you guys make up. Come on in. Come on in.' So I brought him into the house. He came in and we talked for a minute, and they said, okay, we'll be cool. They shook hands. Everything was okay. I thought."

Eighteen-year-old Dennis Marshall, a high school senior, had recently moved in with his aunt, Lucy Brown, a neighbor of Ruth's. He had fled the gangs in his hometown, Aurora, Illinois, a blue-collar city of 100,000, forty miles west of Chicago. It's not that he didn't want to join them. It's that he was in with them too far. A member of the Black Gangster Disciples, Dennis had lost friends to gang violence. He had had a rival place a .357 Magnum to his temple and pull the trigger. Luckily, the magazine was spent. At that point, Dennis worried that they'd come after his mother and younger brother, so at their urging he went to live with his aunt in Benton Harbor.

When I finally tracked Dennis down, he was twenty-four, living in Kalamazoo and working fifty-plus hours a week, tagging clothes at a pricy clothing store. He had, he readily conceded, served time for possession of a gun as well as for robbing a convenience store, but he claimed—and certainly appearances bore him out—to have chosen a new path. We met in a basement apartment he shares with his cousin. Six feet tall and muscular, with a silky complexion, he is a handsome young man. His hair is closely cropped, accentuating the angular features of his face, especially his high cheekbones. Only his droopy eyes detract from his good looks, making him look alternately surly and sad.

Dennis remembered Eric, though he says they weren't particularly close. They shot dice together and played basketball. He said Eric was a wannabe; he acted as if he was in tight with the gangs, when in fact he wasn't. Eric would greet Dennis with a "Whas up, GD?," as in Gangster Disciples, or he'd give Dennis the gang's handshake, which resembles, however slightly, a pitchfork, the Disciples' symbol.

"He try to represent," Dennis said. "I told him don't represent something you don't know nothing 'bout, 'cause one day you might have to go to the penitentiary. He try to impress by trying to be hard, talking big shit, what he can do and what he can't do. Like womens. Like he a player. Like he can have this many women do this to him, and get their money. You know, breaking them. Take you to the mall, buy you clothes. Yeah, he talk 'bout it. He tried to be somebody he ain't."

Eric was a prankster, a bit of a misfit, a kid who hadn't figured who he was or who he wanted to be. "He was cool," Dennis said, "but sometime it get on your nerve. Calm down with all that clowning."

A few days after Ruth admonished Dennis and had him make up with her son, Eric's clowning went too far. On the bus back from school, the two sat across the aisle from each other, and Eric started flagging Dennis's new do, a haircut shaped in a high box, the top dyed burgundy.

"What you doing with a building on your head? Man, that Kool-Aid shit wear off?" And on and on went Eric.

Dennis, who had a temper, stood up, as did Eric. They faced each other in the aisle.

"I'm gonna bust you in the mouth, you don't stop flapp'n them lips," Dennis warned.

"Neh, it ain't gonna happen like that."

Dennis was, to use his word, "shocked" that Eric, who was scrawnier and shorter, didn't back down.

"Fuck'n bitch," Dennis shot back.

"Man, you some punk."

"You need to get the fuck away from me," Dennis growled. "You know you can't hold up with me. Get the fuck out of my face. 'Cause you know and I know you can't do nothing with me. So don't be wastin' my time." Dennis jabbed with his right, hitting Eric square in the mouth. Eric ran home to his mom.

This time, Ruth went to her neighbor's to confront Dennis. She had Eric in tow. The four stood in Lucy Brown's kitchen. As Ruth remembers it, Dennis was defiant.

"I've had it," Ruth scolded. "I cannot let you hurt my baby. I cannot let you hurt my baby."

"Well, you better keep your baby away from me," Dennis said angrily. "I'm gonna fuck'm up." He nodded in Eric's direction.

"What is going on here?" Ruth pleaded. "What did he do? Tell me."

"Naw, he gonna tell me that, you know, if I hit him, he's gonna tell his momma."

"I can't let you do this. I just can't let you do this." Ruth made Dennis apologize and, again, had the two shake hands. Dennis remembered all of this except for having hit Eric. He wasn't sure he had done that. "Eric's mom wanted to know the reason why me and him got into it," Dennis said. "The reason was stupid. But I apologized to him." Ruth, however, wondered whether Dennis hadn't carried a grudge.

At Ruth's insistence, a few weeks after Eric died, Reeves located Dennis. They met at the housing complex's main office. Reeves remembers being struck by Dennis's bravado. Dressed only in bib overalls, his lithe, muscular frame on display, Dennis slouched in a chair and boasted of his ties to Chicago street gangs. He pointedly told Reeves that he didn't care for Eric but had no reason to kill him. He said that on the night in question, he was either at his aunt's or at a music studio, recording raps. Reeves wrote in his report that "when asked to do a slight encore, Marshall immediately broke into a rap session which lasted about 4 minutes."

"He was really cocky about the fight," Reeves remembered, "and told me if he had something to do with Eric, he wouldn't have thrown him in the water; he would've taken care of the issue. He wouldn't be the type to gang up on him later on. If they were going to fight, he would fight right then and there."

Reeves did not think Dennis was involved in Eric's death, though for a long time Ruth did not let go of the suspicion. Six months later, she called Reeves again; she heard that Dennis had been arrested in Kalamazoo. Reeves checked into it and learned that Dennis, on his way to an Ice Cube concert, had been stopped by Kalamazoo detectives, who discovered a revolver in his suitcase. Dennis told me he and his two friends had the gun because they were afraid of getting jumped in a strange city. Reeves never found any evidence that Dennis had killed Eric; in fact, Dennis never visited the Club. He rarely went into St. Joseph.

"That made me mad, you know, they talk about it was an accidental drowning," Dennis said. "I still believe to this day he was murdered 'cause he was messing with that white girl over there."

The week after Eric's death, on a grassy knoll behind the Benton Harbor High School's cafeteria, a group of black students surrounded one of their white classmates and taunted him, suggesting he and all the other whites knew something about Eric's death. The terrified boy dropped his book bag. "I don't know," he stammered. "I don't know anything." Dennis pushed his way through the crowd. "You should of know," he bellowed at the boy, and then punched him in the face.

"They steady hollering that accidental stuff. It wasn't no accident," Dennis told me, his voice rising. Four years after Eric's death, my mention of it still riled him. That happened in interviews with others, too. It particularly bothered Dennis that after the reconciliation in his aunt's kitchen, the two never spoke again. He never had the chance just to say, "Whas up, Eric?" Just something that would have indicated that their dispute was in the past. And, like others, Dennis believed Eric's death was not vigorously pursued.

"Nobody want to do nothing about it. And then after, you don't hear nothing; it like it faded. And I feel if a white boy got killed in Benton Harbor, they'd have the National Guard over here. It don't make no sense."

23.

THE FIRECRACKERS, A GIRL NAMED TERESA, AND OTHER ASSORTED MATTERS

Jim Reeves has visualized the scene many times over. As have I.

Shwoooo . . . Pop! Shwoooo . . . Pop! Shwoooo . . . Pop!

From where he stood outside the Club, Eric could hear the swoosh and then the abrupt report of a bottle rocket. He had, we know, chosen not to pay the $5 entrance fee at the Club that night, because there were so few teens there. He strolled across the street and down the alley alongside the aging, red-brick YWCA. In the city parking lot behind the Y, he ran into four boys, all white, all from St. Joseph or Lakeshore, a bedroom community just south of St. Joseph. They didn't know Eric other than by sight from evenings at the Club. Here's what they said happened.

The five teens gathered behind the YWCA and one of them, John Farrish, distributed bottle rockets to the group. An antic Eric, spotting a parked YWCA van, tried the side door, and found it unlocked. He went in and, while crouched on the floor of the van, lit one of the firecrackers. *Shwoooo . . . Craaaack*. The van's metal amplified the small explosion. The kids, though this is not in the police report, must have reveled in their mischief, laughing, cursing, maybe even high-fiving one another. They were, after all, fifteen and sixteen years old. The five of them then wandered across the street and on top of the bluff overlooking the lake, near a Revolutionary War cannon, shot off another three or four rockets, using the grass as a base for the miniature explosives. There, according to two of the boys, Eric boasted of belonging to a gang and told the awe-struck kids that he could get them any drugs they wanted. They huddled in a small group, as Eric, they reported, pulled out a wad of bills to show them the kind of money he carried. One of the boys told the police he saw the money in a wallet (no wallet was ever found); another said he couldn't make out the money in the dark but heard Eric brag about it.

Much of this is sketchy, based on my reading of police interviews with the teens. The boys, now young men, declined to discuss the evening with me. (One of them has since been killed in a motorcycle accident.) The mother of one, with whom I spoke briefly by phone on two occasions, said she didn't want her son talking with me, because "it's a long time ago and put to rest. I'd like to try to keep it that way. I hate to stir anything up again." She also told me, "We don't know more than what he told the police. It had nothing to do with race. Some people just like to look for a racial excuse. He may have just fallen into the river. It's just too touchy a thing between Benton Harbor and St. Joe. This is a small town and I have to live here." Immediately after Eric's death, she kept her son out of school for a few days; she feared some harm might come to him.

What I can ascertain from the police summaries of the interviews is that the boys crossed the street again, back to the parking lot behind the YWCA. There, Eric, who had not let on about his intentions, entered Ted Warmbein's car. From here, the story picks up as related earlier. The boys told the police they watched, distressed, as a white man in a pink shirt chased Eric past the Elks Club and down State Street, away from them, away from the Club, away from downtown, away from the river. Not knowing the reason for Eric's flight, they ran to the Club for help.

Reeves learned all this within the first week of the investigation. The boys' individual stories jibed, and each took and passed a polygraph test. So there was no question in Reeves's mind that Eric had shot off firecrackers with these boys. It was Reeves's second break in the case, his first having been the discovery that Eric probably was the boy chased by Warmbein. There were still many questions, though, most importantly: what happened to Eric after Warmbein lost him?

The weeks immediately following Eric's death were filled with rumors, innuendoes, mistaken accounts, and outright lies; it was as if Reeves was riding a carnival's tilt-a-whirl. He was going in circles, making little progress. Making matters worse was the unpredictability of adolescents—of the ninety-one people interviewed, seventy-one were teens (one was twelve years old). Reeves often felt the case would come unhinged. Many of those interviewed had no sense of time. What one said happened a week ago had really happened a month ago. They'd pass on rumor as if it were fact. And a few claimed to know more than they did (sometimes they knew nothing), while all they wanted was attention, to know that someone, in this case Reeves, depended on them. Reeves became so frustrated at one point that he considered bringing in a psychic.

To read the police report is to be whipped around with Reeves. Contradictions abound. No one was at the Club that night; it was packed. Eric was a strong swimmer; Eric so feared the water, he would barely wade into the lake up to his knees. Eric got into an argument with some white guys over dancing with a white girl; Eric was too carefree to get into an altercation. On and on.

As I read the report for the tenth or eleventh time, I realized how disoriented Reeves must have felt. It was like asking a group of partying teenagers, "Who broke my antique vase?" They're too bound up in their adolescent cocoon to have noticed; or they won't talk because then you'll know they were partying; or they don't want to snitch on their friends. Reeves was understandably dazed by all the paths that opened up and closed and opened again. But as I read the report and tried to build a kind of flow chart—who mentions whom, who knows whom, who was where when—I was struck by all the dangling threads waiting to be cut or tied.

In the police file labeled complaint #1906–91 is a section entitled TIP SHEETS; it contains scores of assorted leads, rumors, half-truths, and out-and-out fables. Among the more intriguing are the following:

Chriswell works at the Club and saw several black males enter a police car and leave the area after speaking with the officer. Stated that all males were wearing long coats; one had a red coat.

Holly Chriswell, a pony-tailed blonde, attends Michigan State University in East Lansing. Pretty, high-spirited, and athletic, Chriswell, according to others, was one of the more popular girls at St. Joseph High School. Of her hometown, she says, "It's the best place I could have been raised. It's always green. We didn't have to worry about guns or knives in high school; teachers were still concerned about running in the halls. I could jog at eleven at night . . . We were always warned of Benton Harbor. There'd be a rape at the mall—and our parents wouldn't let us go. It's terrible to say, but St. Joe is so white that when you see a black person walking there, you wonder what they're doing there."

So she remembers that night, standing outside the Club at around eleven, and seeing four to five black teenage boys hanging out on the corner in front of Schu's Grill and Bar. Dale Easton, the St. Joseph police officer who earlier that evening had taken the car burglary report from Warmbein, spotted the boys and stopped to strike up a conversation. He had no reason to suspect anything, and he didn't know at this point that their friend was missing. He asked where they were from. They told him. Did they have a way back? No, they said. He offered them a ride over the bridge in his squad car.

"Dale's always telling you how he's connected," said Reeves. "How he's got these informers, how he's working on this big case. He'll try to shuck and jive with people. Dale's also kind. It wouldn't surprise me a bit that he gave the kids a ride home. He'd come up and say, 'Hey, what's happening? What's going on here?' 'Well, we need a ride.' 'Hop in. I'll take you home.' He's probably talking with them on the ride home. Who's doing this, who's doing that."

I tracked down two of the teens, Ollie Horne and Steve Green, both of them friends of Eric. I found them at Horne's home, a small split-level ranch house on a potholed Benton Harbor side street. A Tupac Shakur rap blasted through the brick walls and from the sidewalk I could make out snippets of the lyrics.

Someone turned it down as I entered. Horne stood at the top of the stairs, arms folded across his chest. I walked up two steps and extended my hand in greeting. His arms remained crossed, his eyes defiant.

"Whas this about?" he asked.

Steve Green, a tall slender young man, came upstairs from the basement. He shook my hand heartily.

"Whas this about?" Horne asked again.

I told them about the book.

Horne, who still stood above me at the top of the stairs, made a sweeping motion with one hand. "This is the ghetto," he informed me. "That's my boy. I got a lot of pain." He patted his heart, hard enough so that the gold chain around his neck rose and fell with the thumping. "Why should I let you take my book?" He walked down the stairs and past me to the door. "Come on, Steve. You coming?"

Green seemed hesitant. His friend beckoned again. Green

turned to me and started to talk while Horne stood impatiently by the door, one hand on the doorknob. Green told me that Eric had come by his house after school that Friday to ask whether he wanted to go with him to the Club, but he wasn't home. He said that shortly before—maybe it was the previous weekend; he couldn't remember—Eric had told him about being hassled by some white teens at the Club. When Green and Horne arrived at the Club that Friday night, Green says that the manager, Chris Adams, told them that Eric earlier had been in a scuffle with some white guys. Of course, that may have been a reference to Eric's encounter with Warmbein.

"I don't know who killed him over there. Alls I know he was thrown in the river," Green told me. "Someone chased him by the beach, by the pier, chased him or threw him into the river." Before I could ask why he believed this, Horne's remaining patience gave out. "I got to go. I don't got time for this shit. You com'n, man? I'm leaving." Horne left. Green followed. And I was left in the house as someone, maybe it was Horne's mother or his sister, turned the music up, way up.

Green struck me as holding something back. He seemed to know more. At one point, he was about to tell me something about Lisa Liedke, Eric's white girlfriend, but Horne had glanced at him disapprovingly. Green later moved to Grand Rapids, and no one knows of his whereabouts.

Clayton is daytime railroad bridge tender. Gave schedule reports and persons names working 5/17 and 5/18. Interviews will be conducted.

There was much speculation that Eric, after eluding Warmbein, may have tried to get home by crossing the railroad bridge, and in the dark fell into the river. One of Reeves's friends even suggested that perhaps Eric, while crossing the bridge, stopped to take a leak and got electrocuted. That would have explained why Eric's pants were open when he was found. Reeves learned the bridge was open from 11:40 P.M. on Friday night until 6:30 the next morning, meaning that there was a period when Eric could have attempted a crossing. But Reeves also learned that there were no electrical rails or live wires that Eric could have come in contact with, thereby nixing the speculation that he'd been electrocuted.

Mrs. McGinnis saw Gayles wearing a Task Force jacket, which she thought was that of her deceased son, Eric McGinnis. Gayles indicates he has had this coat for some time, prior to McGinnis' disappearance. Mrs. Gayles, Devon's mother, indicates that she is the one who bought the coat for Devon at Bargain Center & she has a receipt.

This was one of the more promising leads. Eric's missing coat baffled Reeves. The police had searched the St. Joseph arboretum along the river's edge, thinking that if Eric tried to swim across the river, he may have hidden the coat in the shrubbery, beneath a tree, or under the bridge. Three scuba divers from the St. Joseph police and the sheriff's departments combed the muddy river bottom from the seawall out fifteen or twenty feet, where they found splintered planks from an old dock and assorted junk. But no coat.

That Task Force jacket was the one that Eric treasured so much that he had had a fake fur collar added to it. The coat worn by Devon Gayles, a friend of Eric's, had a similar collar.

Reeves, responding to Ruth's call, had Gayles apprehended at church. The police had him sign a Miranda card after reading him his rights, and Reeves met up with him at the Benton Township police station, where they were joined by Gayles's mother. Gayles, it turns out, had purchased the collar from a friend for $5 (the friend confirmed this), and Eric, who much admired the coat, copied the idea. Gayles gave Reeves a list of adults who could verify that this was his jacket. They did.

While interviewing Gayles, Reeves noticed that, like Eric, he had a pinky fingernail painted red. Gayles told Reeves that his girlfriend did the artwork but that he had no idea what it meant. Disingenuous, Reeves thought, so he put out a bulletin asking area police departments for any information regarding the significance of such a marking. No one responded. According to Eric's peers, it was a playful thing, an indication that you were a "player," that you had a girlfriend or girlfriends. Gang members I spoke to said it did not indicate membership in a gang, which is what some assumed.

Jermain said a guy paid Eric $40.00 to do something w/ retarded girl.

[Dale] Cryan [principal of Lake Michigan Catholic High School] was asked to help locate a female by the name of Teresa who would have gone to the club on 05/17/91. Cryan came up with the name of Teresa Budrow.

This may have been one of the more perplexing leads. According to the teens who attended the Club, one of the regulars there, an older girl, maybe twenty or twenty-one, seemed mentally slow. Rumor had it that someone bet Eric money he wouldn't dance with her, or maybe it was that he wouldn't have sex with her. No one knows for sure. The girl's name may have been Teresa.

So Reeves went looking for Teresa. One Teresa he came across was definitely not slow, and besides, she told him emphatically, she'd never date black boys. Never.

Reeves did find a girl who was dull-witted and who attended the Club regularly. And who knew Eric. But her name was Mary. She knew nothing of Eric's death, and wasn't at the Club the night he disappeared. The truth of the matter is that the girl named Teresa may not have existed. "We thought we were looking for a Teresa, but we kept coming up with Lisa Liedke," said Reeves.

24

A THEORY

There was still Steve Marschke and Ted Warmbein and their involvement in the events that followed the shooting of the fire-crackers.

Marschke submitted a written statement to Reeves:

At approximately 8:15 pm on friday May 17, 1991 I was at home and received a telephone call from Jerry Frank. I was asked to meet him at the Silver Dollar for a hamburger. I drove to the area of the Silver Dollar and parked just north of this location on the west side of State Street. As I was exiting my car I noticed running south down the middle of State Street a black male who was running quite fast. I only saw the back of this black male as he ran past my vehicle. I did not pay too much attention to him, but did notice that it appeared he was wearing a jacket with some kind of writing on the back. I then began walking south on the sidewalk toward the Silver Dollar Cafe. A white male sporting a beard was running south on the sidewalk and it appeared he was almost out of breath. I asked this person (the white male), "What is going on?" I was told to "call the cops. I just caught that guy breaking into my car." I immediately went into the Silver Dollar Cafe and telephoned the police. I told the desk officer that a black male was running south down State Street and was being chased by a white male who said his car had been broken into. I then went outside by the Silver Dollar to see if either the white male or black male could be found. I could not see either person, however, I noticed a St. Joseph patrol car turning onto State Street a few blocks down from the downtown section.

Later that evening a St. Joseph policeman came into the cafe on a bar check. I asked him if they had located either the white male or the black male. The officer told me that the white male had made a report regarding his car being broken into, but that the black male was not caught by the white male.

I did not obtain a very good look at the black male, but I have seen the white male before. If you have any questions regarding this report, please feel free to contact me.

Marschke's dinner companion that night, Jerry Frank, the director of Berrien County Social Services, confirmed that, yes, he had met Marschke for burgers at that Silver Dollar, that Marschke had mentioned the chase, that a police officer on a bar check did stop by, and that Marschke had asked the officer whether anyone had been caught.

Marschke later recounted the same story for Ruth and her brother Bennie, who met with him to hear firsthand what had happened that night. He told them, as he later told me, "People want to make it a racial situation. Why would I think that was unusual that a black man was running down the street? . . . I saw the guy running and that was the extent of my involvement."

Bennie, the state trooper, was in disbelief. "I don't know any police officer who would have done that," Bennie said. "I know police officers who have seen fender benders in a parking lot and would wait for the police to arrive so they could take a report. If I had seen someone chasing a kid, I probably would have gotten in my truck, followed him, got on my car phone, and told them where the kid is, what direction he's running. And he's an experienced police officer. He did nothing. That sticks in my mind as something that's just not clear. The more and more I get involved in this thing, I can almost paint a picture in my mind of what happened. But that's different than proving it."

Ruth added, "The thing that bothers me the most is why they didn't give Marschke a lie detector test and why they never found the 911 tapes where he called in."

Reeves kicked himself for not listening to or impounding the tape of Marschke's call. It was, as a matter of course, erased after thirty days. Reeves didn't think he would have found anything new. On the contrary, its existence might have helped allay suspicions and put closure on another line of speculation. Reeves believed Marschke's account. He had no reason not to. But privately he scorned his fellow officer's decision not to give chase.

In those few weeks after Eric's death, Reeves would periodically ask his wife, Denise, "Why didn't he do anything?" Denise, trying to be helpful, would suggest, "Maybe he didn't want to get involved."

"Why?" Jim would ask again. "But *why* wouldn't he want to get involved."

Denise couldn't answer. "Jim will jump to the aid of someone no matter where we are," she told me. Once at a McDonald's in Chicago, where Reeves had taken his family to see the musical *Joseph and the Amazing Technicolor Dream Coat,* a boy, maybe ten or eleven, started choking on his hamburger. Reeves ran to the boy, grabbed him from behind, and pounded hard with his fists just below the boy's rib cage. The boy regurgitated the food, and Reeves then hugged him tight until he was sure he was okay. Another time, outside the Hilltop grocery, an elderly lady fell and broke her hip. Reeves, who was shopping there, knelt by her side and slipped his jacket under her head. He held her hand and talked to her as he waited for an ambulance to arrive.

Reeves doesn't like discussing Marschke's inaction that night, but once when I pressed him, he conceded, "Yeah, it raised questions. I won't be judgmental of Steve, but I think I would have done differently."

Where Marschke's indifference bothered Reeves, Warmbein's fury haunted him. Could Warmbein have caught up with Eric by the river and confronted him? Could Warmbein, in his pique over the burglary, overcome someone half his age and twice as agile? And, if he had done all that, could he then lie about it so convincingly?

Warmbein's story about that evening never wavered. Not to Reeves. Not to me. And not to the polygrapher. And he had an alibi. After losing Eric and filing a report with Dale Easton, Warmbein drove his friend, Dee Cunneen, to her car and then went home, where his thirty-eight-year-old cousin and her daughter were watching television. He tried calling Cunneen to make sure she had got home safely, but he couldn't reach her until later, because she had stopped to buy groceries. He joined his cousin and niece in front of the television. The cousin, Chris Warmbein, confirmed all this to the police, and said that Ted had come home around nine-thirty, which would have been shortly after the police report was filed.

At the polygraph test, attended by both Reeves and Warmbein's attorney, Warmbein was asked a series of questions, including: "Are you withholding any information regarding the death of this boy?" and "Do you have any knowledge of or did you have any involvement with the death of Eric McGinnis, the boy who broke into your car?" He passed, convincingly.

Two summers later, Reeves bumped into Warmbein at a reception during the town's Venetian Festival; it was on the deck of the *U.S.S. Boulder,* a naval ship anchored in the river. Earlier that day, Warmbein, while driving his prized 1987 Monte Carlo Supersport, got struck by an elderly driver, and the Monte Carlo spun 180 degrees. The passenger-side door and entire rear panel would have to be replaced. "I was pretty shook up," recalls Warmbein.

By the time Reeves ran into him, Warmbein, according to Reeves, "had been drinking heavily." Reeves continued, "He was drunk when he got to the reception and continued drinking there. I said something—I don't remember the exact words I used—but something about Eric. And I didn't get a defiant reaction. He says, 'Oh, yeah, I remember everybody thought I did it.' He was almost sobbing about how he had been accused. I chose my opportunity to ask him that. His guard was certainly down. He couldn't tie his shoes, much less think of a quick response. I said, 'Well, were you this drunk when you were chasing Eric?' He said 'No. I sure was accused on that one. Boy, that was a real mess.' " Reeves believed him.

I hooked up with Warmbein more recently. It was not an interview I was looking forward to. On each of my visits to the towns, I'd stay at the Best Western directly across the street from Warmbein's office-equipment repair store. I saw it every time I left the motel, and yet it was months before I could get myself to visit him. Despite all the rumors to the contrary, I had come to the conclusion that Warmbein did not have anything to do with Eric's death. He was, as the cliché has it, in the wrong place at the wrong time. When we did finally meet—over drinks at, of all places, the Silver Dollar Cafe—he was wary but gracious. Word of my quest had spread. "I've been expecting this," he said of my visit.

We sat across from each other, cautious and tentative. He drank coffee and smoked his Marlboros; I sipped an O'Doul's. His clothes, a white dress shirt, blue blazer, and chinos, fit his paunchy frame awkwardly. The shirt and blazer seemed too small and tugged and stretched with every gesture he made, as if the two, the body and the clothes, were tussling with each other.

He started by recounting the sequence of events that night, and what he said was consistent with what he had told Reeves, the polygraph examiner, and me years earlier. "Did I lose a lot of sleep?" he asked rhetorically. "Sure. But the fact that I lost a lot of sleep is minuscule compared to what happened." He recounted the loss of his twenty-six-year-old sister in a car accident eighteen years earlier. "I've thought back on what my parents had to go through. Parents shouldn't have to be subjected to something like that. I kind of understand how Eric's family might feel.

"I'm not sure why I'm sitting down with you," he continued, his face barely changing expression. It contained a certain sternness. I'm sure he felt affronted by the unspoken reason for my being here: that he had been, for a short while, the most obvious suspect in Eric's death. He told me that one of his customers, a corporate client, discontinued his service because of that. "They have a very racially mixed workforce, and they had some people who were still venting.

"Please be responsible," he asked, as our conversation wound down. "I don't want my business to burn . . . There are still a lot of frustrated people . . . Do I think that someone deep in their heart would like to have a little revenge? Yes. When you write this book, if my store gets torched . . ." He trailed off as he sipped the last of his coffee and lit another cigarette. He said that if I needed to call, I should leave a message and he'd get back to me. He didn't want to talk with me from work, because only one person there knew about his part in the case.

Warmbein drove me back to the hotel in his station wagon, which has the store's name, Great Lakes Office Supply, stenciled on a side window. As we sat there with the engine running, I told him I felt confident that he had played no role in Eric's death. He seemed relieved. The hardness cracked slightly, and he smiled, briefly. His shirt by now had come untucked and his blue tie hung to one side. The scattered papers and empty Marlboro packs on the car floor added to the sense of disarray. He seemed a lonely man. As we shook hands, he pleaded with me one more time: "Do the right thing, Alex. I've got my business." And then he added, as much to himself as to me, "It's never going away. Never."

A few days into the investigation, Reeves had realized that he needed help. First he invited detectives from neighboring departments to assist in the interviews of potential witnesses and tipsters. Then he went to a local FBI agent, who met with Benton Harbor leaders, including the NAACP head, to assure them they were doing all they could and to urge them to pass on any tips they might get. And Reeves read through the interviews, again and again.

Finally, that summer, Reeves sent the collection of interviews, tips, autopsy results, and rumors to the Michigan State Police, where it was read by two police psychologists and a detective. They wrote back that their analysis, based on "statistical data, training, our experience in other death investigations," concluded the following:

> . . . Unfortunately rumors and innuendoes have occupied much of the investigators' time and efforts. These rumors circulated among Eric's classmates and seemed to grow as they were passed from person to person. This phenomenon is not unique to this case. When an adolescent dies, there is a feeling of victimization which spreads throughout the community. People struggle to assign a reason for the death of someone so young. Another dynamic of a case such as this involves the police investigators. When the police become involved, there is an implication that a crime has occurred and persons

occasionally will recall information that may help the police solve the crime.

The final scenario involves an accidental death . . . Eric was in flight or flight mode when he escaped from the car owner. He knows that he is being pursued and he likely knows that the police will be summoned . . . All indicators are that Eric had been raised with strong moral principles and a sense of right and wrong. He is keenly aware that his coat is easily identifiable. If the coat was hidden, it is likely that it would be . . . in a place that Eric could later find it.

Given this flight mentality, Eric needs to get across the river to Benton Harbor. The vehicular drawbridge is manned, therefore making a crossing at that point riskier. The railroad bridge could be utilized, however this is more dangerous. It would be mere speculation as to what actually occurred next. If Eric was wearing the coat when he went into the water, the extra weight would be extremely burdensome and it is likely that he may have removed it. It is possible that an attempt was made to remove the pants as well. Eric was described as a good swimmer. The distance across the river is somewhat deceptive. The temperature of the water at the time of this incident would preclude all but a very short exposure. Even though Eric was feeling healthy, it is likely that he still had not fully recovered from the chicken pox.

Whether Eric fell in the river or attempted to swim across it the best scenario involving the death of Eric would have to be an accidental death . . . The investigators have searched tirelessly for physical evidence, and interviewed numerous persons. The media has given this investigation a great deal of attention. Yet, nothing other than rumor has surfaced which would point to a murder or suicide . . .

Given the events of the evening, it is likely that Eric knew he had made a mistake and was in a state of mind where he was desperately trying to get back to his safe haven, his home.

That was the coda in St. Joseph. Eric McGinnis, having been caught breaking into a car, panicked. Maybe he jumped into the river, thinking he could swim across. Or maybe, to avoid the cruising police cars, whose spotlights were scanning the riverfront, Eric hid by holding on to the breakwall, his feet dangling just above the river. Maybe his grip weakened and he dropped into the frigid waters. Maybe he was urinating by the river and stumbled in. Or maybe he tried crossing the railroad bridge, slipped, and fell.

"I'm really doubtful it was foul play," asserted Anne Morrisset, the widow of one of the town's more powerful financiers. "When anything happens to a black boy, they raise the roof. If the police said there was no foul play, then I believe them. I can't believe that anyone would have purposely tossed that kid in the river."

Tom Sparks, a former mayor, was just as certain. "There was no question in my mind about it," he told me. "If he drowned, he drowned himself. To escape from the repercussions of these incidents. You'll notice, they always say 'But he's only robbed two places' or 'But he's only shoplifted four times.' They really don't have an excuse for their actions . . . He just got into a river that was too wide for him."

Reeves publicly referred to Eric's death as an accidental drowning. "There's been no physical evidence to support anything other than a drowning," he insisted, almost apologetically. "We keep hearing about race. If race was the issue, if somebody had some information, wouldn't they have told one of the officers about it? If they saw something, heard something? I don't know. Look, people are going to believe what they want to believe. I don't think there's anything else out there to find out . . . This is not the first body turned up in the river."

"Is the case closed?" I asked a few years after Eric's death.

"Based upon the information we've received so far, I'd say, yes, the case is closed."

I spent many moments with Reeves—at his house, over lunch, in his office, trailing him while he conducted investigations—going over the case. We rehashed it piece by piece, person by person. We looked at the photographs a second and third time, dissected the various tips, spun out the possible sequence and then poked holes in the theories. Yet through it all, I had the sense that Reeves was not fully convinced he had found out everything.

Periodically, when some event reminded Reeves of the case, he would tell his wife, "I wish I could put this one to rest." Something nagged at him.

25.

THE RIVER

The Benton Harbor community doesn't buy the official explanation of Eric's death. Blacks, I was told again and again, don't go to water. Simple as that.

At Clementine's, a St. Joseph restaurant that sits alongside the Pier 33 marina, I listened to a conversation between Carolyn Graves, the school bus dispatcher, and Mamie Yarbrough, the school board member.

"We don't swim," Yarbrough asserted. "We don't run to the water. That's in our history. When people wanted to get black people, they'd drown 'em."

"They'd put you in a crokersack and put bricks in the bottom," Graves added.

"There aren't a lot of black people who can swim. My parents told us to keep away from the water. That it was too much to drink." Yarbrough laughed at the memory.

"They say Eric's death was an accident," Graves offered.

"That's what they say," Yarbrough said. "We know Eric Mc-Ginnis didn't go to the water on his own. We know that."

"That's what we believe," Graves agreed, "that somebody held him down and drowned him . . . They'll come forward. They won't be able to live with it."

I heard this a lot in my conversations with adults from Benton Harbor: black people don't go to water. Especially, they'd stress, rivers. At first, it struck me as both farcical and sad. Here, blacks were repeating the same stereotypes uttered by those on the other side of the river. Who can forget Al Campanis, general manager of the Los Angeles Dodgers, who remarked on national television that blacks lacked the natural buoyancy to swim well? Why give credence to such nonsense? Why this myth that blacks viewed rivers as un-friendly, if not the enemy? And why suggest that Eric, who was fit and could, according to his mother, swim, wouldn't attempt just about anything, including crossing the river, to flee the St. Joseph cops? A little history might help.

Edward Hoagland has written: "Rivers have carved the world, and because they never stop moving—gray, brown, blue, black, or green on a single day—they seem infinitely reassuring." There is much truth to that, particularly in the history of the white Europe-ans who settled this country. Consider the St. Joseph River.

The St. Joseph starts as not much more than a trickle out of BawBeese Lake, in Hillsdale, a small town in the center of the state. Narrow enough to leap across, and barely ankle deep, the river, even at its genesis, is clouded by sediment, giving it a distinctly toast-brown tint. From here, it flows south through the hamlets and farms of southern Michigan into Indiana, where, at South Bend, it angles sharply west, then back north. This is the southernmost tip of the river; hence the city's name. The river winds its way back through Michigan, snaking its way, sometimes doubling over itself, to its ultimate destination, Lake Michigan. Over its course of roughly two hundred miles, the river accommodates ten hydroelectric dams, all upstream of the Twin Cities; but because its waters are not very swift—like most midwestern rivers, it travels a relatively short distance on fairly flat land—it creates barely enough electricity to power a town of three thousand.

By the time the river reaches St. Joseph and Benton Harbor, it has become a wide, sluggish stretch of turbid water; here, it is vast enough for water skiers and speedboats, and calm enough for canoeists and fishermen. And it's here, at its mouth, that the St. Joseph, like a siren, seduced first explorers, then traders, then entrepreneurs, and eventually vacationers. It's here that the river became a center of conquest and commerce, a gateway to points east and south.

Jacques Marquette, missionary, poet, and priest, became the first white man to enter the river when he traversed it in 1669 on his way to the Mississippi. He baptized the river the Miamis, after one of the Indian tribes that hunted and cultivated the fertile land along its shores.

Ten years later, René-Robert Cavelier de La Salle, a swashbuckling French explorer searching for land for his mother country and for places that might enrich his own pockets, came across the Miamis. He had arrived from Montreal with a large force of men and supplies, and quickly saw the land along the Miamis as prime real estate, so he wintered there, clearing away brush on the bluff to build Fort Miamis, not far from where the Elks Club now stands. St. Joseph thus became the first white settlement in southern Michigan, and La Salle soon changed the river's moniker, naming it after the patron saint of Canada.

Over the next century, the post was, in turns, captured and destroyed by Pontiac's Indians, recaptured and rebuilt by the French, surrendered to the English after the fall of Quebec, and finally turned over to the United States in 1812. By 1831 so many were living by the river's mouth that the settlers laid out a village and built a tavern on the bluff. St. Joseph became the port of entry for all freight from Detroit and Chicago to the midsize cities along the river, including Kalamazoo, Niles, and South Bend. Steamers and keel boats hauled goods upriver, and industrialists built saw mills and flour mills along the route. By the 1840s, it had become a more heavily trafficked shipping point for grain and flour than Chicago. And land speculation was so unbridled that some lots in St. Joseph sold for fifty times more than lots in Chicago.

But as the railroad became the main form of transport, in the mid-nineteenth century, the town's importance as a port declined. Undeterred, enterprising entrepreneurs capitalized on its location—the magnificent lakeshore and natural river port—and lured vacationing Chicagoans, running daily steamers between the two cities, boats with names like *Lady Franklin, Skylark, St. Joseph,* and *Benton.* Families came for the sandy beaches, and, in time, for the amusement parks at both Silver Beach and at the House of David. By 1890, three steamship lines brought nearly 370,000 passengers each summer into the two cities.

The early land boom boosted speculation across the river, as well, and led to the birth of Benton Harbor, dubbed Bungtown, after a factory that produced the wooden stoppers used to seal barrels. The villages eyed each other with caution; after all, they were competing for industry and business. The rivalry became so intense that annual baseball contests between the St. Joseph Clippers and the Benton Harbor Shoo Flies had to be discontinued for a number of years because of the brawls between fans. But the biggest source of conflict was the river itself. Benton Harbor originally did not front on the river; St. Joseph owned that strip of shoreline. Benton Harbor citizens, intent on gaining access to the waterfront, adopted the slogan "To the river or die." Eventually, Benton Harbor, which threatened to run a sewer line through St. Joseph's land so as to reach the water, paid $5000 to extend its city limits to the middle of the river, which to this day is the boundary between the communities.

The river forged the character of the two towns. Benton Harbor for many years boasted the nation's largest outdoor fruit market, and the land along the river became both towns' most valuable real estate. In summer, St. Joseph and St. Joseph Township host over eight hundred boats moored at their four marinas. And freighters still ply the river, dropping off their loads at one of two cement plants near the waterway's mouth. The St. Joseph River, to borrow from Hoagland, carved these two communities.

But for African Americans, the St. Joseph and other rivers have taken on a more ambiguous role. The St. Joseph River was a final crossing for fugitive slaves. In the small town of Cassopolis, thirty-three miles southeast of the Twin Cities, a band of Quakers harbored runaways whose last barrier to freedom was the St. Joseph, which they would cross under cover of nightfall. Some continued their flight into Canada, but a large number settled there, creating what became the largest concentration of black farmers outside the South. There are also accounts that an ardent abolitionist in Benton Harbor housed fugitive slaves who, after crossing the St. Joseph, could enter his home through an underground passage leading to the river's edge.

For fugitive slaves, a river was a friend—and a foe. In escape after escape, they waded the rocky beds of streams and rivers so that the pursuing hound dogs couldn't pick up their scent. The river, particularly under the cover of darkness, was also a navigational tool, a natural trail that guided fugitive slaves through deep brush and woods. But what was perhaps most notable, rivers like the St. Joseph marked, metaphorically and literally, the last leap to liberty. It was the final obstacle. "Crossing the River Jordan" came to mean completing the run north.

But for much of this century, rivers served a decidedly unambiguous role, particularly in the South. Rather than a source of life, they became its extinguisher. Lynched bodies, weighed down by cement blocks or chains, were deposited in rivers throughout the Deep South. Emmett Till's mangled body—a bullet in his head, an eye gouged out, and his forehead crushed in on one side—was found in the Tallahatchie River when the barbed wire holding the cotton-gin fan around his neck became snagged on a tangled river root. Nine years later, when the civil rights workers Mickey Schwerner, James Chaney, and Andrew Goodman turned up missing near Philadelphia, Mississippi, FBI agents and two hundred sailors scoured the surrounding waterways, and though they didn't find the three activists (the bodies were eventually discovered buried in an earthen dam), they did find the bodies of other blacks long missing.

I mention this history because I think it helps explain why people like Carolyn Graves and Mamie Yarbrough felt so certain that Eric, whom Graves knew only peripherally from church and whom Yarbrough didn't know at all, did not voluntarily enter the St. Joseph River. Maybe he fell in. But swim it? To get home? No way. Not in the minds of Graves and Yarbrough, both of whom—like many in Benton Harbor—have deep connections to the Jim Crow South. Graves grew up in Fountain Hill, Arkansas; Yarbrough's parents hailed from Tennessee and Mississippi. Memories of Klan rallies and tales of lynchings remain vivid and to this day seep into the routine of everyday life. But there were other reasons to believe that Eric did not try to swim the river, as the state police had suggested.

The St. Joseph is a patsy of a river—at least in terms of its flow. The slope of a river's bed determines the current; the steeper the drop, the faster the surge. The St. Joseph, west of the Blossomland Bridge (which is where Eric is presumed to have entered the water), barely surges at all. There's almost no incline. It's been dredged to a level of twenty-five to thirty feet for the freighters, so it's like an extension of Lake Michigan, which has a similar depth where it meets the river.

The U.S. Geological Survey has measured the river's velocity near its mouth at roughly half a foot per second; that can double after several days of rain. Even then, at its swiftest, the river toddles along; a series of riffles in a small stream is moving three to four times as fast. Consequently, the flow of the St. Joseph west of the Blossomland Bridge is determined not by the pitch of the river bottom, which barely slopes at all, but by the gusts blowing in off the lake.

This is not to say the river is easy to swim. It isn't, particularly the closer you get to its mouth. Winds out of the west blow lake water *into* the river, and that creates a sloshing effect, not unlike the result of plopping into a bathtub. It also creates powerful undertows. The winds push the surface water upstream, while the river itself is gently pushing downstream toward the lake. On gusty days, the river appears to flow the wrong way, upstream, producing swells between the piers that can reach twelve to fifteen feet, capable of upending small craft. Once, a combination of waves and ice tore the foghorn off the lighthouse.

On May 17, 1991, the day Eric entered these waters, a stiff breeze blew in from the northwest, generating two-foot waves in the lake and stirring up the river at its mouth. It had rained off and on all day, and the temperature had hovered in the 50s. By the time Eric might have made it to the river's edge, it had dipped into the 40s.[1] The water itself was a frigid 49 degrees, cold enough that the Coast Guardsmen wore flotation survival suits, wet suits to guard against hypothermia, in case they fell in. Most swimmers without

1. There are two weather stations in the Twin Cities, one at the Benton Harbor Airport, the other at the Coast Guard Station. For particular days, like May 17, the two stations reported conflicting data. The temperatures sometimes varied by as much as 20 degrees. At the advice of people at the National Climatic Center, I relied foremost on data provided by the Benton Harbor station. It was more in line with readings from nearby weather stations.

protection in such cold waters would cramp up within ten minutes. It was an unlikely night for anyone, even a panicked teen, to enter the river voluntarily.

Moreover, Eric was not an experienced swimmer. One of his friends said that when Eric was at the beach, he would wade up to his knees and no farther. Another said he and Eric used to hang out together at the YMCA pool—in the shallow end. His mother, though, says that Eric could swim. Ruth remembers visiting her brother Bennie when he attended college in Arkansas. There was a pool at his housing complex, and Eric, who was six at the time, would leap into the water. "He wasn't an Olympic swimmer," Ruth says, "but he was not afraid of the water." My sense is that Eric could manage in deep water but wasn't an especially powerful or savvy swimmer. There's nothing to indicate, for instance, that he ever took a life-saving course or swam laps for recreation or swam much in lakes or rivers. I don't believe that Eric would have looked out over the St. Joseph River, contemplated the 350-foot crossing, and thought to himself, No problem. The sight of the choppy waters at night would have been intimidating to him, as they would to the strongest of swimmers. What's more, entering the river is no easy matter. The steel pilings create a sheer drop into the water. There is no sandy beach or gently sloping bank.

Then there's the question of Eric's untied shoes and open pants, as well as his missing overcoat. According to Eric's friends, he often wore his shoelaces untied. It was the fashion, a cultivated nonchalance. But his friends were equally adamant that Eric did not wear his belt unbuckled and hanging loose, nor did he cavort around with his pants open. He was too natty a dresser for such unkemptness, his friends said. So what could have happened to cause his pants to become undone?

David Smith, a retired Coast Guard commander who now works as a water safety consultant, often testifies in cases involving drowning incidents. I ran by him what I knew. Smith chuckled.

"It's not at all unusual to find bodies partly unclothed," he told me. "The joke is that they often find fishermen with their pants at half mast." The men may have tumbled off their boats while urinating; or, as is more often the case, they frantically tried to disrobe in the water in order to gain some freedom of movement. And the first item they usually try to pull off is their pants. Even before trying to kick off their shoes.

Most drowning victims, however, don't try to remove their clothes. "Most people who die in the water do so within ten feet of safety," Smith noted. "Their big problem is getting back out of the water. Usually they don't try to take their clothes off but try to get back to where they came from. If someone slips off a dock his primary move would be to get back to the dock." Fishermen who fall in try to disrobe because their boat has blown away.[2]

Smith theorizes that Eric was in a situation similar to that of a fisherman: getting out of the water was not an immediate option. Eric, he suggests, could not exit the river. "A person who tries to take his clothes off usually realizes that he has to swim somewhere and that safety is not near at hand. Eric did not drown immediately, because he tried to undo his clothing . . . And the indication would be that he wasn't near safety; for example, if he'd fallen off a nearby bridge or if someone pushed him in and he had to move away from where they were."

What Smith suggests, without saying as much, is that Eric probably did not choose to enter the water. If he had, given the water's iciness and his water-logged shoes and jeans, he would have tried almost immediately to clamber back out. If he had gone in at the arboretum, he would have had trouble pulling himself up over the breakwall or, in the dark, finding the safety ladders built into the

---

2. When the Coast Guard pulled Eric's body out of the water, they did so by hooking a boat hook onto his belt. Reeves theorizes that that might explain the open belt and pants, though, unless the belt was undone, the maneuver would not have caused the pants to unbutton and unzip. Also, some speculate that Eric may have been having sex by the river or was about to have sex, which would explain the open pants.

wall, but that's how he would have drowned: desperately clawing his way out. It would not even have occurred to him to try to disrobe.

And the missing coat? If Eric had tried to swim the river, he first would have hidden his coat along the shoreline, as was suggested by the state police profilers. But it was never found. If Eric had gone in the water involuntarily, he probably would have had it on. And if that was the case, it would have been the first item he ripped off. It's conceivable that it sank and to this day remains submerged.

These weren't the only open questions about Eric's death.

26.

THE BODY

The dead man, a fifty-five-year-old Taiwanese immigrant whom I'll call Li Ying, looked dignified even under the fluorescent light and against the stainless steel of the autopsy table. His narrow shoulders pulled back; his skimpy chest pushed out. He was wearing a pinstripe dress shirt, still neatly tucked into his black polyester pants, which barely reached his ankles, revealing white athletic socks. He had topped it all off with a handsome pair of black wingtips. He dressed neatly for his end.

Li Ying was a suspected suicide. The day before, a group of factory workers eating lunch under the summer sun had spotted a body floating in the Kalamazoo River. Police officers fished it out, identified the man from a prescription for pain medication he carried in his pants pocket, and tracked down his wife, who had just found the suicide note. Writing in Chinese, Li Ying had apologized for disgracing her and begged her not to disclose to family or friends that he had taken his own life. He wrote that he still had extreme discomfort from his recent gall bladder operation, and despaired at having been laid off from his job as a cook. His employer had told him he was too weak to perform his work. The police speculated that Li Ying, who according to his wife couldn't swim, walked into the mild currents of the Kalamazoo until he could no longer retain his footing, and drowned.

His body was brought to what the pathologists and police obliquely refer to as Ward 20, a euphemism used on the hospital's paging system. There are no Wards 1 through 19. Ward 20, the morgue, is located in the labyrinthine basement of the Grand Rapids Blodgett Memorial Medical Center. It is here, on one of the two steel beds, that Dr. Stephen D. Cohle, deputy chief medical examiner (the chief medical examiner is the director of the county public health department and does not perform autopsies), cuts and slices bodies, some of which have already been cut or sliced, in the hope that he will be able to tell loved ones and the police precisely why the person died.

Sometimes everything is not as it seems. Once, Dr. Cohle performed an autopsy on a two-year-old boy who the police suspected had been beaten by his father. The father had come home drunk the night before and, finding his son soaked in pee, gave him a bath. The grandparents, who lived in the house, heard two loud thuds. The next morning, they found the toddler dead in his crib. They and the police assumed the father had killed him. But Cohle couldn't find any injuries. What he did discover, though, were seven potassium chloride tablets in the boy's stomach. The grandmother had been taking them to offset the side effects of high blood pressure medicine. Unbeknown to anyone, the boy had swallowed the pills and accidentally poisoned himself.

Cohle is a forensic pathologist: part doctor, part biologist, part sleuth, and part anthropologist. He is well respected by his peers. In his fourteen years at Blodgett, he has performed four thousand autopsies—and did another thousand when he was a resident in Houston. He's so good that law enforcement officials from thirty-five

Michigan counties have at one time or another sent him bodies to examine or, in some cases, re-examine. Berrien County is one of his more regular clients; it frequently ships bodies the eighty miles north to Grand Rapids. In one year alone, Benton Harbor police sent him half a dozen corpses, all suspected homicide victims.

I had a standing request with Cohle to view the autopsy of a drowning victim. Drowning is a diagnosis of exclusion. Although physical changes, such as water-filled lungs, can indicate drowning, there is no single body change that would lead a forensic pathologist to conclude categorically that drowning was the cause of death. For example, saturated lungs indicate that the person spent time under water, but the lungs of someone who was dead before being thrown in could, under some circumstances, fill with water as easily as those of a person who entered the river while alive. Moreover, some drowning victims don't take any water into their lungs; on occasion the upper airway closes reflexively, preventing water from entering the trachea. (This happens most often in young children, which accounts for the ability of some to survive after being immersed in cold water for many minutes.) So, in concluding that a person died from drowning, a forensic pathologist wants to rule out all other possibilities, including heart attack, poisoning, a blow to the head, strangulation, stabbing, shooting, and any other means of assault.

Cohle's secretary called me one summer night to say they had not one, but two floaters. Cohle would dissect one of them; his colleague would examine the other. I headed for Grand Rapids that night.

When I arrived at Ward 20 the next morning, Cohle hadn't yet returned from a meeting, so I took refuge in a corner, my vision partly obscured by a plastic replica of a human skeleton. Through the ribcage, I watched Cohle's assistant plop a large plastic garbage bag into the open chest cavity of a seventy-year-old fisherman who had apparently suffered a heart attack before falling into the Muskegon River north of here. The bag in place, the assistant, with what looked more like cord than thread, made wide, lazy stitches, sewing the chest wall shut. The bag, I was told, contained the gentleman's essential organs.

A Kalamazoo detective, Michael Werkema, here on the Li Ying case, must have noticed me grimace. He gently asked whether I'd ever observed an autopsy before. I told him no. "You want a piece of advice?" he asked. "Don't stare. Just glance." He didn't have to do much convincing.

Cohle scurried in around eleven, an hour late, and, after a few cursory pleasantries, donned his green gown and white surgical mask, walked over to the corpse, and gently brushed a few grains of sand off Li Ying's pants legs. It was a respectful gesture. Cohle stepped back. His eyes focused on Li Ying's belt, which he then unbuckled.

Cohle is, by his own admission, "compulsive and obsessive." He is fiercely focused on his work. Forty-four years old, of medium build and height, he appears disheveled and perpetually preoccupied: his shoulders hunched, almost touching his ears; his black hair uncombed; his mind so focused on the minutiae of his work that every week his secretary makes two copies of his weekly schedule, one for his desk and the other for his refrigerator at home.

He began what would ultimately be a two-and-a-half-hour dig by listening to the detective tell him of the suicide note and of discovering the body face down in the river. The officer also mentioned a small knot or contusion on the back of the victim's head. While Werkema spoke, Cohle removed the belt, which, he noticed, had three extra holes punched in it, reducing its original size by six inches. Cohle speculated that Li Ying had lost much weight recently, most probably, given what was known of his medical history (through the police's interview with his wife), as a result of the gall bladder operation. Indeed, once Cohle had removed all of Li Ying's clothes, the unnaturally gaunt frame was apparent; the dead man's legs were spindly, and his ribcage seemed intent on bursting through the skin.

Fully undressed, Li Ying looked fully dead, his joints stiff with rigor mortis, his skin rubbery and chalky. Fortunately for us in the room, the body was neither bloated nor malodorous, since it had been in the water no more than a few hours at most. Cohle's assistant, a bearded, rotund man, climbed onto the steel table, straddled the dead man, and, looking not unlike a frumpy fashion photographer, snapped photos of the head, the torso, and all that lay below, his groin and legs, creating a kind of triptych of the human corpse. Finished, he dismounted and took blood and urine samples, both of which were to be sent to a toxicologist for analysis.

Cohle, his face only a foot or so from the body, scanned it closely, beginning with the feet and ending at the head. He looked as if he were searching for lost contact lenses. His fingers massaged the skin softly, exploring for bruises. He made note of the small healed incisions just above the stomach, presumably from the recent surgery. Then he rolled Li Ying onto the right side, probing with his fingers along the back of the head for the lump. He couldn't find it. Water, discolored by blood, drained from one ear. I was still just glancing, so the procedure took on the jerkiness of a 1920s motion picture. I missed some frames.

Cohle had now completed the first stage of the postmortem: the external examination. (On occasion, if a shooting is suspected, he will have the body x-rayed for bullet fragments.) The assistant, with an oversize scalpel, made a Y-shaped cut through the ribcage and abdomen. This I couldn't watch at all, so by the time I refocused my gaze, the body had been emptied of all its organs. Cohle now began the internal search.

I stood with him in a corner of the room, my back to the hollowed corpse, my eyes focused on Li Ying's heart, lungs, and trachea. Cohle weighed them, as well as the liver, spleen, and kidneys. It was here, as I watched Cohle pull apart the body's gears, that I came to admire his thoroughness. Given the suicide note, there was, after all, little question as to the cause of death. But Cohle took no chances. What if the note was a fraud? What if someone had forced Li Ying to write it and then killed him? Or, if it was suicide, maybe Cohle could find a physiological explanation for the man's depression. If he could, he told me, it would certainly make matters easier for the family.

With his gloved hands, he picked up the neck organs, which still had the tongue attached, an unrecognizable mass of reddish tissue. He sliced into the muscle tissue extending along the larynx and pharynx, making half-inch-deep cuts with a scalpel. He was looking for signs of internal bleeding, which would indicate possible strangulation. He also sliced into the thyroid gland, looking for the same, and then sectioned it into small chunks, scanning them for signs of disease. If the thyroid wasn't functioning properly, that could cause depression or excitability and help explain why Li Ying took his life. But it appeared normal. He sliced open the pharynx and upper esophagus, looking for internal hemorrhaging. Nothing.

He then cut the tissue away from the hyoid bone, a fragile structure that looked like a rounded wishbone. If it was fractured, that would almost certainly indicate that the person had been choked. He held it up for me to see. It was in one piece. Finally, to eliminate any possibility of Li Ying's having been strangled, he scanned the cornua, hornlike protrusions of the thyroid cartilage, to see whether they'd been fractured. They were intact. He now explained that he was going to probe for signs of illness or disease.

The spongelike lungs crackled as he gently squeezed them in his hands. "They feel pretty heavy," he said. "I think they're going to be the usual drowning lungs." It turned out that they weighed about twice what they should. The liquid bubbling from the lungs, Cohle explained, was both water and the body's own fluids, which had been forced into the lungs because of what he called "circulatory overload." He pointed out the carbon stains, small black blotches on the lung's surface. Anthracosis, he told me. Most likely from smoking.

He then held the heart, life itself, in his left hand as he carefully sliced into it at quarter-inch intervals, looking for signs of disease. He did the same with the arteries, which were, in fact, slightly clogged. Meanwhile, I heard the buzzing of an electric saw, so I turned and glimpsed his assistant cutting away the top of Li Ying's skull. The scalp had been pulled down over the face, as if someone had peeled back a Halloween mask. I turned away. The assistant called Cohle over. In the lining of the skull was a benign tumor as wide as a quarter and a quarter-inch deep. He also discovered a small gelatinous cyst, the size of a thumbnail, at the base of the brain. Cohle paged a neuropathologist to take a look at the growth, which he called an incidental finding. The neuropathologist, a woman in her thirties, told Cohle it was a rare embryological remnant, an extension of the spinal cord. "This is wonderful; I don't have any in my collection!" she exclaimed, and asked Cohle's assistant to remove it and preserve it in formaldehyde. She also examined the benign tumor. "I don't think either of those would cause him to be depressed," she told Cohle.

Cohle turned toward the detective, Werkema, who was also turned—away from the body. "I'm sure it'll go asphyxia by drowning," Cohle alerted him. "There are two benign growths in the brain, but they wouldn't have caused depression—I'm sorry to say for his wife."

"It's sad," Werkema said. "He just moved her here, and his whole family's back in Taiwan. Okay, Doctor, until next time."

"And there will be," Cohle offered as he went back to kneading the heart.

After lunch, he completed that day's work on the autopsy by checking the liver, spleen, and kidneys. In another ten days, he would explore the brain. And a week after that, he would examine microscopically the slides of the liver and other major organs, and would inspect samples of the bone marrow for leukemia and red blood cell abnormalities, either of which could explain Li Ying's extreme fatigue.

When I asked Jim Reeves whether he'd do anything differently regarding Eric's death, he answered tersely, "I should have sent the body to Cohle."

Eric's body had been examined by Dr. E. Arthur Robertson, one of three pathologists at St. Joseph's Mercy Memorial Medical Center. Each serves a week in rotation as the county's medical examiner. None is a forensic pathologist. None has spent the requisite extra year of training or taken the boards in forensic pathology. Before his arrival in St. Joseph, in 1982, Robertson had been a pathologist at the National Institutes of Health, in Bethesda, Maryland.

He is a tall, angular-featured man who appears so narrow and elongated that one almost suspects he could walk upright between prison-cell bars. Robertson tells me that nearly half of all suspected homicides are sent to Cohle, who, he readily admits, is better trained for such cases. Robertson also adds that suspected murder victims can be unusually time-consuming, to say nothing of controversial.

"What was your most controversial?" I ask him.

"The Maben shooting," he says without hesitation.

He remembers that the body was brought to the morgue late in the day, and prosecutors, local cops, and state police crime experts hovered around, demanding that Robertson perform the autopsy immediately. He did. He examined the two bullet holes, exit and entrance wounds, and concluded that the bullet had entered through the chest and, in a downward trajectory consistent with someone's having shot from a second-floor window, exited the lower back. Just to be certain he wasn't missing anything, he excised the two wounds, preserved them in formaldehyde, and sent them along to Cohle for a second opinion. Cohle, he told me, couldn't come up with anything definitive after examining the two bullet holes.

But I got a very different story from Cohle. Maben had not been shot in the chest; he had been shot in the back. Despite the fact that Cohle performs over two hundred autopsies a year and that it was four years since he had examined Maben's wounds, he remembered the case quite well. He rifled through his files and took out slides of the wound, which he projected on a wall in a conference room adjacent to Ward 20. The sample from the lower back is a square-inch piece of skin in the middle of which is a nearly perfectly symmetrical opening, as if someone had carefully pushed a pen through soft tissue. That is typical of an entrance wound; the bullet carves out a neat round hole. The other sample, taken from the chest wound, is irregular in shape, almost like an oval tent flap. That is typical of an exit wound, after the bullet has been slowed and redirected by the body's tangle of organs. The entrance wound, Cohle concluded, was in Maben's back, not his breast. Cohle speculated that Maben had been leaning over when Fiedler shot him, and the bullet had entered his lower back and exited his chest.

Cohle knew that the shooting had caused strain between St. Joseph and Benton Harbor, and he didn't want to register his opinion without double-checking his findings. He consulted Dr. Vince DiMaio, the chief medical examiner of Bexar County (San Antonio) in Texas and the author of a book on gunshot wounds. DiMaio confirmed Cohle's judgment. Cohle remembers calling Wiley, the Berrien County prosecutor, who, on hearing of the possibly botched autopsy, said, "Oh, shoot." Cohle also sent a letter to the prosecutor, outlining his discovery—though the language hedged a bit, since, Cohle says, he hadn't seen the full body and since formalin can cause tissue to shrink slightly, sometimes distorting samples. He wrote that it was impossible "to definitively state which wound was the entry and which the exit." Nonetheless, Cohle told me that he was "ninety percent certain" that, contrary to Robertson's conjecture, Maben had been shot in the back. Wiley never disclosed this, nor was it mentioned at Fiedler's trial—though, to be fair, Cohle seems more certain of his findings now than he did then.

If Eric's body had been sent to Cohle, would it have made a difference?

When Robertson received Eric's body and heard that the deceased may have been last seen in St. Joseph, he knew right away that "this had the potential to be a high profile case." The corpse was placed in one of the morgue's nine cooler trays. Like Cohle's Ward 20, Mercy Memorial's morgue is located in the basement. Robertson says that the stench of floaters often seeps into the air ducts of the hospital, permeating the other floors, and so I can only suspect that, given the decay of Eric's body, doctors, nurses, and patients walked around much of that day holding their breath.

Robertson, with Detective Dennis Soucek observing, dissected the body. He took x-rays, looking for bullet fragments and broken bones. And he withdrew urine and blood samples for testing. The autopsy report is just over a half-page long, with none of the thoroughness or rigor evident in the examination of Li Ying, a case in which there was little question as to the cause of death. Cohle's report on Li Ying ran to eight pages, including a critical discovery made three weeks after the actual dissection: while microscopically examining slides of liver sections, Cohle noticed evidence of inflammation; further tests revealed that Li Ying had had hepatitis C, which could have accounted for the man's unusual tiredness and pains.

Robertson's description of Eric's body makes no mention of the pockmarks that covered his face. Many who knew the boy, including his math teacher Bobbie Nadus, said that the disfiguring from his chickenpox had bothered Eric. It is possible, though, that the decomposition concealed the marks. The report has no mention of an examination of the neck's hyoid bone for possible fracture. Nor is there mention of incisions made in the skin in a search for possible bruises. Or of the bloody ligature along Eric's neck, which is clearly apparent in the photographs. (Reeves later learned that it was likely the result of a rope used by the Coast Guard to tow Eric's body to shore.) When I showed the report to Cohle, he diplomatically replied, "It's cursory." Others I have showed it to were not so restrained.

Bob Kirschner, the former deputy chief medical examiner for Illinois's Cook County and now the Physicians for Human Rights' lead forensic investigator on human rights abuses, said of the report, "This does not meet the standards of a forensic autopsy . . . He [Robertson] shouldn't have been doing this case. He's not qualified to do this kind of autopsy. He should have said no." At a minimum, Kirschner told me, the postmortem should have included an examination of the tongue for bite marks, which might have indicated Eric had been struck in the mouth or on the head, as well as a thorough exam of the neck to rule out strangulation. Finding bruises or lacerations on a decomposed body can be like looking for juice stains on a Jackson Pollack painting. During decomposition red blood cells break down, changing the skin color to a purplish blue, obscuring bruises. And so, Kirschner told me, one must make incisions through the skin into the fatty subcutaneous tissue to see whether there has been any hemorrhaging. This procedure isn't mentioned in Robertson's report on Eric's autopsy. Nonetheless, Robertson concluded there were "no obvious injuries."

The toxicology report lists .04 percent of alcohol in the blood, an amount so small that it may have been a byproduct of the body fermenting; it also mentions traces of N-desmethyldiazepam, a mild tranquilizer. But because of the small amount, it was probably ingested at least several days before Eric's death.

27.

ANOTHER THEORY

Flaubert once wrote that a critic is a failed artist. So it might be said that I spent my energy puncturing the theory that Eric tried to swim the river because I failed to produce evidence that something else had occurred. But then there's Daniel Thornton.

Thornton, a convicted burglar, provided Reeves with the only proof, however tenuous, that Eric may have been murdered. Two years after Eric's death, Reeves was on to other matters, including a $78 theft from the local McDonald's by a teenage employee. On occasion, though, he received tips. Usually they led nowhere. Once, two insurance agents called to report that a colleague who they believed was a distant relative of Eric's exhibited strange behavior, disappearing for days at a time. Maybe, they suggested, he had had something to do with Eric's death. He was at the time of Eric's disappearance at a veterans' hospital for mental illness.

In August 1993, Reeves received a phone call from Abbott Taylor, a deputy sheriff. Taylor had been approached by an inmate at the county jail who maintained he knew what had happened to Eric.

The inmate, Daniel Thornton, offered to exchange the information for leniency in his sentencing on charges of stealing $695 worth of jewelry and CDs from a house trailer.

A few days later, Reeves drove the two blocks to the county jail. Thornton claimed to have witnessed a white teenage boy berate Eric for dancing with a white girl. Thornton said the boy chased Eric down to the river, where he pushed him into the frigid waters. The story, like Thornton himself, was a bit off kilter. But as with all the tips he'd received, Reeves felt obliged to pursue it. Besides, Thornton mentioned a young man, whom I'll call James, who had come up earlier in the investigation, someone with a professed dislike of blacks (a relative had been killed by a black man in California)—and a connection to Lisa Liedke, Eric's former girlfriend.

Thornton is white and had a reputation that can best be described as unsavory. He boasted of his affiliation with the Insane Gangster Disciples, a mostly black street gang, and has the tattoos to prove it, twenty-two in all, one of them a six-pointed star above his heart. A smiling Yosemite Sam on his right forearm has GD, for Gangster Disciple, inscribed on its cap. A gargoyle gazes menacingly from his other forearm; it has a tail in the shape of a pitchfork, also a Disciples' icon. When I met Thornton a couple of years after his first encounter with Reeves, he informed me that he soon planned to engrave a dotted line on his neck. "It'll say, 'Cut on the dotted line.'" I couldn't tell whether he was joking. His street name, I learned later, was, appropriately, Mad Hatter.

Of sinewy build, he has a shoulder-length mane of jet-black hair. His eyebrows, thick as a rainforest, make his brown eyes look dark and hermetic. They never wander, never let go. He's hard to read. When he talks of his heroes—Charles Manson and Jim Jones, because of their ability to manipulate others—one can't tell whether he's playing mind games himself, trying to keep others guessing as to his own sanity. Is this guy really crazy? Or is he trying to test your reaction, measure your candor and honesty? One fellow inmate said,

"I feel like every time I'm looking at his eyes, I'm looking at the devil."

Reeves already knew Thornton. Most of the cops did. Previous to the recent burglary charges, he had been convicted of stealing money and lottery tickets from a Mobil gas station, for which he received probation. Reeves himself arrested Thornton when he threatened to stab an assistant principal at St. Joseph High School. After he'd been expelled, he and a group of friends lived in one of St. Joseph's marinas, staying on an old cabin cruiser that suffered from dry rot and was parked on land. Reeves suspected the band was responsible for disappearing radios, liquor, and assorted odds and ends from the other boats.

On this warm summer afternoon, Reeves, along with Taylor, the sheriff's deputy, greeted Thornton at the jail, where they removed his handcuffs and replaced his jailhouse-issue slippers with sneakers. The jail garb, a drab green outfit, hung loosely from his lanky frame. The three climbed into Reeves's Pontiac Sunbird and drove to Pleasant Street, to the building that had once housed the Club.

Thornton said he had attended the Club the night Eric disappeared. "It was packed," he said. "I didn't really associate with anyone in there. I just went there to get some pussy, to get drunk afterward." He said he recognized Eric from when he'd attended a program for troubled youth at King Preparatory School. (King shared some facilities with McCord Rennaisance Center, which Eric attended.) Eric, Thornton said, got into an argument with a white girl he was dancing with. Through the din of the music, Thornton couldn't hear what they said to each other, he told Reeves, but it was clear from their facial expressions and their gestures that they were having a disagreement. Eric, he said, slapped or pushed her.

Thornton instructed Reeves to drive to the corner, to the top of the bluff at Silver Beach. Here, he said, just to the right of the bathrooms with the new aqua-blue tin roofs, he had seen Eric and James exchange words. James, Thornton said, was the white girl's cousin, friend, or boyfriend. He wasn't sure which. Eric took off down the bluff as James and two of James's friends pursued him. Thornton, who couldn't identify the other two boys, followed them down the bluff and was met by a friend whom he only knew as Dallas. Dallas is black. Thornton hopped into Dallas's old Bonneville and joined the chase. Thornton said he just wanted to witness the action. This all happened sometime around midnight, well after Eric had broken into Warmbein's car.

Eric, with James and others in pursuit, sprinted across the railroad tracks, past the waterfront condominiums, through the knee-high dune grass, to the south pier—all according to Thornton.

Thornton guided Reeves through this route, and the three of them—Reeves, Thornton, and Deputy Sheriff Abbott Taylor—left the car at the foot of the breakwater, where a yellow sign warns in large black letters: "Structure is not designed for public access. Proceed at your own risk." Joggers and lovers nonetheless venture out on the wharf, usually staying near the center to avoid the cold surf. For the more adventuresome, a blue metal railing lines the sides, out to a hundred feet or so, at which point the pier drops three feet and sits just inches above water level. Here the warning sign shouts: "CAUTION. This structure protects navigation. Insure your safety. Use with caution. KEEP OFF DURING STORMS OR HIGH SEAS." Thornton told Reeves that James and his two friends chased Eric just beyond this spot, just beyond the end of the blue metal railing, just beyond the warning sign.

"James will fight quick and fast, 'cause he knows he can," Thornton said. "He's a fuck'n brickhouse. He's huge, hundred percent muscle. He ain't no gangbanger. He ain't been in no trouble with the law that I know of." Thornton said he knew James only from drinking and partying, mostly on the beach. "I don't hang with no one but gangbangers." He recounted that James and Eric had argued loud enough for him to hear some of what they said even from where he stood, a basketball court–length away. "A lot of 'fuck you's' " is what Thornton remembered.

"James kicked him in the head. Eric was standing. Just brought his foot up and kicked him in the head right where the ladder's at. Eric went right back over a chain. He didn't die an accidental death. What'd the autopsy say? Man, there should be boot marks on his head. There should be bruises. Did they find bruises? . . . We [he and Dallas] left as soon as he went in and they went to yelling and throwing rocks at him. We got outta there. We didn't want any part of it. They knew they were going to beat his ass. I don't think they meant to kill him."

Such is the story of Eric's death as told by Daniel Thornton to Jim Reeves and Abbott Taylor—and later told to me. On separate occasions. Three years apart. The exact same story.

There are a few tantalizing asides, which by themselves don't mean much, but together lend some credibility to Thornton's story. Thomas Page, a friend of Eric's who is now in the military, told me that earlier that week in school Eric had asked him to join him at the Club Friday night. "I'm going to meet a female there," he told Page. Could that girl have been Lisa Liedke, his former white girl-friend? Eric's peers said they would wear jeans and high-tops instead of the fancier silk pants and dress shoes when they thought they might be going somewhere with a girl, another indication that Eric may have had plans that night.

Charles Ash, who danced with Eric in their group the Untouch-ables, told Reeves that white boys had made threats against Eric and others in the past about dancing with white girls. Steve Green, another friend, told me that sometime in the previous week Eric had told him he'd been hassled by some white guys. Another boy, Dajuan Hodges, said he was at the Club that night and that Eric had danced with a white girl. "The dude stepped up and said, 'She's my girlfriend,' " Hodges told me. "And Eric said, 'No, she's mine.' Then they calmed down . . . I had my mom's car, so I said to Eric, 'C'mon let's go.' I left around ten-thirty. I came back around twelve, but he was gone."

Both Larina Robbins, his former girlfriend, and Bobbie Nadus, his math teacher and gymnastics coach, said that during that last week Eric seemed unusually agitated and upset. Could he have been distraught over his breakup with Liedke? Or was he already involved with another St. Joseph girl and having troubles? In the police report, a number of people mention that they'd heard Eric had made a bet about dancing with a white girl, not Liedke, and that a group of white guys got angry with him about the wager.

I tracked down Liedke in Missouri, where she's now married to a naval enlistee. She said she was not at the Club the night Eric disappeared. "I just barely knew the guy. There was nothing between us except for innocent flirting. I just saw him for a few hours once a week at the Club for a few weeks. I really didn't care what his life was like. I wasn't that interested in him. We didn't date at all." She wanted, it seemed, to put distance between herself and Eric. Or maybe it's a matter of semantics and she didn't, in fact, believe that she and Eric had "dated." In her interviews with Reeves back in 1991, Liedke had said, "Well, we weren't necessarily going out. We were just seeing each other."

I asked Liedke whether she knew what had happened to Eric.

"I don't know. I really don't know. I have no clue." Her exasperation with my inquiry was clear.

"This is so long ago. I'm happy. I'm married. I don't want to deal with it." She concluded our conversation.

Reeves, long before he heard Thornton's account, had questioned Liedke extensively. Liedke said she was at a friend's party that Friday night, that she spent the night with her new boyfriend. She passed a polygraph.

Maybe it wasn't Liedke at the Club that night. A few remember her being there; most don't. If Thornton's story is true, perhaps the white girl they saw was someone else.

A few months before Reeves met with Thornton, he received an unsigned, typed letter. It read:

> I am responding at the request of a friend about the murder of a black boy last May 1991. Please look into a young man whose name is Richard Teller [not his real name]. He told several people he was involved or knew who was involved with this murder. I do not know if he was fabricating this story to "fit in" or if this was the honest to God's truth. Richard may be living in the St. Joseph area, or at this time may be in trouble with the law . . . I would rather not state my name. I hope this information will help you in some way.

Reeves tracked down Teller, who had served time for forgery, and Teller said that he hadn't known Eric, and that he was willing to take a polygraph. He never did. Reeves believed his story.

I spent many months trying to find Teller and Dallas, who allegedly had witnessed Eric's drowning along with Thornton, but could find neither. I always seemed one address behind Teller, whom I last looked for, without luck, at a ramshackle cottage in Stevensville. I did learn, however, that Teller had dated James's sister. Could Teller have been on the pier with James? As for Dallas, I could find no one in the area who went by that name. The only Dallas I came up with was through some sources at the Benton Harbor Police Department, but he was a man fifteen years older than Thornton.

Reeves was skeptical of Danny Thornton's account; soon after the guided tour of the south pier, Reeves said the tale was "full of bullshit." There were inconsistencies in the yarn and a few matters that were out-and-out wrong. Lies? Or just misplaced memories?

Thornton distinctly remembered that Eric was wearing a black-

and-red Chicago Bulls overcoat. According to Ruth, Eric had on his green Task Force jacket. Thornton seemed certain of this detail, but memory can, as Reeves has learned, play tricks. Five years after Eric's death, one of the Coast Guardsmen who had fished Eric out of the river told Reeves that, over the years, two details about Eric had stayed with him, both indications to him that Eric may have been involved in the drug trade: one, that Eric had a gold chain around his neck, and, two, that he wore British Knights basketball shoes, which the Coast Guardsman associated with drug traffickers. He was wrong on both counts. There was no gold chain. And Eric wore Nikes.

Thornton says the Club was packed that night. A few have agreed. But according to its owner, Chris Adams, and others, it was particularly slow that evening because it was the season's first good weather and many of the kids were at pregraduation parties.

But the part that raised the most doubt for Reeves was Thornton's specifying that Eric was pushed into the river *downstream* of the Coast Guard station. The body, Reeves argued, could not possibly have drifted a thousand feet upstream.

Despite his misgivings, Reeves returned to talk with Thornton again—three times. And as he listened to the story again and again, he thought, "Danny seems to be connected some way, like there's a thread of truth in there . . . He may be repeating something he n]heard, but I'm open. If I was able to prove what happened to Eric McGinnis, I'd walk into City Hall and tell everyone to kiss my ——. I'd just walk out. That would be the end of my career. I'd be so elated. I'd leave on a high note." Reeves liked to say his job was "to sort out the truth," but he certainly believed in hunches, and his hunch told him there might be something to Thornton's tale. But there was one "truth" that Reeves was wrong about: the body could have floated upstream.

28.

THE HANGING:
A TALE IN ONE PART

On the granite of hard fact grows the moss of legend, and even pure myth contains its grains of stony reality.

—Allan Nevins, historian

This much is not in dispute.

Marcus Cooley, a twenty-one-year-old petty thief, was found hanging by his red necktie in a Berrien County jail cell.

It's here where people begin to disagree.

It is common wisdom that myths help people make sense of the world. Indeed, they may explain the inexplicable. They can serve as a compass to the present, though the navigational forces are neither magnetic nor a measure of veracity, but a considerably more variable force, which mutates over time, according to one's dealings and place in the world.

During the four years I spent visiting Benton Harbor, I occasionally heard murmurs from old-timers about a lynching in St. Joseph. No one had many details, though a few conjured up images, albeit hazy ones, of whites attacking a black church. It happened in the 1930s, I was told. Or maybe the 1920s. Or maybe it was as late as the 1940s. No one was sure. It was always mentioned in the context of Eric's death. An elderly woman, Rita Wagner, whispered to me once, "I know how people are over there [in St. Joseph]. This is the second black that come up dead. Well, I mean there was that other fellow that was lynched. They have ways of getting around stuff."

I didn't pay it much mind at first. Most lynchings occurred in the South. Michigan, a fairly progressive state, witnessed one lynching of a black between 1882 and 1934. By contrast, during that same period Alabama recorded 296; Georgia, 478. Moreover, St. Joseph's elders had no recollection of such an incident. The handful of books and pamphlets written on the area make no mention of a racial crime—though, to be frank, there's barely any reference at all in these histories to blacks. In one book, *History of St. Joseph,* published in the 1920s by the town's Chamber of Commerce, the author makes only one allusion to blacks, and that is in the context of a yarn about a river boatman named Stormy Davis.

"One time a big, burly negro made the mistake of calling Stormy a liar," L. Benjamin Reber wrote. "Davis hit the nigger just once, but that coon was knocked fifteen feet across the boat and into the river."

That's not to say the history isn't there. Whites have killed blacks before. Or killed because of blacks. The stories have passed from generation to generation, over supper or over a beer, on stoops and in parlors, told by grandmothers and by pastors, the narratives shaped and reshaped by people's prejudices and blurred memories and by their own experiences. And while they may not be recorded in history books, they exist just as powerfully and vividly in these oral tales.

There's the story of Henry Burkhard, a St. Joseph building contractor, who in 1948 shot and killed his neighbors, Robert and Helen Stevens, because they'd sold their home to an interracial couple. Or Cecil Hunt, a black teen who eighteen years later, on the third night of civil disturbances by Benton Harbor youth, was shot with a .22-caliber rifle in a drive-by. The shooters, people believed, were white. Around the same time, police found the mutilated body of seven-year-old Diane Carter. She was, the story goes, killed by a white doctor in search of body organs. And there's the tale of Steven Smith, a local black college student who in 1985 was found dead behind a department store, over 90 percent of his body charred. People say he was torched in retaliation for his dating a white girl.

While myths can help us make sense of the incomprehensible, they can also confine us, confuse us, and leave us prey to historical laziness. Lore becomes shrouded in the glow of inarguable fact. Truth, though, is not always scientifically discernible—and even when it is, the prism, depending which side of the river you reside on, may create a wholly different illusion. It's an odd calculus. Consider the tales of murder. The first two happened just as people remember, though no one was charged with Cecil Hunt's death. The third is pure fiction. The police did at first speculate that Diane Carter's killer was a well-educated white male skilled in dissection; six years later a forty-two-year-old black man who was already serving a 320-year sentence was held responsible for the murder. And the last, as with Eric McGinnis, is, well, fiction or fact, depending on whom you speak to. The police concluded that Smith accidentally set himself afire after igniting his car to collect insurance, though some confuse his death with that of a young black man discovered near a tomato patch, his body burned beyond recognition; to this day the police have been unable to identify the victim, let alone arrest his assailant.

As David Walker, Benton Harbor's police chief, bluntly told me,

"Facts don't mean shit. Perception is the truth." And thus it becomes easy to dismiss one another's experiences.

The prosperity of St. Joseph, for example, when contrasted with
the poverty of Benton Harbor, has only reinforced the myths of old.
St. Joseph's civic leaders say the fundamental reason for Benton Harbor's erosion is that blacks moved to Benton Harbor from neighboring Indiana and Illinois for the welfare benefits. "Michigan was very
generous with welfare benefits, and they kept increasing those benefits without making many requirements," a former Berrien County
judge instructed me.

Migrant farm workers came "and then they found within six
months they could get a nice welfare check and if three or four
families moved into one apartment they could get more money, and
if they had children they could have even more money. There
wasn't much to do in the winter but multiply—and then we had
white flight." I received that analysis from Bill Johnson, an executive
at Gast Manufacturing.

"People used to go and apply in Gary or South Bend, and they'd
say, 'Why don't you move up to Michigan and get it right away—
and you get more money.' That actually happened. That was a fact,"
explained William Gillespie, a former drugstore owner and St. Joseph mayor. "People came into the store and wanted to know where
the courthouse was."

It is certainly true that many single moms with kids in tow
moved to Benton Harbor, and other Michigan cities, to receive
public assistance. In 1981, at the height of this concern, Berrien
County's Department of Social Services processed 787 out-of-state
families applying for aid, up 70 percent from two years earlier. But
these figures neglect history; they discount St. Joseph's part in its
neighbor's decline.

In the 1930s and 1940s, the factories advertised in the South,
particularly in Arkansas, for workers. Some Benton Harbor old-
timers say that employers sent trucks to pick up prospective laborers.

A few remember railroad cars arriving in town, filled with Southerners who'd been promised jobs.

In the 1970s and 1980s, the factories fell like dominoes. In 1977, the V–M Corporation, maker of record changers, closed. The next year, the Superior Steel Castings Company filed for bankruptcy. In 1979, Michigan Standard Alloys shut its doors, as did Clark Equipment's Benton Township plant three years later. In 1985, after a lengthy strike, Auto Specialties shut down. And by 1987, the Whirlpool Corporation, provider of over two thousand blue-collar jobs at its peak, closed the last of its local assembly plants. Whirlpool has since funded the Cornerstone Alliance, an economic development group, part of whose mission is to revitalize Benton Harbor. The very industries that had once lured Southern blacks were gone, and many families had no option but the public dole.

The historian Spencie Love has written a book, *One Blood: The Death and Resurrection of Charles R. Drew,* that deconstructs the fable of the renowned black surgeon's death in 1950. The story goes that Drew, director of the nation's first Red Cross blood bank, bled to death after an automobile accident in rural North Carolina because the local whites-only hospital refused him treatment. The tale, retold in newspaper columns, in classrooms, and even in an episode of TV's *M*A*S*H,* was false, yet blacks held on to it because the truth was that many hospitals in the Jim Crow South had a limited number of beds for blacks or didn't take blacks at all. In that context, the story about Dr. Drew made sense to them.

Love writes, "There are different kinds of historical truth, and the history that people pass on orally—a group's legends—is an important clue not only to how they feel and think about their past but also to the very substance of that past." Love might have added that the legends also serve as an important clue to how a group feels and thinks about the present—and to the very substance of the present.

And so I listened closely and took seriously the distinct but dimming memories of the Benton Harbor elders. A lynching? In St. Joseph? Within their lifetime? Maybe.

Marcus Cooley, alias Marcus or Harold Lewis, was running from the law. The authorities in his hometown of Des Moines, Iowa, wanted him for violating probation; he had been arrested for breaking and entering.

I don't know much about Cooley, other than that he lived with his grandmother, Ardy Lewis, and that he had his troubles with the police. I tracked down a distant relative who as a kid remembers hearing stories of Cooley's athletic prowess, including the time he eluded Des Moines police by swimming the width of a local river under water.

That summer of 1934, in the heart of the Depression, Cooley, like many others, headed for Benton Harbor, where he knew he could get work picking berries. The reason I know this much is that on his way, the South Bend police arrested him for vagrancy and Cooley told them of his destination. He fled the Indiana city before the local authorities learned he was wanted in Des Moines, but they alerted the Des Moines sheriff that Cooley was headed for the Twin Cities. The Des Moines sheriff mailed his Berrien County counterpart, Charlie Miller, a photo of Cooley, accompanied by a note: "This Lewis will do anything to escape arrest, but doubt if he carries a gun. However, it will be well to watch him closely if you locate him. We are anxious to get this man into custody. Will extradite if necessary."

The correspondence got misplaced and wasn't discovered until after Cooley's death.

Sheriff Miller was a glad-handing, free-wheeling, oversize figure in Berrien County politics. At his death, in 1953, his obituary referred to him as "one of Berrien County's all-time most colorful political figures." Everyone called him Charlie. A Republican, he won his first of three terms as sheriff in 1932, the year of a Democratic landslide. At well over six feet, big-featured, and broad-shouldered, Miller cut an imposing figure. He loved hunting big game in the Canadian north woods, and twice won the state's trap-shooting contest. He became best known, though, for his annual picnics, at which he fed and entertained thousands of his loyal constituents. He dished out free ice cream and drinks, held games for the kids, and sponsored burlesque shows and boxing matches for the adults.

One of the local newspapers wrote adoringly: "A hard worker when he gets on the job . . . Charles Miller is . . . clean, honest, fair at all times [and] would enforce the laws impartially." Those living in the Flats, though, didn't think so.

Benton Harbor's black population lived on the swampland along the river. The wooden shanties, many with dirt floors, housed families recently from the South. The neighborhood was like a town to itself. The Flats had its own stores, its own churches, its own leaders, and its own gambling. One of its spiritual and political leaders was the Reverend Edward Burrell Williams, pastor of the Union Memorial A.M.E. Church. Williams was a new arrival; he had grown up in rural Mississippi and entered the ministry by way of Kansas's Western Theological Seminary. Though a newcomer, Williams immediately became involved in electoral politics and, along with others, was instrumental in steering the county's black vote from the Republicans to the Democrats. Though I can't find any mention of it, I assume that Williams supported Miller's Democratic opponent in the 1932 race for sheriff.

Williams was short and sturdy; his square jaw and balding pate made him look distinguished, if not stern. His church was the most prominent African-American institution in the county, and with it as his base he reached out to the area's youth. He gave boxing lessons in the church's basement; his wife taught piano. Williams was also what some called "a race-conscious man." He took positions for President Roosevelt's courtpacking and fought vigorously for blacks to be included in the county's delegation to the state Democratic Convention. He produced a play, but when the ads described it as "depicting the true life of a southern darkey," Williams canceled the production. "I'd rather lose everything than to sacrifice even one of the principles for which I have fought and labored for over twenty years throughout the United States," he told a local reporter. In later years, he would return to school and become Notre Dame's first black graduate.

Rose Burkett, who is white and now ninety-nine years old, remembered Williams as "quite radical, always stirring up racial tension." Raymond Robbins, founder of Robbins Funeral Home and grandfather of Eric's girlfriend Larina, described Williams "as a Martin Luther King of his time." He continued: "He didn't bite his tongue about anything." Including the death of Cooley.

In September, shortly after his arrival, Cooley was arrested for stealing a car in Benton Harbor. He was housed at the county jail, located on the first floor of the county courthouse. A few weeks later, Cooley pleaded guilty to the crime and, while awaiting sentencing, attempted a breakout, as the Des Moines sheriff had presciently warned he would.

At four thirty in the afternoon of October 29, after being fingerprinted, Cooley, on his way back to the bullpen, bolted. The deputy accompanying him hesitated before giving chase; he first had to lock the door to the holding cell so that the other inmates couldn't follow. Cooley hurdled a five-foot fence, sprinted over the bluff behind the jail, and disappeared into the thick underbrush. All available sheriff department personnel as well as the St. Joseph police and a score of neighbors scoured the woods and the area around a nearby canning factory and railroad depot, to no avail. Cooley, it turns out, waited for darkness, crouching in the corner of a small private woodshed, hidden by tools and cut logs.

Three hours later, the sheriff's department received a report that a truck belonging to a St. Joseph plumber had been stolen. Two deputies spotted it in Union Pier, a beach town at the southern end of the county, twenty miles from St. Joseph. They pulled up beside the truck on the Red Arrow Highway, which ran parallel to the lake, and immediately recognized its driver as Cooley. As they yelled for the escapee to halt and sounded their sirens, Cooley slammed his foot on the accelerator. The deputies kept pace and shone a spotlight in Cooley's face, but he veered left, scraping against the squad car in an effort to crowd it off the road. Fearing for their safety, the officers slowed down; they trailed the truck and shot twice, blowing out the rear left tire. Cooley lost control, hit a gasoline pump, and flipped. He emerged from the toppled vehicle wielding a three-pound hammer, ready to do battle, but under threat of being shot by the pistol-toting deputies, he surrendered. They drove him back to the jail, where they placed him in what was called the insane cell, a small isolated room lit by a bare lightbulb and closed by a steel door with a small window, instead of by open bars.

A couple of hours later, John R. Shram, a St. Joseph doctor, received an emergency call from the sheriff's department. He later testified that when he arrived, a deputy was administering mouth-to-mouth resuscitation to Cooley, who lay motionless on the concrete floor of his cell, dressed in overalls he'd stolen from the woodshed. Shram injected an adrenaline-like serum into Cooley's arm, but it had no effect. He pronounced Cooley dead shortly after midnight. The doctor later told a coroner's jury that he noticed a deep mark on the inmate's throat and, beside him, a portion of a red necktie, which apparently had been lashed around his neck. There was no slip noose. Shram noted that another portion of the tie hung, fastened by wire, from a heating pipe that snaked across the ceiling.

The Reverend E. B. Williams read about Cooley's death the next day. The article in the paper called it a suicide. Neither Williams nor the other leaders in the Flats believed that, given the events of the previous decade.

Though the Reverend Williams didn't arrive in Benton Harbor until 1931, certainly he heard about the attempted mob lynching eight years earlier in St. Joseph, an incident that, like Cooley's hanging, is absent from all written histories of the area. On a hot summer night in 1923, nearly a thousand men and women gathered on the courthouse lawn. Some had been drinking. They demanded that Sheriff George Bridgman turn over two young black men who had been arrested for raping an eighteen-year-old white woman.

"We want those niggers!" people shouted. "Where are they?"

"If you want to find out, just try and rush this door," Bridgman calmly warned them. He and a deputy stood on the courthouse steps, each with a shotgun by his side.

One man approached Bridgman, coaxing the mob to move forward with him. He dared the sheriff to remove him from the grounds. The crowd hissed and roared their approval. The lone deputy stepped in front of the sheriff and, with a quick right roundhouse, floored the man. The deputy and sheriff then handcuffed him. The crowd was silent. "Boys, I don't know just what you hope to do," Bridgman said. "But we sometimes have to get out of here in a hurry, so y'all just move back, please. I don't want anybody hurt, but in case of emergency there'll be no hesitation on my part . . . Now this has gone on about far enough. I'm here to protect my prisoners from mob violence, and you can bet I'm going to do it."

Sheriff Bridgman and the deputy held the mob at bay until, as it grew late, the people slowly dispersed, a few mumbling that they'd return the next night. They never did. "I would have killed somebody, even if I had lost my own life," the sheriff later told a reporter.

The two black men were eventually found guilty by a jury that, for the first time in the county's history, included a black.

Six weeks after the attempted lynching, the Ku Klux Klan gathered fifteen hundred followers at St. Joseph's Silver Beach; there, they set ablaze a twenty-foot-high wooden cross wrapped in gasoline-soaked burlap while a minister from Marion, Indiana, decried any mixing of the races. Within weeks, there were cross burnings in two nearby towns, an indication that Klan membership in each of those hamlets had reached five hundred.

When the Depression came, whites felt threatened by blacks who, like Cooley, had come looking for work. Two years before Cooley arrived, a group of white men had burned a cross in nearby Sodus as a warning to blacks who had come to pick berries to push off. Fifty blacks who had recently arrived by train heeded the warning and headed south along the highway. And a year and a half later, a few months before Cooley arrived, sheriff deputies arrested sixty-one itinerant workers, fifty-six of whom were black, who had arrived on a single freight train in Benton Harbor. They were told to leave town or face charges.

The day before Cooley was found dead, one of the local papers carried a front-page, banner-headline story about the lynching of Claude Neale, a black Floridian accused of killing a white woman. The article reported that Neale was shot at least a dozen times, dragged behind a car for several miles, and mutilated by men with knives before being strung up on a tree at the courthouse square in Marianna, Florida.

In the context of all this, it is understandable why Williams, on viewing Cooley's body and noting that the jaw was bruised "as though punched with a fist, and one side of his face was swollen," could so quickly become suspicious about the true cause of the prisoner's death. Williams and fifty other black leaders—including ministers, laborers, a foundry worker, and a pharmacist—crowded into the chambers of the county supervisors, demanding a formal investigation into Cooley's "suicide." Williams was the first to speak. He told Sheriff Miller and the other county officials that he did not believe that someone could hang himself with a necktie. He also denounced the county coroner, Lewis Kerlikowske, for refusing the request of one of his church trustees to view the body. He became suspicious when a funeral home owned by the white coroner was assigned to embalm and bury Cooley, who had no local family. Williams insisted that a black physician be allowed to examine the body and that he be permitted to visit Cooley's cell.

Others then testified, including Kerlikowske, the coroner, who suggested that Cooley's facial injuries could have been incurred when the stolen truck overturned. Shram, the doctor who had attended to Cooley, told the officials that, in his opinion, Cooley "came to death by strangulation and by no other cause."

Williams, in his trademark double-breasted suit, rose from his seat. "Can we see his clothes?" he asked in his deep, resonant voice. Kerlikowske responded that he had had them burned because they were soiled. "How about the tie?" countered a disbelieving Williams. A jail trustee, it was explained, had mistakenly thrown it away. This further enraged Williams, who continued to interrupt and question the witnesses himself, all of which, according to a newspaper account, "led to constant wrangling and confusion."

That afternoon, after the hearings had adjourned for the day, Sheriff Miller pulled together a small group of reporters in the courthouse lobby. I can picture Miller, who was clearly admired by the local press, resting his hand on the back of a reporter or winking at another. I can imagine him warming them up by telling jokes or inquiring about their families. I can imagine him casting a glance at Williams, standing off to the side, to let him know who was in charge. Certainly loudly enough for Williams to hear, Miller, having soothed the scribes, excoriated the minister.

"The investigation is wholly political in character," he proclaimed. "But I welcome the inquiry, which exonerates my men from vicious rumors spread for political reasons. I wish it to be understood that I do not in any degree blame my opponent, but I do place the responsibility squarely on the shoulders of the Reverend E. B. Williams. He has plenty of reason for having a personal dislike of me. He has not been fair to members of his own race, and I wouldn't tolerate his chiseling from members of his own race who happened to be in jail."

Williams, from what people say, couldn't remain quiet, not when he felt strongly about something—and surely he felt strongly about Miller's innuendoes. He broke into the group of journalists and confronted Miller, who towered over him.

"Is the third degree used in your jail?" Williams queried, as reporters furiously recorded the exchange.

"It is not," Miller replied.

"Then why was the prisoner's mouth swelled up?"

"If you ever had been in an auto accident where your car turned over, you might be able to answer that," observed Miller before stomping off.

That night, in the basement of Williams's church, twenty-five black leaders gathered. Offended by Miller's insinuations that Williams was acting alone, they talked and debated and put together a statement, which they issued the next day.

We, the undersigned committee of 25, resent this. The presence of over 50 outstanding negroes at the courthouse yesterday should show to Mr. Miller and to everyone else that this is not a one-man proposition, but rather the outcry of a people constituting one-tenth of our population who want to know why a colored man facing a 10-year prison sentence would want to commit suicide, how he could hang himself with so flimsy a thing as a necktie, why that same necktie cannot be produced, why the clothes were burned in which he is alleged to have killed himself, why on Wednesday of last week, a day after the embalming was completed, Thomas Jones [a church trustee] was denied the opportunity to see the body, and why others who appeared to see his body later in the week were required to get the consent of the sheriff before they could see the body. We want it made clear that instead of this idea of a one-man proposition, that last Sunday afternoon, nearly 400 people who had jammed the AME church to hear an assistant attorney general of the United States, Robert L. Vann, selected a joint committee of 50, representing every negro church, political and economic organization, to investigate this matter, and the Rev. E. B. Williams was merely selected by the group at large as the spokesman for this committee.

Bowing to pressure from the black community, the prosecutor, a Democrat who in part owed his election to the support of Williams, called for a coroner's inquest. The jury, which consisted of three Republicans and three Democrats, convened four days later. On the first morning, they heard testimony from three doctors, one of whom had been chosen by the black community and all of whom, after examining the body, concluded that Cooley had died of as-phyxiation. Williams and others had speculated that Cooley may have been beaten unconscious or killed before he was hanged.

That evening, the Reverend Myron C. Everett, pastor of the First Evangelical Church and a representative of the Twin City Min-isterial Association, asked to take a look at Cooley's cell. While examining it, he found a message scrawled in pencil along one of the walls:

Some may think I am crazy, but I ain't. To the state of Micigan—Plice send me home is all i ask.

Plice send this to [here an arrow pointed to an adjacent note]

Dear Granmam. I now take my own life because of so much trouble. Tell all i say hello. God be with you all, from marcus. Mrs. Ardy Lewis Cooley, des moines, iowa, 113 ridge st.

A deputy accompanying the Reverend Everett found a pencil stub on the cell's floor. The coroner's jury brought in a handwriting expert, who, after comparing the cell note with Cooley's signature, concluded it was in the same handwriting. How, Williams wanted to know, could he, two other church members, and a slew of deputies, all of whom had inspected the cell for blood stains (they found none), miss these penciled notes? Too much didn't make sense to Williams. The missing clothes. The missing tie. The delay in letting blacks view the body. Williams continued to insist that Cooley had been beaten and then hanged. But the jury, after deliberating for twelve minutes, concluded that Cooley had "met death by self-inflicted strangulation at the county jail between the hours of 10:30 pm and midnight on October 29."

In a service led by Williams, Cooley was buried in the county's infirmary cemetery, which, unmarked, is now partly covered by a new hospital building. The only family member present was Cooley's uncle, who traveled from Des Moines. His grandmother was too ill to make the journey.

Three days later, shortly after dusk, eighteen-year-old Anna McCaster, on her way home from choir practice at her church in the Flats, saw a rocket of flames soar into the sky. "I never saw anything like it," she told me sixty-two years later. "I was scared to death. I thought maybe we'd all be killed." The wooden cross, erected in a vacant lot, stood twelve feet high, the orange glow of the flames reflected in the stained glass windows of Union Memorial A.M.E.'s new home, a brick building with oak and gumwood interior, and Williams's wood-frame house, both of which sat directly across the street. Families came out of their homes to see the spectacle. They gathered along the edges of the vacant lot and by the steps of the church. A band of children stood mesmerized by the scene.

Williams, coming from the parsonage, was dressed in suit and tie, even at this hour of the day. He walked to within a few feet of the blazing cross and turned to those who had gathered. "This is the wrong thing to be happening here," he said slowly, as the flames behind him licked at the darkness. "We are not troublemakers. We are Christian people. We will not stand for this happening to our young people. Now, let's go home. Please, let's get the children home."

McCaster heeded Williams, but at a measured pace so that she could watch the men of the neighborhood take axes to the cross and chop it into pieces. They then doused the embers with water. Meanwhile, the church became a fortress. Fearful of an attack, the church deacons, armed with hunting rifles and shotguns, took up residence in the sanctuary, where, in shifts, they remained for the next week. They sat with rifles in the bell tower. And three to four men each night patrolled the land around the church, shotguns at their side and pistols in their belts. There were no other incidents.

"Everyone loved the Reverend Williams," recalled McCaster. "He wasn't afraid of dying."

"Among blacks there's still a feeling that Cooley was hanged," Warren Mitchell tells me. Mitchell, whose father helped defend the church with his one-shot shotgun, refers to Cooley's death in a short prose poem he wrote about growing up in the Flats: "They took certain men to jail. They don't know how he died in his cell." Other than the newspaper stories, it is the only written account of the incident, however brief, that I can find.

Miller, who won re-election, never investigated the cross burning, and a short time later, despite numerous death threats made against Williams, denied the minister a gun permit. Williams, belea-guered and harassed, vowed that he would never again use his church as the setting for a political gathering. He moved on to another church in another city five years later.

But the suspicions lingered. "Things were never the same after that," McCaster said. "Before that, you didn't notice much about race." She added, pensively, "I heard that someone ran that boy, Eric McGinnis, off into the river. That really shook up both of the towns, and I don't think Benton Harbor ever recovered from that either."

29.
FAMILY

New Year's Eve, 1996.

Ruth and her friend Kathy Miller, each single, each looking for a way to celebrate the New Year, purchased a Las Vegas–night package together. The event was held at a local hotel, where the two played blackjack and roulette and drank the Kamikazes recommended to them by a friendly waiter. They listened to a rhythm-and-blues band and chatted with a few acquaintances they'd bumped into. Ruth went up to the hotel bed before midnight, before the champagne bottles were uncorked. Kathy followed a few hours later. They both remember thinking how few blacks there were, maybe ten or fifteen, among the hundred or so revelers.

The next morning, they rose at nine-thirty, early for a New Year's day, and headed down to the dining hall for their buffet breakfast. It was there, Ruth told me, that she began to think, really for the first time, that just maybe Eric had been killed because he'd dated a white girl. It wasn't because of some new evidence. It wasn't because she now realized something new about Eric. It was, rather, that for the first time she felt stung by what she believed was someone's animosity toward blacks. When she told me the story of that breakfast a week later, she was near tears. And the thing about it was that the insult, certainly in contrast to more egregious injustices, seemed so slight, almost insignificant, maybe not even at all related to race. But, then again, such personal pricks, swathed in ambiguity and nuance, often leave us aching the hardest. All that anger. Where to direct it? And who will believe you?

Here's the story as told to me by both Ruth and Kathy. Ruth had gone through the buffet line and filled her plate with strips of bacon, sausage links, and hashed browns. Kathy followed right behind, her plate equally full. As they headed to a table, a young waitress, who was white, stopped them.

"Can I have your ticket?" the waitress asked, loud enough for those around to hear.

"It's in the hotel room somewhere," Ruth explained, keeping her voice low, a clear contrast to the waitress's shrillness. "I have no idea where it is. But I do have the envelope we got from this place. Because we did get it. We're not trying to get a free ride."

"I didn't say you were trying to get a free ride," the waitress shot back. "All I'm telling you is I got to have the ticket."

Ruth turned to Kathy. "Obviously," she told her friend, "I got to find the ticket, 'cause all I have is this envelope." She turned back to the waitress. "I guess we won't eat, then." The waitress grabbed the plates out of Ruth's and Kathy's hands.

"I do want to tell you that you could have waited till we sat down and then you could have come over to get the tickets," Ruth admonished her. Both Ruth and Kathy had by then noted that the waitress waited for the white patrons to take their seats before collecting their tickets.

Ruth went to her room, found the ticket, and returned to the dining hall. It was clear that the waitress, who was emerging from the kitchen, had been crying, her eyes red and swollen.

"Here's the ticket," Ruth said, handing it to her. "I told you I had it, but I just couldn't find it."

"I didn't say you didn't have it. I just said I had to have it."

"Okay, fine."

"Well, it doesn't matter anyways; you said you weren't gonna eat."

"Since I found the ticket, we might now. Since our food's sitting there."

Ruth and Kathy sat down at the table where the waitress had put their plates and began eating. Ruth was seething. And then the waitress and her colleagues made a visible display of not heeding the women's request for coffee, though they served diners all around them. And, in tones loud enough for Kathy and Ruth to hear, the waitresses inquired of neighboring patrons whether they could bring coffee or orange juice. Ruth left her meal unfinished and complained to the hotel manager.

When Ruth first alluded to this incident, she asked that I have Kathy recount it first. It still hurt too much. She worried she'd get too emotional. And I believe she didn't want to appear as if she were whining. If the story came from a third person, I might be more likely to believe it.

"Ruth was hurt," Kathy told me as we sat at the dining table in her Benton Harbor house. She smoked Mistys and drank a bottle of Schlitz. "I just wanted to take Ruth out of there. She was, you know, almost in tears . . . What hurt her is that you could be treated like that in the nineties in Benton Harbor, where she was born and raised. I'm sure she's come into contact with racial mistreatment, but years ago, below the surface. And with the kind of status she has at her job and traveling for the company to Mexico, I think it made her sit and think."

Particularly about Eric. I'd known Ruth now for four years, yet I didn't feel that we had formed a particularly strong bond. As I mentioned earlier, she often avoided me, not returning phone calls, sometimes canceling appointments. Kathy, who handles the switchboard at Modern Plastics, often had to deliver the news. "Ruth says it's been a horrible day," she'd tell me. "She wants to know if you can come by another time." Kathy would always apologize for Ruth and reassure me. "Try her in a week," she'd urge. "She's had a tough few days thinking about Eric." Yet on the occasions when Ruth and I did meet—at her apartment or over a meal—she was open and gracious, extending herself in ways she certainly didn't have to. Once when I called to set up a lunch date, Ruth suggested I ask my questions over the phone instead. But I persisted, so we eventually did meet, and what was to be a quick half-hour meeting turned into nearly two hours.

I think Ruth herself had ambivalent feelings about my work— not my writing the book but my delving into her son's death. Sometimes I felt she'd rather not know. That there was some comfort in being unaware of all the facts. I had thought the converse would be true, that closure would make it easier on her. But by not possessing clear images of Eric's last moments, she was not consumed by that awful instant when her son stopped breathing. Maybe the last minutes were peaceful. Maybe Eric slid into death unaware of his fate. At least Ruth could think that. Also, Ruth is a forgiving person. I sometimes wondered what she would do with all her wrath if, indeed, she believed that someone had murdered her son. I wasn't the only one who felt this. Shortly after Michael Green wrote the guest editorial on Eric's death, he met Ruth at a retreat for selected local leaders. Green introduced himself and asked whether there was anything he could do. He was, at the time, intent on pursuing the case. "I got the impression that she wanted the whole thing dropped," he told me. "Talking to her kind of changed my feeling about the whole issue. She wanted it to heal; she wanted some closure. I gave her my phone number and asked her to call me. Then I ran into her a few times and she said, 'I know I should get in touch with you. I'll give you a call.' But she never did."

Eric had become a symbol for many, a kind of reference point on a racial map. But for Ruth he was, plainly and simply, her son. He represented her life, her love, her contribution, her legacy. In the end, did it really matter for Ruth whether he was killed by whites or by blacks, or whether he drowned accidentally? Anyway she cut it, he was gone. Ruth could still not bring herself to display the picture she and Eric took together at J. C. Penney.

Even now, five years after his death, a few weeks after the New Year's morning incident, Ruth seemed uncertain about what to do. She talked for weeks of filing a complaint with the Michigan Civil Rights Commission, but never did.

"I called everyone in my family," she told me. "I started with Bennie first. He could tell I was very upset. I felt that I was stripped in there . . . To be treated like that, it just killed me.

"I wondered; I always told Eric you treat people like you want them to treat you. What if he wasn't able to question it like I was able to do? If that's what happened, I'm okay with that . . . It made me look at things differently. You see, I never realized it was like that. I knew from what I read over the years that the prejudice and racism was there, but it never hit home close like that. I could totally not believe it. It was to a point where I was so mad that I was just ready to call up Reeves over there and tell them how I felt, that you guys were just so rotten and dirty. And then I pulled myself together and said that's not really fair, because you really don't know. It made me stop and think. If Eric had gotten loud and obnoxious . . . but that's not enough to take his life from him like that, just because he might have cursed someone out."

Ruth did call Reeves. She told him that she was collecting Eric's belongings, placing them in storage, and wanted a copy of the police report to put with his possessions. She confided in me that in reality she wanted to read it through tip by tip, lead by lead. She wanted to test her own theories against what the investigation had come up with. Reeves obliged and passed on a copy of the report.

"I don't know if I regret it or not, but I don't know why I didn't make a big fuss when Eric died," she said. "I guess I didn't want any parent to have to go through what I did, and I knew what the tensions were like between these towns. I chose to stay in the background. I don't know if it was a good choice.

"I'm more at peace now, though. I just think I'm going to get some answers one day."

been involved in a coverup of Eric's death. Would I portray him that way? When I reached him, he was feeling jittery, as he did from time to time.

"I know everyone doesn't feel that way," he said, looking for reassurance. "I figure it's best to be open with you. I'm an open guy. I've got nothing to hide." He paused. "Ohhhh, I don't know what I'm getting myself into," he said, as much to himself as to me. And he asked the question he always posed, sometimes more seriously than at other times. "Am I going to be able to show my face around here after the book comes out? I'm probably going to have to move." He laughed nervously.

I couldn't blame Reeves for feeling defensive. Every time I called him with one more hypothesis or one more name of someone he hadn't interviewed, he must have thought that, directly or indirectly, I was questioning the thoroughness of his investigation. But more to the point, I was, intentionally or not, questioning, or at least examining, Reeves's relationship with the black community. He often urged me to talk to the two black officers who worked on the task force, Bill Elliott from Benton Harbor and Bobby Simmons from the St. Joseph Township force. They would, he assured me, confirm his conclusion that Eric had either fallen in the river or tried to swim across. They would dispute the murder speculation in their own community. Or he'd suggest I speak with one of two black friends, Archie Carpenter, who worked at a printing company, or Joshua Ndege. Carpenter and Reeves played golf together on occasion, and Reeves told me that Carpenter wasn't angered by Eric's death. He was much more bitter about the shooting of Norris Maben. Give him a call, he urged. Or call Joshua. Ndege and Reeves had never discussed the case, but Reeves felt they shared an outlook on the world, that they particularly shared a take on Benton Harbor. Both believed that a degree of irresponsibility and of dependency (primarily on government largess) was, in large part, the cause of the town's bleak outlook. Give him a call, Reeves would urge. I never did. Reeves did it for me.

"What you doing now? Right now?" he asked me over the phone.

"Nothing," I said, a bit on guard. "Making phone calls."

"How would you like to meet Joshua? Let me call him." Reeves hung up and called me back a minute later. "Meet me at McDonald's in twenty minutes." He didn't wait for an answer.

Ndege, a devout Seventh Day Adventist, came to this country from Zimbabwe in 1991 so that he could attend one of the church's schools, Andrews University. It's located in Berrien Springs, fifteen minutes from St. Joseph. He now runs a computer-training center.

When I met Ndege at McDonald's that morning, what struck me most was how distinguished, how professorial he looked, particularly in his tweed sportcoat. I noticed his erect posture; even sitting down, he exuded confidence. His southern African lilt belied his moxie and single-mindedness. "I knew what America is all about," he said, speaking of his youth. "I knew all the states when I was ten years old. Oklahoma. Nebraska. All of them." He was, at a young age, determined to make his future in America.

Reeves and I sipped coffee; Ndege drank orange juice. The restaurant was nearly empty, so we had some privacy at a Formica table smack in the middle. I told Ndege about my book.

"People take advantage of race, on both sides of the river," he said. Without prodding, he began to recount a stream of incidents in which he had felt mistreated because of his skin color. The first tale involved a shopping excursion to a local department store, just the past Saturday, that he had made with his fourteen-year-old son and his son's friend.

"You know my son is real big," he said. "We bought a video editor. We paid for it at the cashier and then started to go out. When we got to the door, a lady stopped us and asked to see our receipt. I asked her, 'Why do you need to see our receipt?' She told me, 'I need to check it.' 'But what about all these other people? They were just walking through the door. Why me? Why not them?' The cashier who had served us came up and whispered to her that we had bought it. She just turned around and walked away. Nothing. No apology. I followed her."

Ndege smiled at Reeves. "You know me, Jim, I'm stubborn. I said, 'Don't you want to see my receipt?' She thought she had caught a thief. It had everything to do with race. All those people going out through the door were white. Me, look, I'm black. This kind of stuff has not affected my thinking. There are stupid white people and there are stupid black people. It won't change me."

Reeves then took on the role of interviewer, asking Ndege, for my benefit, why he chose to settle in St. Joseph rather than Benton Harbor. Ndege explained he had done so for his kids' safety. "Who doesn't like that peace?" he asked rhetorically.

"Joshua, why do you think Benton Harbor's so down?" Reeves asked, again for my benefit.

"It's the government's fault. They perpetuate it." But he didn't continue with the subject. Instead, he recounted another personal experience. These encounters clearly ate at him. While nodding at Reeves, he said, "I've had experiences here but I haven't told Jim because he'd try to find out who did it." And he proceeded to describe a heated exchange he had had with a clerk at a car electronics store. The clerk called the police, who calmed everyone down and escorted Ndege from the store. After Ndege drove away, the officer followed and pulled him over a block later; he ticketed Ndege for not carrying car insurance. "It all had to do with race," he said.

He warmly placed his hand on Reeves's shoulder. "This guy is a good person," he said. "He's a person, not a cop . . . He is my friend. He is my friend . . . This racial thing, people take advantage of it."

I asked Ndege about Eric's death.

"It pained me," he said. "Because I know the truth behind it. I believe that boy was killed."

Reeves's face turned crimson. He tugged at his tie. He swatted at a fly. He swiveled in his chair to face his friend.

"You do?" he asked, trying to sound unruffled. "Why?"

"I've been that route."

"Do you think I covered anything up?" All pretense of composure was gone.

"No," Ndege calmly told him. "You worked with what you had. But logic is not always the truth."

Reeves started to question Ndege, but Ndege held up his hand.

"At Andrews University," Ndege interrupted, "a black student was hassled for dating a white girl. It's the same thing. You should know as a white that not all whites feel like you."

"If you think Eric was killed," Reeves asked, his eyes locked on his friend's, "do you think a black could have killed him?"

"I come from Zimbabwe. Whites feel supreme there. I've been trying to find out why you're my friend. Because I am black? So that people won't think you're like others? No."

They talked past and over each other, Ndege philosophical, Reeves still puzzled that his friend didn't share his views about Eric's death. "What part of the case disturbed you that much?" he asked.

"That they caught him stealing. Was he? It's easy to set people up."

"But in the case of Eric," Reeves responded, "we had information from his mother and father that he borrowed five dollars from his mother to go to the Club. And we had this guy, Ted Warmbein, who reported his car broken into and had forty-four dollars taken. And he took off running after Eric. Eric was never found again. In the hospital they took forty-four dollars out of one pocket and five out of the other. So my question is, how did he end up with that money?"

"How good do you know this guy, Warmbein?" Ndege probed.

"I didn't know him, but he talked to the police for half an hour after his car was burglarized. I don't know how he would have had time."

"I don't blame you for thinking no one killed Eric. You worked with the evidence. Logic. But not always." Ndege smiled.

"But I take it personally," Reeves shot back. "We couldn't have done any more. People believe it's a coverup. Do you believe it's a coverup?"

Ndege laughed softly. "No. No."

"Then I don't feel so bad," Reeves said, relaxing some.

"You worked with what you had," Ndege assured him. "I'm talking from experience. I've seen these things happen." He went on to tell of a store manager who had accused him of shoplifting a set of tools when, in fact, he was at the store to return them.

"And this guy offers me a gift certificate, as if he could buy me out." Ndege snorted. "An apology would have been enough. I thought about taking him to court, but I wouldn't waste my time on such nonsense. What I believe is that people like that will meet their match."

Reeves, now on his second cup of coffee, wasn't listening closely, his mind still fixed on Ndege's earlier remarks. He tugged at his tie, kept swiping at the persistent fly. How could his friend, someone whose children have been to his house, doubt him? How could he think Reeves was wrong to conclude that Eric had died accidentally, that no criminal act had been involved? It burned Reeves. Absolutely burned him. What I didn't tell Reeves is that the two black police officers who worked on the task force with him, as well as his friend Archie Carpenter, believed that Eric may have been killed—and killed at the hands of whites. Reeves would not have understood that either.

31.

Ripples—

and Whitecaps

On unusually gusty days, the lake—and the river at its mouth—whip themselves into a cycle of fury. The wind molds waves that pound into each other with such force that they create a fountain, spouting water high into the air. And then the wind, still blowing hard, casts new swells, perhaps from a slightly different angle or at a slightly different height, and these again pound into each other, only to break apart and start anew. Thus, whitecaps appear, the splashing of the waves, sometimes two or three at a time, crashing into each other over and over and over, like a roomful of young boys run amok.

When I think of the story of Eric's death, I think of its effect on the lives of individuals as well as on the lives of the towns. It's everlasting. For some, it's like ripples, the gentle, symmetrical rollers formed by the dropping of a pebble into water. For others, it's more like whitecaps, turbulent and unpredictable, and at times strong enough to disorient and, in certain situations, capsize. These are a few of those stories, the ripples and whitecaps, resulting from Eric's death.

The Mayor

Sometimes you can tell more about a people from the exceptional than you can from the routine. Two days before Eric's body was recovered, an exceptional event occurred: elected officials and top administrators from Benton Harbor and St. Joseph spent the day together. They toured St. Joseph's public works garage and Benton Harbor's water-filtration plant. They shared lunch at the Captain's Table, a restaurant in Benton Harbor, and barbecued dinner at St. Joseph's Riverview Park. It was such an extraordinary event that it made front-page news. Among those attending was Jeff Richards, a brash young veterinarian who at the time was a St. Joseph city commissioner.

After the discovery of Eric's body, Richards sat in on a task force meeting led by Reeves. "I was satisfied that as much as possible was being done," he said. "But I think we should have been as candid as we could from the beginning." Of course, they weren't, which only contributed to Benton Harbor's distrust of its neighbors. The fallout from Eric's death, though, spurred Richards to run for mayor. He did, and he won. And he then extended an olive branch to Benton Harbor.

His efforts as St. Joseph mayor were, for the most part, symbolic gestures to let his neighbors know that he cared about the well-being of their community and, moreover, about the two towns' relations. He publicly invited people from Benton Harbor to his town's Venetian Festival, an event at which many blacks had felt unwelcome. He invited Benton Harbor's mayor, Emma Hull, to spend a day in St. Joseph. He participated in Hands Across the

Bridge, an annual event in which members from both communities would form a chain across the Bicentennial Bridge. (The event ended for lack of participants.) He convinced the St. Joseph commission to observe Martin Luther King, Jr. Day by canceling its regularly scheduled Monday meeting. He attended events in Benton Harbor, including the ten-year celebration of Dial-a-Ride, a free bus service that operates in both communities. He was the only white to attend.

Eric's death "might be the starting point for these communities to come together so that we never have an incident like that in the future," he told me. "I wanted them to know that there are many people in this community who care."

The Uncle

What first strikes you on meeting Bennie Bowers, Jr., is his size. He's enormous, all brawn, his biceps easily the size of most men's thighs. I wasn't surprised to learn that he had at one point considered a career in professional football and had tried out with the Houston Oilers. (He was cut after four days.) Bowers, who lives with his wife and children in Kalamazoo, sixty miles east of Benton Harbor, has been a state trooper since 1987.

Bowers and Eric were unusually close. "Why would he want to come live with us on weekends, with me?" Bowers mused out loud one evening as we sat in his living room. "He'd come here and we'd have to eat at a certain time; he'd have to use a napkin on his lap. He couldn't talk to me like we were roadies. He couldn't swear and disrespect me. He had to treat my son, Jonathan, with respect. I was really, really strict, discipline-wise.

"The peace of mind I'd like is, you know, maybe he just wanted to be around his uncle. But I don't think so. My kids were much younger than him, so it wasn't like they had the same interest. Eric was interested in girls; Jonathan, who was ten, was interested in his toys. I missed a lot of things."

What Bowers thinks he missed were signs that Eric was hovering on the periphery of Benton Harbor's street gangs. Eric wasn't tough; he wasn't streetwise. In hindsight, Bowers believes that's why Eric came to stay with him on weekends: to flee the pressures of his peers. Bowers doesn't believe that those pressures had anything to do with Eric's death, but sometimes he's not sure. He started, with his own money, a gang-awareness program. He visits schools across the state to talk with kids and warn them of the dangers of the street.

Here's how he opens those sessions:

"The reason I got involved with this issue is because five years ago I got a phone call and my nephew was missing. I told my sister, 'Hey, he'll be back in a couple of days.' A couple of days later I got a call that he'd been found in the St. Joe River. He was dead. Before that, he'd come stay with me on weekends, and I'd run a bootcamp compared to his life at home. But there were a lot of things I missed in regard to his lifestyle, from his fingernail being painted to things being spoke. He'd make references to what the gangs were down in Benton Harbor. One particular sect he'd talk highly of was the Vice Lords. To this day, I don't know . . . Just his wanting to come live with me. I missed it totally. And something that bothers me is, I can't remember how he wore his baseball cap." The Vice Lords wear their cap visors to the left; their rivals, to the right.

Bowers, despite his size, is a gentle man. Nonetheless, it's hard for me to imagine his losing control, which is what happened in those months immediately following Eric's death. He had a recurring dream in which Eric would visit him at the state police post. He'd stand in the doorway. "Uncle Junior," he'd plead, using the playful nickname, "find out what happened to me. Please, find out what happened to me." Bowers would hear Eric's voice as he drove to work. "Luckily," he says, "it takes me twenty-five minutes to drive to work, 'cause I'd cry for the first fifteen minutes."

Bowers is leery of St. Joseph, though his contact with his former neighbors has been minimal. As a senior in high school, he participated in an exchange program with St. Joseph High School, so he spent a day with his rivals across the river. His host was Hank Fullman, also a football star. Bowers hung out with him that day and ate at his home. Bowers liked Fullman, and to this day regrets that the two never stayed in touch, but more to the point he regrets—and wonders why—the two never saw each other off the football field, other than on this one day when the town fathers extended a welcome.

"For fifty years it's been St. Joe this and Benton Harbor that," he says. "If we didn't have this separation, maybe we'd solve the case. It's always so hard for me, 'cause I know someone killed Eric. As a police officer, I see death. But the death isn't so bad. It's the dying. To see someone trying to breathe, with all the blood that's entered their lungs. To hear that death rattle. To hear them struggle to live. And when I think what Eric had to go through, to actually suffocate under water. That tears me apart for a moment. And then I try to talk to him and say that you've given me the motivation to do what I've done with these kids. You've touched my life. Then I drive off." But not before reassuring Eric that he'll persist in trying to find out what happened to him.

Little Eric

Bennie Bowers is always alert to leads. One morning in the fall of 1995, his partner responded to a complaint of possible child abuse. It turned out that the complainant, Jane Austin, the child's mother, was originally from Benton Harbor. She was about the same age as

Eric, so after the interview, as an afterthought, the officer asked her whether she knew Eric McGinnis.

"I thought no one would ever ask," she said with a sigh.

She went on to tell him that she had been with Eric at the Club when he got into an altercation with a group of white boys. A few days after meeting with the officer, she visited the Battle Creek state police post, where she gave Bowers a tape-recorded statement. A few weeks after that, she relayed the story to me.

Austin lives in a trailer home on the outskirts of Battle Creek. A soft-featured, open-faced woman, Austin sat on her sofa, her bare feet tucked beneath her, a Danielle Steel novel at her side. It was Halloween, and her four children, all in their costumes, noisily devoured fried chicken and slices of bread at the kitchen table, eager to go trick-or-treating.

Austin spent her early years in Benton Harbor and knew Eric from school. She remembers that he once had Ruth bake her a birthday cake. Another time, Eric protected her from a boy who had been bullying her. "He was a really good friend. He was my Urkel," she told me, referring to the cuddly television character. "Always on me. Always wanting to do things for me. We kind of had a crush on each other, but, I don't know, nothing ever came of it." They lost touch, though on occasion in high school Eric would cut classes and join Austin and her friends by the railroad tracks, where they would smoke cigarettes and swap gossip. But it had been quite a while since they'd seen each other when they met that night at the Club.

It was a Friday night. No, maybe a Saturday night. Before the Blossomtime parade. No, afterward. While Austin is certain she ran into Eric the night he disappeared, the date seems uncertain. Another person there the same night as Austin says it was a few weeks before Eric's death. But here's what Austin says happened, a story confirmed by another who was there that night: Eric was slow-dancing with a white girl.

"I remember he was wearing new tennis shoes. I commented on

it. He was just dressed for dancing. Anyway, I guess the girl's ex-boyfriend, these guys got mad because he was with her and he was black. Maybe four or five guys. They just asked, 'Why are you in St. Joe? Why you with one of our girls?' Eric was starting to get upset. The other guys called him a 'nigger.' He was, like, 'Fuck you.' They said, 'Go back to your own side of the bridge.' The lady that sold pop, she asked us to leave, me and the people we were with."

Austin says she then left the Club with Eric, and on their way home to her mother's apartment, just south of downtown, Eric went to urinate behind a car, and a white man began chasing him. That's the last she saw of Eric. Of course, this doesn't quite jibe with the story related by Warmbein and the four boys who shot off bottle rockets with Eric.

I talked with Austin for a couple of hours and pressed her on certain points. Did she remember what Eric was wearing that night? No. Did she know the girl he was dancing with? No. Why didn't she go to the police? Because she'd been in some trouble of her own. Could others confirm her story? She gave me the name of her sister, with whom she doesn't get along. The sister, Angel Leighty, confirmed the part about Eric leaving with Austin, but doesn't remember an altercation in the Club. Leighty insists also that that was the night Eric disappeared.

As Austin and I talked, her children became more restless; they wanted their mom to take them trick-or-treating. The two-year-old boy, who had a red rope tied around his forehead and a red sash just below his black vest, insisted he was a Ninja. "No, you're a pirate," Austin told him. The three-year-old, who was dressed in black, boasted, "I'm a Ninja. Haa-haaa." The two, pirate and Ninja, went at it. Meanwhile, the oldest of the bunch quietly stood in the kitchen, his thoughts elsewhere, oblivious of the karate kicks of his brothers. As he made his way to his bedroom, through the flailing arms and legs of the Ninja and the pirate, Austin called him over to meet me. His Batman cape dragged behind him.

"This is Eric," she said by way of introduction. We shook hands. "I kind of named him after Eric." Eric—like Jane—is white.

The Shooter

The finding by the medical examiner, Steve Cohle, that Norris Maben had probably been shot in the back never made it into Dennis Wiley's report, nor did it become a part of the trial. Assistant Attorney General John Walters, who tried the case, felt "it didn't really matter whether the kid had been shot in the front or the back. That was irrelevant. He was the wrong guy. You didn't have any reason to shoot him, period."

The attorney general charged Fiedler with two crimes: involuntary manslaughter and reckless discharge of a firearm. The trial got off to an inauspicious start when, of the fifty prospective jurors chosen, not one was black. That infuriated the Reverend Johnson and others. A Berrien court officer responded that it was just chance that no blacks were selected.

It was during the three-day trial that it surfaced that Fiedler had, eight months before the shooting, sat in on a two-day trial in which Maben faced charges of assault. Walters argued that Fiedler should have recognized Maben from that encounter when they met in the second-floor apartment on Pavone. Also, Walters pointed out that Tracey Hibbler, the one Fiedler thought he was pursuing, had been described as wearing a blue-jean jacket with fur collar, black sweat pants, white tennis shoes, and a brown hat, while Maben wore a black leather jacket, blue pants, blue tennis shoes, and a gray hat. Fiedler, Walters argued, should have known that he had the wrong man.

A few days before the trial, the Reverend Brown told a local reporter, "I'm not saying because he was a black man the officer wanted to shoot him. I think it's more bad judgment and maybe being on the force too long. I can't think the shooting was racist. But what made it racist was the way it was handled after the shooting. All I'm saying and all anybody is saying is let it go to trial and let the trial speak for itself." It did.

After four and a half hours of deliberation, the jury acquitted Fiedler of the manslaughter charges, but found him guilty of recklessly discharging his gun. The judge sentenced him to six months of house arrest and ordered him to perform 120 hours of community service.

On the day of the verdict, the Benton Harbor police prepared for the inevitable: that Benton Harbor's residents would vent their rage, ripping through the town's streets. In recent months, the police had acquired riot gear from various departments, and now placed it in the trunks of their patrol cars. But they had no need for the steel helmets, shields, long batons, and gas masks. Nothing happened. In fact, despite the all-white jury, there was a sense in Benton Harbor that justice had been served. And, as was pointed out by several people, at least someone was being held accountable for Maben's death, unlike Eric's.

As for Fiedler, he and his wife eventually moved to a small southern town, where he has taken up work as a bricklayer. He politely declined my repeated efforts to talk with him. "It's behind me," he said several times during our one brief phone conversation. "The people in the community know who I was."

The Prosecutor

In the fall of 1996, Dennis Wiley applied for a judgeship; a local judge had resigned. The only public opposition came from people in Benton Harbor.

I had met Wiley once, a year after Eric's death. When I asked him how he would characterize relations between the two towns, he had replied, tersely, "I don't want to talk to you on the record about that. I think they get along fairly well." It is how many feel in St. Joseph.

"Race is an issue to those people who make it an issue," the former mayor William Gillespie once told me.

Or consider Ben Butzbaugh, one of the town's city commissioners, who said, "I think we're pretty fair in this community. I don't know that I can say I know of any out-and-out racial-type things that occur . . . I just think people like their own better than others. I think that's pretty universal. Don't you think? . . . For white people who live in a community where they're not around other races, it's not an issue. We're not a bunch of racists. We're not anything America isn't. Now maybe that's good, maybe that's bad." Butzbaugh proudly pointed to his friendship with Renée Williams, Benton Harbor's new school superintendent. "Renée was in our home three, four, five days a week," he noted. "Nice gal. Put herself through school. We'd talk all the time." Williams and her sister cooked and cleaned for Butzbaugh's family.

Wiley's connection to the Benton Harbor community is tenuous at best, though he attends monthly Rotary Club meetings there.

I have since tried on numerous occasions to interview Wiley. I ran into him at the courthouse, at a county Republican gathering, and at a Rotary breakfast. Each time he told me he was too busy, but suggested I call in a few weeks. I did. And he still didn't have time. So I wrote him letters and finally sent along a copy of my first book, knowing that he has a great love for children. Wiley wrote back, referring to my story, which had run in the *Wall Street Journal*:

. . . It has been my experience that past practices are the best
predictors of future behavior. Your previous malevolent portrayal
of this community in the *Wall Street Journal* contradicts your
self-serving assertion of fair, accurate, and unbiased reporting.

For the above reasons, I see no reason or obligation to contribute to your private commercial endeavor. Your request for an interview is denied.

> Yours very truly
> Dennis M. Wiley
> Prosecuting Attorney

P.S. Your book is returned; I do not accept gifts from non-friends.

There was much I wanted to talk with Wiley about, including what he thinks happened to Eric. But it was never to happen.

The only public opposition to Wiley's judgeship application came from Glenn Yarbrough, a county commissioner and Mamie Yarbrough's brother-in-law. He publicly denounced Wiley as "a poor prosecutor" and cited Wiley's alleged mishandling of two cases: the deaths of Norris Maben and Eric McGinnis. The *Herald-Palladium* ran a story with the headline YARBROUGH: DON'T MAKE WILEY JUDGE.

On November 15, Governor John Engler of Michigan appointed Wiley to fill out the term of the resigning judge. Within a matter of days, there was talk as to who might run against him in two years.

The Editor

Steve Pepple, the *Herald-Palladium*'s managing editor, sent me an article that had run in the *Detroit News* on July 5, 1983. The story recorded the financial difficulties of Benton Harbor and the conspiracy theories harbored by some of its leaders. But that's not what Pepple wanted me to see. He had circled a reference to Willard Banyon, the former publisher of the paper. Banyon was quoted as saying that blacks' "mental processes are definitely inferior—except if you look at the basketball teams."

Pepple still flinches at that remark. "We're living with our past," he said. "We're the white newspaper in St. Joe. It's hard to get past that." But Pepple, who is in his mid-forties, has tried to do so, in large part because of Eric's death. While Pepple firmly believes Eric died accidentally, he says, "It taught me there is another perspective out there. I don't know that I understand it. Many firmly believe that Eric was murdered and there was a big coverup. We missed that . . . So as issues have come up we've tried to cover them a little differently."

After Pepple was picked to run the paper, in 1992, he increased the coverage of Benton Harbor, much to the chagrin of a handful of readers, who have threatened to cancel their subscriptions, and he cosponsored two communitywide symposiums on race. Pepple is most proud of the paper's coverage after Benton Harbor experienced ten homicides in a twelve-day period, starting on December 29, 1996. He sent a team of reporters and photographers into the neighborhoods, knocking on doors for a series of stories about the impact of the town's crime and possible solutions. "It gave our readers a different perspective. It put a human face on it. What I hoped it would show is that there are a lot of good decent people living in Benton Harbor. They're scared. They want help. I think sometimes there's a perspective that everyone over there is a drug addict or a criminal."

Pepple has since left the *Herald-Palladium* for a position with another newspaper. His two biggest frustrations, he said, were the paper's inability to attract black reporters (it has had only one, and he was a one-year fellow) and its inability to attract readers in Benton Harbor. Benton Harbor accounts for less than 10 percent of the paper's circulation.

Shortly before his departure, Pepple received a voice-mail from Michael Green, who had written the op-ed piece on Eric and now worked for a local bank. Green has grown increasingly frustrated with the politics of his community and the indifference of St. Joseph. "I'm sorry to see you leaving," he told Pepple in his message. "I just want you to know that I thought under your leadership the paper actually made an effort to build some bridges." Green later said of Pepple, "Not living in Benton Harbor, there was a limit to what he could do, but I noticed a willingness on his part to cover stories from all angles. He actually tried."

The Tumbler

Leigh Ann Bender helped teach gymnastics at Bobbie Nadus's gym in Stevensville. There, she met Eric. With her closely cropped hair, her doll-like features, and tight gymnastics body, Bender looks perky, but she is actually a shy girl. She was charmed by Eric's easy way with people. "He brightened the gym up," she said. "I looked forward to coming to the gym when he was there."

Bender lived in Three Oaks, a quaint hamlet south of St. Joseph. She did not know any black people personally, and she had her stereotypes. "I've never been to downtown Benton Harbor," she told me. "I've heard stories. You drive through with your windows rolled up and you don't stop for stop lights." Eric was the first black person with whom she was friends. The two would flirt, and Eric once called her at home to ask her out, but Bender's parents didn't let her date. She and Eric saw each other only at gymnastics.

When Nadus told Bender that Eric's body had been found in the river, Bender went home and cried herself to sleep. The next day, she cut out the newspaper article and placed it in her scrapbook. The following September, she went off to college in Rhode Island, where she became friends with a number of black students. Her friendship with Eric had opened her up to such relationships. "Eric helped me," she said.

The Activist and Her Children

At a vending stand in the parking lot of Benton Harbor High School, Carolyn Graves squirted ketchup on a hot dog. "More," the young customer demanded. Graves cast him a you-don't-talk-to-me-like-that glance, her eyes bearing down on his. "Please," he added, and Graves burst into her signature hearty laugh. She dished out franks and pop while helmeted boys and girls zipped down a nearby hill in the town's annual go-kart competition. She loves this small-town life.

A single mother of two children, Jared and Gia, Graves is engaged with her community. She attends Rotary Club breakfasts and has sat on the school board. She took in a teenage boy whose mother had become addicted to crack. Graves's reputation was sullied, though, when she was caught a few years back underreporting her income so that she could qualify for a rental subsidy. She said it was the only way she could help put her children through college. She pleaded guilty and spent thirty days in jail. But it hasn't diminished her involvement in the town's affairs. Nor has it silenced her.

When a local minister asked her to participate in a rally protesting the shooting of Norris Maben, she declined. She knew Fiedler and thought him kind and just. Moreover, she wanted to know why the protest wasn't about the escalating black-on-black violence. "I asked 'em the question, 'Tell me, when is a murder a murder? This week, we already had one over in the Buss projects, a young man killed, then we had a young lady get killed over in the same area where Maben had gotten shot. Nobody said a word. But the minute Mr. Fiedler shoots this boy and kills him, the whole community gets outraged.' I said, 'I ain't marching nowhere, not until we decide that every time somebody gets killed we gonna march against it.' "

Graves had equally strong feelings about Eric's death. He was, she firmly believed, murdered. She had attended the same church as Eric and is a friend of his grandfather's. And her daughter, Gia, was Eric's classmate and friend. Gia, like her mother, does not shrink from what she thinks is right. When classmates were beating up white students, Gia and two companions hovered over a fourth friend who was white. They escorted her to and from classes. They ate lunch with her. They walked her home. They made sure no one touched her.

Gia's brother, Jared, is the most reserved of the three, though he has his mother's easy laugh. After attending Wilberforce University, he returned to Benton Harbor and hired on as a police officer. In his rookie year he was named officer of the year. One spring afternoon, Jared let me ride with him as he patrolled the town's streets. As we passed an abandoned gas station with FUCK DA LAW scrawled across its boarded-up windows, Jared veered to avoid a pack of half a dozen scraggly, hungry dogs. Two boys, maybe thirteen years old, came careening down the street on their bikes; one performed a wheelie. Jared rolled down his window. "Hey, guys," he yelled. The kids looked up, thinking for a moment that they were in trouble. "Hey, guys," he said again, "why don't you help those ladies?" He nodded toward two women struggling to carry a dresser into their house. The boys laughed—as did the women. Both boys parked their bikes and went to assist. Jared continued driving. He told me that during the past weekend, he had spotted a group of black teenage boys flirting with a group of white girls.

"I told them, 'Look, you guys, as soon as you get all you want and you don't call them no more, they're gonna call out rape and you're going to be hit.' I told these guys in their own best interests, it's not worth it." He continued, "McGinnis was dating a white girl at the time."

Eric's death lingers for all the Graveses—as it does for most in Benton Harbor. Gia, now a student at Northwestern University, says, "It stopped me from going over to St. Joe socially . . . It just opened my eyes to the situation between Benton Harbor and St. Joe. Before, I was pretty much oblivious to it. If I was followed into a store, for instance, I didn't pay it much attention. Now I do."

Her mother, Carolyn, says, "If I don't have to go across that bridge, I don't. The electric company is over there. The courthouse is over there. And they have restaurants over there. I won't shop there, though. You walk into a store, and you're automatically followed. Questions asked of you. 'Are you new here?' I'll say no. They say, 'We haven't seen you here before.' "

Jared and I drove down a side street. "I have to ask you something," he said.

"Okay, go ahead."

"You're still looking for what happened to Eric?" he asked.

I nodded.

"Think you'll break it?"

"I don't know," I said.

"You ain't afraid or nothing?"

32.

A FINAL NOTE

I canoed the last twelve miles of the St. Joseph River; it was in early June, after an unusually rain-soaked spring, so the waters were high. Where my friend and I put in—down a gravel road, behind a dairy farm—the waters had risen over the tree-lined banks, engulfing a cornfield that now resembled an Asian rice paddy. A dozen or so blue herons, their willowlike necks silhouetted against the rising sun, stood crowded in the knee-deep water, plunging their long beaks into the soil for snails and worms. A snapping turtle waddled across the muddy road, traveling from one fresh cornfield-turned-lake to another. And mosquitoes, early and energetic, swarmed about us, forever unsatiated. The animal life had swollen along with the river.

The deluge had quickened the water's flow, though even in floodstage, the river thick with mud was easily navigable. There were no stretches of whitewater, and with only a little effort we could paddle upstream, retracing our path. I was surprised to learn later that just the day before, the high waters had pushed a freighter, emptied of its cargo, into the railroad bridge, denting one of the steel girders.

It took us three hours to paddle the twelve miles, at first past thick woods hiding open croplands, then past steep bluffs atop which sat half-million-dollar homes, replete with private docks and regal watercraft. As we approached the two towns, we paddled under the heavily trafficked I-94, its thick cement pillars adorned with the Gangster Disciples' six-pointed star and pitchfork. We reached St. Joseph and Benton Harbor by late morning. Here, the river widens, and here it is said that long after the spring rains have subsided there are places where one can wade across. It is also here that the river cuts not only through the landscape but also through the soul.

Much has happened in the six years since Eric died to affect race relations. Nationally, Rodney King's attackers were first acquitted, then found guilty. A jury rendered a verdict in the O. J. Simpson criminal trial that, like a freeze-frame, caught America in full undress, exposing its racial wrinkles and underbelly. And as I write, President Clinton, who recently apologized to victims of the Tuskegee experiments, has just called for a year-long dialogue on race.

Here in the Twin Cities much has happened as well. The St. Joseph fire chief resigned after he allegedly told two black youths they weren't welcome in St. Joseph and after it was learned he often used the word "nigger" in the fire station. Benton Harbor leaders objected to warnings given sailors from a naval ship docked in the river; they were told to be careful about going into Benton Harbor. And while state troopers have been invited into Benton Harbor to help patrol the streets, the big news in St. Joseph is that there's now a coffee war: the number of downtown coffee shops has doubled from three to six.

"This is a strange place to live sometimes," a St. Joseph High School teacher once told me. But perhaps no stranger than anyplace else, at least when it comes to race.

I continue to obsess over Eric's death. So does Jim Reeves.

Reeves is still a detective. To his disappointment, he didn't get appointed police chief after the former one retired. Another detective, John Nolan, got the job. Reeves wasn't even considered for the post. He had got into some trouble when, as a favor, he tried to post a $15,000 bond for the son of the former city manager. The son, a grown man, had been arrested for failing to pay child support. Reeves's efforts had the appearance of impropriety, since departmental regulations forbid officers from posting bond. The newspaper suggested that the money came from the city coffers. (It didn't—nor did Reeves end up posting bail once he learned his money could be confiscated to pay the child support.) Wiley launched an investigation, and though he cleared Reeves of any wrongdoing, he suggested that Reeves had showed poor judgment.

I called to tell Reeves I hope things work out for him under his new boss, with whom he has had a somewhat wary relationship. His thoughts, though, seemed elsewhere. "I had a dream last night," he said, apropos of nothing. "I wasn't on the ground. I wasn't on the bridge. I was just above, looking down. I remember it was the St. Joseph River. I saw the steel pilings. Eric was floundering in the water, yelling for help. There's no doubt it was Eric. He was wearing that white turtleneck he had on in the picture.

"I remember the bank of the river, and there were two other figures there," he continued. "I don't know if they were going to help him or were going to run away."

The dream, like so many, was hazy, but it disturbed him. He'd had trouble sleeping in recent weeks because of the mess with the city manager's son, and this time, as on those other nights, he slid out of bed and, so as not to disturb his wife, went downstairs to the family room, where he stretched out on the sofa. About fifteen years ago Reeves had had another upsetting vision. He dreamed that a body had washed up on Silver Beach. Several days later, the police did discover the body of a middle-aged woman, covered in sand and ice, along Lake Michigan. He acknowledged, as he told me this, that many people might consider such a premonition cockeyed, but he said, "I put some stock in dreams." And so as he lay there on the couch, he thought to himself, "I've got to talk to Thornton again." Daniel Thornton hadn't been in the dream, not that Reeves remembers, but that's what he was left with as he rewound the vivid image of Eric grabbing at air as he slipped beneath the river's surface. "I believe that sometimes in one state or another we can be more intuitive," he told me. His intuition told him to talk to Thornton. In time, he did.

In the six years since Eric's death nothing seems settled. If I am asked the inevitable question: What do you think happened to Eric?, I could give the glib response that the truth doesn't really matter. It's all about perspective. It's all about myth. As Reeves once said to me, "People are going to believe what they want." But the truth does matter, especially in the death of a young boy. And in a big way. It's just that sometimes it's not easy getting to it.

Anaïs Nin once wrote that "there are very few human beings who receive the truth, complete and staggering, by instant illumination. Most of them acquire it fragment by fragment, on a small scale, by successive developments, cellularly, like a laborious mosaic."

How much of the mosaic have I pieced together? I don't believe that Eric tried to swim across the river, as the state police psychological unit suggested. It was too nasty a night, the river itself too intimidating. And there's no indication that Eric felt completely confident in the water. If he did, then maybe—with the emphasis on *maybe*—he removed his coat, hid it somewhere along the shoreline, and lowered himself into the river to swim the width of 350 feet. But I've been on those banks many an evening, in spring and in summer, and there is nothing inviting about the waters. I consider myself a fairly strong swimmer, but I would never attempt that crossing, not even during the day, not even when the river appears calm. Moreover, if Eric voluntarily entered the river, what happened to his coat? Why does it appear that he tried to disrobe once he was in the water?

I believe Eric either fell in accidentally—or was forced into the water. Maybe, as has been suggested, he stumbled while urinating, which might account for his unzipped pants. Or he tried to cross along the railroad bridge and tripped. Or he got into an altercation.

Like Reeves, I too have dreams. I read and reread my interviews. I pester Reeves for one more look at the photographs. I find one more person to talk to. I pursue yet one more tip. I paddle the river.

As my friend and I passed under the Blossomland Bridge that summer morning, Lake Michigan now in sight, I found myself daydreaming, fantasizing that I was about to break the case. I do this often. I find someone who saw Eric fall in. Or I confirm Thornton's story. And then I think to myself, Where does that leave me? Where does that leave us? Is the lore more powerful, more lasting than the truth? Are our perceptions of the world so radically different that we can't agree even on fact?

For Eric's family, at least, the truth does matter. It's everything. Somewhere between this bridge and the lake is where Eric supposedly entered the water—and perhaps here lie some answers. Reeves initially discounted Thornton's story on two counts: Thornton failed a polygraph, and the body, Reeves contended, could not have drifted upstream.

First, Thornton voluntarily submitted to a polygraph and, in answers to questions about his story, showed deception. Afterward, he told the polygrapher that in fact he had not seen Eric killed but instead had heard about it through James, the fellow who allegedly had chased Eric. Reeves entertained the notion that Thornton was passing along a true account, albeit secondhand.

Second, the body could have drifted upstream. That became

apparent as my friend and I paddled between the two piers. It was an exquisitely sunny day, with only a slight breeze blowing in from the southwest, yet as we neared the blue waters of Lake Michigan, we charted a course away from the wharves. Waves ricocheted off the breakwaters, creating enough of a slosh to upend us. But the water appeared to be going the wrong way, as if it were flowing upstream. Eric Niedlinger, who has run a charter fishing service on these waters for twenty-seven years, says, "If you have a strong wind from the west, the river may be almost dead, though it never actually flows upstream." It just looks that way as the surface water is blown away from the lake. The night Eric McGinnis went into the water, the wind blew in from the northwest in gusts up to sixteen knots, and conceivably could have pushed the body back *up* the river. Reeves, though, wonders whether it could have pushed it nearly a thousand feet to the Coast Guard Station.

Nonetheless, Reeves recently revisited Thornton in the county jail, where he was awaiting trial for attempted escape, and then went back a second time to record him on video. Reeves also took Thornton back to the pier, this time in cuffs and with jail guards. Thornton's story was the same as what he had told me and what he had told Reeves four years earlier.

Reeves has a list of people he plans to interview again. Among them are Lisa Liedke and James. He hasn't spoken to either one in nearly six years. He wants to pinpoint exactly where the body was found. He intends to send the video to a voice specialist in Palm Beach, Florida, who apparently can assess, through Thornton's speech, whether he's being truthful. Reeves was charged up.

So the digging continues. But slowly. When Reeves called Ruth to let her know about his dream and his intentions to interview Thornton again, she told him about the interview her brother had conducted a year earlier with Jane Austin. She promised to send Reeves the transcript, but never did.

"That really bothered me," Reeves said. "I don't think she trusts me at all." Ruth's distance stung and drained Reeves of some of his drive. Maybe, he said, Ruth has come to terms with the loss of her son and doesn't want the emotional tumult of opening the investigation once more.

Reeves told me that Eric, a boy he never knew, has had a deeper effect on him than has any other black person. That says a lot.

And it bothers Reeves that in all the finger-pointing and speculating no one—outside Eric's family—has had time to mourn the boy's death. "You know what the tragedy of the whole thing is?" he asked me rhetorically. "Eric is dead and gone, and we remember him for the wrong reasons." Indeed, Eric has come to embody what both sides of the river deem to be true—as seen through each one's unique prism. For these two towns, Eric has come to mark the divide, a reference point. To those in St. Joseph, Eric's death is proof that race blinds their neighbors to the obvious. To those in Benton Harbor, it is proof that because of race even the obvious is never what it seems.

One day I hope to visit Eric's gravesite at the Crystal Springs Cemetery. I've been there before, but always with notebook in hand, inquisitive, observant. I've noted its placement among the fifty-five thousand graves, at a far corner of the century-old graveyard. I've noted the red, yellow, and white tulips planted at the foot of the tombstone. And I've recorded the epitaph, etched in the stone above a pair of praying hands:

My Beloved Son
Eric F. McGinnis
Dec. 6, 1974
May 17, 1991

I'd go next time to mourn his loss, as Reeves suggested. In doing so, maybe I can acknowledge that the river, while wide and, in places, turbulent, is in the end our most profound connection.

On the Reporting

Over the course of five years, I interviewed over two hundred people, from politicians and business leaders to teachers and teenagers. Some met with me just once; many sat down with me on numerous occasions. These interviews were my primary source of reporting. A few asked for anonymity, a request I honored.

Wherever possible, I confirmed someone's account of events with others who were also present or with public documents. The police report on Eric McGinnis's death was obtained through a Freedom of Information Act request submitted to both the St. Joseph Police Department and the Berrien County Prosecutor's Office. The following items were also obtained through the Freedom of Information Act:

—the investigation by both the Sheriff's Department and the Prosecutor's Office into the shooting death of Norris Maben;

—the State Police investigation into the suspected arson at 586 Pipestone Street;

—the State Police investigation into Sherwin Allen, the Benton Harbor schools' superintendent;

—the investigation by the Prosecutor's Office into the use of absentee ballots in the Benton Harbor School Board recall effort.

The Benton Harbor Police Department shared certain files, including homicide records and police logs for the time around Eric's death. They also allowed me to search through records from the 1930s for information pertaining to the hanging death of Marcus Cooley.

As a matter of course, the courts in Berrien County videotape their proceedings, so I was able to procure tapes of the trials of Marvin Fiedler and Cleve Smith. I obtained transcripts of the case against Jim Rutter.

For historical events, the newspapers of the area were invaluable, especially the *Herald-Palladium* and *The Michigan Citizen*—as were a number of books and pamphlets I found at the local libraries. Michigan State University's Center for Urban Affairs had for a period of years worked closely with Benton Harbor leaders in an effort to revive the town. The files kept by the University were helpful in understanding the town's recent past, as was material at the Berrien County Historical Society.

My reading for this book was varied. It included numerous books and articles on race, as well as Tim O'Brien's *In the Lake of the Woods,* Sherwood Anderson's *Winesburg, Ohio,* and Rian Malan's *My Traitor's Heart,* all of which helped me think about how best to tell this story.

The Cast

Sherwin Allen—*superintendent of the Benton Harbor schools*
Marion Bady—*Cleve Smith's girlfriend*
George Barfield—*Benton Harbor School Board member and former ally of Sherwin Allen*
Bennie Bowers, Jr.—*Eric's uncle*
Gladys Peeples Burks—*Benton Harbor School Board member*
Stephen D. Cohle—*forensic patholigist in a nearby county*
Marcus Cooley—*in 1934 found hanged in the Berrien County Jail*
Dale Easton—*St. Joseph police officer*
Dan Ertman—*Benton Harbor School Board member*
Marvin Fiedler—*Benton Harbor police officer who shot Norris Maben*
Carolyn Graves—*Benton Harbor activist*
Gia Graves—*Carolyn's daughter and friend of Eric's*
Jared Graves—*Carolyn's son and Benton Harbor police officer*
James—*white teen who may have had an altercation with Eric*
Alfred Johnson—*Eric's minister and Benton Harbor activist*
Lisa Liedke—*St. Joseph girl who dated Eric*

Norris Maben—*Benton Harbor teen shot by police officer Marvin Fiedler*

Excell McGinnis—*Eric's father*

Ruth McGinnis—*Eric's mother*

Stephen Marschke—*deputy sheriff (and briefly sheriff)*

Dennis Marshall—*Benton Harbor teen who had an altercation with Eric*

Bobbie Nadus—*Eric's math teacher and gymnastics coach*

Joshua Ndege—*Jim Reeves's Zimbabwean friend*

Steve Pepple—*managing editor of the* Herald-Palladium

Jim Reeves—*St. Joseph police detective who headed the investigation into Eric's death*

Larina Robbins—*Benton Harbor teen who dated Eric*

Gary Shaffer—*state policeman who investigated Sherwin Allen*

Cleve Smith—*Benton Harbor man accused of murdering a young gang member*

Dennis Soucek—*St. Joseph police detective*

Daniel Thornton—*jailhouse informant*

Ted Warmbein—*had his car broken into the night Eric disappeared*

Burton Weisberg—*dentist and friend of Marvin Fiedler's*

Dennis Wiley—*Berrien County prosecutor*

Ken Woltman—*Benton Harbor School Board member*

Mamie Yarbrough—*Benton Harbor School Board member*

everyday discourse. It is, as cultural observers might note, part of the local Zeitgeist.

While the publication of *The Other Side of the River* undoubtedly contributed to this conversation, it was an event this past spring which pushed the subject of race once again to the fore. In the weeks following the book's publication, I was invited back to the two towns to speak: at a luncheon sponsored by the St. Joseph Rotary Club, at Whirlpool to a group of employees, at a gathering sponsored by Benton Harbor's former police chief, and at the local community college. At one of these events, a luncheon at the Union Memorial A.M.E. Church, my presentation was overshadowed by a story which just that day had begun to unfurl. Before my remarks, Frank Walsh, the St. Joseph city manager, asked if he could take a few minutes to address the crowd, which included people from both sides of the river, a complement of local politicians, ministers, and other civic leaders. Walsh is an unassuming man who gives little of himself away in public, and so it was unusual when he got to the microphone and had to pause to collect himself. He cleared his throat several times and then began by talking about how hard this was for him. Two weeks earlier, Levarst Hullett, Jr., a forty-year-old black man, had been riding his bicycle from St. Joseph, where he'd been drinking at Tsar's (previously the home of the Club), to his home in Benton Township. It was two-thirty in the morning. Two St. Joseph police officers, who later said they were concerned for his safety given that he was weaving as he rode and had, in fact, at one point fallen, followed Hullett in their squad cars. (One of the officers said that he had offered Hullett a ride home.) As Hullett pedaled across the Bicentennial Bridge into Benton Harbor, one of the officers, Sergeant Rick Smiedendorf, got out of his vehicle and, standing in front of the intoxicated bicyclist, stuck out his right arm, knocking Hullett off his bike. Smiedendorf said he was motioning for Hullett to stop; Hullett contends he was clotheslined. "You wouldn't stop a white man like that," Hullett declared. Though shaken and scraped, Hullett wasn't seriously injured. The incident might have gone unnoticed had it not been for a video camera in the second squad car which recorded the sequence, a television moment which in days to come would be broadcast on news programs as far away as Chicago.

At the A.M.E. church, Walsh's voice quivered as he apologized to the people of Benton Harbor. He promised swift and just action. Walsh had viewed the videotape for the first time just the day before, and was so unsettled by the incident that he invited reporters from the *Herald-Palladium* to view it. He also showed the tape to Benton Harbor's mayor and city manager. Walsh later compared the incident to the beating of Rodney King, and though many thought he was overreaching—after all, King was brutally beaten—he meant only that both moments had been caught for posterity on videotape. The officer in the case was soon suspended for twenty days without pay and demoted in rank from sergeant to patrol officer (though this was later reversed).

Benton Harbor leaders, most of whom were appreciative of Walsh's openness and sincerity, remained relatively quiet on this issue. Maybe it was resignation. Maybe it was a feeling that Walsh would do the right thing. The clamor, instead, came from the other side of the river. A large number of St. Joseph residents, indignant at Walsh's comparison to the King beating and angry at the treatment of Smiedendorf, a popular officer, took to the streets. Three hundred chanting citizens marched from the county courthouse to city hall in protest, and then organized an unsuccessful campaign to recall the town's commissioners, who had supported Walsh in his actions.

"This incident made people retreat back to their camps," Dave Brown, the *Palladium*'s new editor, told me. "Many white people supported the white police officer and many black people felt that an injustice had been done." But, Brown continued, "we lived through it without a lot of damage to the two communities." Indeed, it further sparked conversations, contentious at times, about race and how it does (and doesn't) impose on our lives, on our friendships, on our perceptions of the world. And, in fact, the St. Joseph community was divided over the issue, many publicly and privately supporting Walsh's swift actions.

When the next squall blew in, and the next opportunity to talk about race came along, people seized upon it. It became a clarifying moment for these two towns. The occasion in question came a few months after the bicyclist incident when twelve members of the Ku Klux Klan—all of whom traveled from the South—staged a rally on the steps of the county courthouse. (They reportedly came to St. Joseph having read the book, figuring, I can only assume, that they would get a friendly reception.) The rally, coincidentally, occurred on the same day the Klan demonstrated in Jasper, Texas, where two white men had been charged with murdering a black man after dragging his body behind their pickup. In Jasper, tensions ran high. The police had to keep the Klan and protesters apart. Some protesters showed up armed with rifles and shotguns. In St. Joseph, though, the rally was a bust. Nobody came. Jim Reeves, who stood on the courthouse roof videotaping the event, counted 37 spectators, most of whom arrived purely out of curiosity. And while the Klan fumbled, across the river an interracial crowd of 250 packed the pews of the Ebenezer Baptist Church for a unity prayer service. The twelve Klansmen, unsettled by the low turnout, canceled their rally, vowing to return. "It was like throwing a party and nobody showing up," Reeves told me with some pride. "I thought it was great."

In the meantime, the Rotary clubs in St. Joseph and Benton Harbor have convened an initiative on race, an effort on the part of these traditionally conservative groups to talk about racial diversity. A similar effort has been undertaken by a group of civic leaders from both communities. Former civil rights hero Congressman John Lewis came to speak. The newspaper has run a probing yearlong series exploring race in the Twin Cities. And individuals on both sides of the river have found their own ways to span the bridge. Bennie Bowers, Eric's uncle, got assigned for a time to the Benton Harbor police department, where as a state trooper he assisted in efforts to reduce the town's still high violent crime rate. Jim Reeves, who continues his work in the St. Joseph police department, has found opportunities to speak privately—and on occasion publicly when interviewed about the book—on the need for greater racial tolerance and understanding.

As for the case itself, Reeves—and I—had thought the book's publication might spur a flurry of tips, but despite Reeves's willingness to pursue any new leads, none have surfaced. On occasion he will arrest someone who used to frequent the Club, and will question him about Eric, but time now is a foe since people's memories are fading. "You just don't hear anything, nothing," Reeves says. "Either we've covered everything and we've done a good job and there ain't no more—or someone's keeping their mouth shut."

But if Eric's death left any legacy, it's that the people of his town and their neighbors across the way have found connections. Indeed, the changes in St. Joseph and Benton Harbor have been incremental, and there are those who point to the book and accuse it of just stirring up trouble, making an issue of something that, at least by their accounts, would otherwise lay dormant. I've been called a troublemaker and worse. But these past months as I've revisited the towns, my faith in most people's desire to do right by each other has been reaffirmed. At my presentation to the Rotary luncheon—a mostly white crowd of 600—I was presented with a gold Cross pen with the inscription: ALEX "THANKS," and at a book signing in a mall outside Benton Harbor a black former detective from the town presented me with a box of chocolates. A number of residents have told me that the book got them thinking of their neighbors in a different light. One wrote me that at the sentencing of a friend for tax fraud, the judge cited the book. "The essence of what he said was that

Acknowledgments

This is a book whose main protagonists are two towns, and so I relied on the openness and candor of the people of St. Joseph and Benton Harbor. There are too many to mention by name, but some deserve particular thanks, especially Jim Reeves and Ruth McGinnis. Both had their own reasons not to talk with me, yet each acknowledged the divide and hoped in their own way to bridge it. They trusted me with their stories. And for that I am forever grateful. For Eric's parents, Excell McGinnis and Ruth, my presence undoubtedly reopened old wounds, and so I'm particularly thankful for their willingness to talk about such a painful episode in their lives.

The following townspeople were especially helpful, as well: Bennie Bowers, Bennie Bowers, Jr., Denise Reeves, David Kirshenbaum, Ted Kirshenbaum, Ken Overley, Carolyn Graves, Gia Graves, David Idinopulos, Jim and Wendy Keller, Mamie Yarbrough, Amy and Harvey Johnson, Jack Banyon, Andy Burch, Michael Green, Sherry Collins, Larina Robbins, Tom Nelson, Rev.

Alfred Johnson, Stan Lapekas, Joyce Leuty, Bill Elliott, Tanya Ryshiad, Sister Mary Jo Holmes, Rick Taylor, Gary Ruhl, Kathy Miller, David Douglas—and all of Eric's friends.

The staffs at the Benton Harbor and St. Joseph public libraries steered me through their respective archives and located books and articles which helped flesh out the towns' histories. Members of both police departments made themselves accessible, lent their perspectives, and turned me on to stories. To David Walker, Milt Agay, Ron Singleton, Tim O'Brien, Mark Lundin, Mary White, Diana Goff, Jared Graves, Dale Easton, Janet Owsianka, and Ted Fleisher— thanks. Steve Pepple, former managing editor of the *Herald-Palladium,* generously gave me access to the newspaper's extensive clip files. It made my research immeasurably easier. There were others at the *Palladium* who also guided me, including Dave Brown, Bob Tita, Rick Brundrett, Ron Leuty, and Jim Dalgleish.

Steve Cohle, Kent County's deputy chief medical examiner, invited me to look over his shoulder as he performed an autopsy—and then patiently answered what I'm sure seemed to him the most elementary of medical questions. Bob Kirshner, the lead forensic investigator for Physicians for Human Rights, read my account of the autopsy to help ensure that I knew my anatomy. Any errors, needless to say, are my own. In Chicago, private investigators Paul Ciolino and Grace Castle, criminal defense attorney Jed Stone, and police captain Tom Cronin all helped me ask the right questions.

At the beginning, when I was unsure whether there was, indeed, a book here, the John D. and Catherine T. MacArthur Foundation sponsored me for eight months by anointing me a Distinguished Visitor. My thanks to Adele Simmons and Rebecca Riley for making it possible. My former bosses and colleagues at *The Wall Street Journal* let me run loose—and gave me what was undoubtedly among the best jobs in daily journalism. It was while at the *Journal* that I initially stumbled upon the idea for this book.

Research assistants Eugene Raikhel and Lucas Waltzer combed

archives, sought court documents, tracked down sources, and fielded my panicky calls, all with great aplomb. Their work was invaluable. Also, Ian Zack, before moving on to a full-time journalism job, conducted some initial research. David Sanders of Jenner & Block and Kathy Trager of Doubleday once again provided me with invaluable legal advice. David assisted me in filing numerous Freedom of Information Act requests.

Nan Talese, ever wise, has been both editor and friend. She saw things I didn't see. She posed questions I hadn't asked. She made this a better book. She always does. What more can one ask. Others at Doubleday have been supportive along the way, including Martha Levin, Marly Rusoff, Alicia Brooks, and Claire Roberts. Frances Apt copy edited the manuscript with her usual care and deliberation; with purple pencil in hand, she sharpened my prose. I feel blessed to have as my agent David Black who, with exuberance and a generous spirit, has stood by me from the beginning. Also, thanks to Susan Raihofer and Gary Morris of David's office.

Writing can be an extraordinarily isolating experience, but I've been fortunate to be surrounded by a group of writer friends whose unflagging support kept me afloat. Isabel Wilkerson, Sam Freedman, and Melissa Fay Greene read all or parts of the manuscript. John Conroy listened, with great patience, to my reporting tales. They poked and prodded, challenging my assumptions—and assured me I was onto something when I wasn't so certain. Isabel, with whom I shared regular lunches at Erik's Delicatessen, admonished me early on: "You need to figure it out for yourself. How you feel. What you believe." I took that to heart.

I am also indebted to Kevin Horan, John Houston, and Michael Greene, who provided criticisms and suggestions on various permutations of the manuscript. Kevin, in particular, read drafts early and often. Numerous friends nurtured me along the way, including Jim Adler, Maureen Nelligan, Kathy Read, Pat and Mike Koldyke, Nancy Drew, Beverly Donofrio, Jacki Lyden, Frank James, Erik

Larson, Don Sharp, and John Koten. Special thanks to my brother, Dan Kotlowitz, and his wife, Kathleen Cunneen. Dan's gentle humor and wild fishing tales were a welcome relief, especially in the last months of writing.

My father, Bob Kotlowitz, instilled in me a love for the written word. A novelist and memoirist, he is, in my mind, the finest wordsmith out there. He's given me something to aspire to. A month after I began work on this book, my mother, Billie Kotlowitz, died of cancer. She was a woman filled with passion. She spoke her mind. She wrestled injustices to the ground. This book never could have been written without the lessons she passed on.

Pharoah Walton occasionally accompanied me on reporting trips. I welcomed his company and his incisive observations. I treasure what we have, and know I'm better for it. Madeleine, now two-and-a-half, arrived in the midst of reporting this book, and so we spent our first summer together at a rented farmhouse just south of Benton Harbor and St. Joseph. Her full-throated laughter made the end of those long days blissful.

Finally, there is Maria. My love. My best friend. My bluntest critic—and biggest champion. She is my compass. This book is for her.